For Packers Fans Only

By Rich Wolfe

Published by Lone Wolfe Press.

ISBN: 0-9748603-2-8

Interior photos
Back cover photo:
Cover Design: Dick Fox
Photo Editor: Dick Fox
Cover Copywriter: Dick Fox
Interior Design: The Printed Page, Phoenix, AZ
Author's Agent: T. Roy Gaul

The page count skipped 16 pages on page 192 to reflect the number of full-page photos.

The author, Rich Wolfe, can be reached at 602-738-5889 or at www.fandemonium.net.

DEDICATION

To

Steve Schmitt of Black Earth, Wisconsin—
Whose enthusiasm for the Green Bay Packers,
the Madison Mallards, the St. Louis Cardinals, the
Wisconsin Badgers, and life make him an absolute
joy to be around.

Chat Rooms

Chapter 1

The Land of Ahs

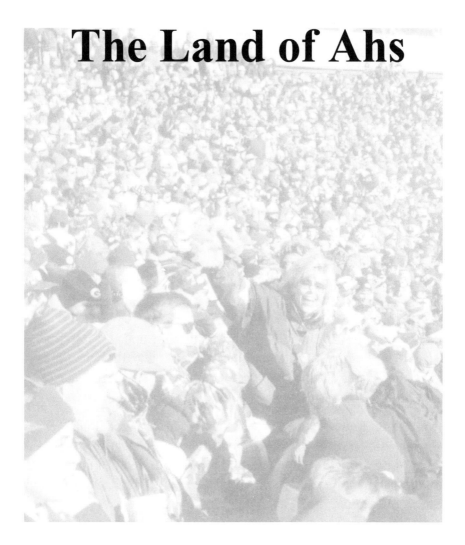

Sweet Home Lambeau

WON'T YOU COME HOME, ROCKY BLEIER, WON'T YOU COME HOME?

ROCKY BLEIER

Rocky Bleier grew up above a bar in Appleton, dreaming of playing for the Packers. After a stellar stint as a halfback on Notre Dame's powerhouse teams of the sixties, he was badly wounded in Vietnam, almost losing a foot. His incredible rehab and comeback was deftly chronicled in Fighting Back, *which was both a best-selling book and a highly-rated movie. He currently sends volley cheers on high as a motivational speaker in the Pittsburgh area.*

I grew up in Appleton, Wisconsin, about 25 miles south of Green Bay. Living there, you had no choice but to be a Packer fan. You really have to think about "pre-Lombardi" and then "post-Lombardi." He came in and developed the team, and by 1960, when I was a freshman in high school, the Packers started to win—meaning…they weren't losing like they had in the past.

There was no Super Bowl at that time—although they eventually won **Super Bowls I and II**—but they won the national championship in '61, '62 and '65. Everybody there was a Packer fan. As a young man in high school, watching this evolve, not knowing the importance, until you start looking back at it, of the Packers in your life…how important it was to the people in Wisconsin. Eventually, the winning was something you could be proud of, that you could hang your hat on, that you could be associated with. No matter what else might be going on, you could always relate and say, "Well, yeah, but we've got the Packers. You don't have anything."

> **The first Super Bowl, in 1967 at the Los Angeles Coliseum, had 32,000 empty seats even though the most expensive ticket was $12.**

Some of my high school friends had parents who became so involved and wrapped up in Packer games. They were going to the games on Sundays. They were tailgating. They had their green and their gold, their colors, and they talked about the players as if they were part of their own family. They talked about Wee Willie Wood and Bart Starr and Ray Nitschke and **Paul Hornung** and Jimmy Taylor—the offensive line, the defensive line. It became a very personal thing, and they had a personal interest in the game.

During that period of time, in the sixties, even with the emergence of the Packers, television was still a relatively new phenomenon, and Ray Scott was the broadcaster. My recollection is very spotty at times, but I think Ray Scott did the whole game by himself. There wasn't tape. There wasn't a booth. There wasn't a color analyst, instant replay or slo-mo. Ray Scott had a great knack for explaining the game. The picture was there. He just gave down and distance, and what might happen. There were silent periods in between. There was only one game—the Packer game. There weren't multiple channels, there wasn't cable, there wasn't the afternoon game at four, or the Sunday night game, no Thursday game—just the *one* game. So we'd crowd around that television to be able to watch that game. God forbid, if you were so lucky as to have tickets—to actually go and see it would be amazing. The broadcast was brought to you by Hamm's. I can remember that "sky-blue water."

All that is part of my memories of being a Packer fan and seeing it evolve. The other thing, from my point of view, is that I was born and raised in a bar—our apartment was above the bar. This was very important because it was a constant. When you're in a bar, what do

> **The Super Bowl was not called the Super Bowl for its first three years. It was called the World Championship of Professional Football.**

> **At Notre Dame, 1956 Heisman Trophy winner Paul Hornung played halfback, fullback, and quarterback; punted, kicked-off, kicked field goals; ran back punts and kickoffs; and was a starting safety.**

you talk about? You talk about sports. There were always people there to talk about the Packers and/or the high-school teams and/or college teams. My life was kind of constantly involved with sports— like you might not get in a normal household. If you're working, cleaning tables in the bar, or helping dad take the beer bottles out, or stocking the refrigerator, you're just there. The older you got, you started talking to people about the Packers. To this day, my nephews are avid Packer fans. Their parents may live in California...but they're Packer fans. The older ones live back in Appleton, and the youngest of my immediate family are going to the University of Wisconsin. Their folks live in California. It's still kind of inbred. I was talking to my mom and she had just gotten a call from her grandson, "Jeremy's on his way to the game," or "Jeremy's ensconced in front of the television." Jeremy's thirty-something years old. It has an ongoing effect...and it passes on. If you run into those Packer fans, it's still there.

Before Lombardi, I don't think people were as die-hard a fan. What Lombardi brought was winning. What he brought was a whole philosophy. What he brought was "old school." And, he became an icon in the community. To this day, he's still being quoted. His players became larger than life because of him. The stories that evolved out of communities become legendary.

Winning covers a multitude of sins. No matter what one may do, as long as you bring a winning program, then you start building on a winning program...a winning program over a decade—1960 through '69. And now, to bring it back with Favre has been great. We were kind of lulled in between with some changes, and then the Packers came back in full force. Winning becomes the important thing.

The Braves won the World Series in 1957 with Adcock, Eddie Matthews, Warren Spahn, Lew Burdette. Baseball was baseball. In Appleton, as well as Green Bay, we had our minor league teams, the Appleton Foxes, associated way back then with the Washington Senators, which became Minnesota. Then, Green Bay had a minor league team with the Dodgers. Baseball had its place here. If you go back, *Sports Illustrated* had an article, written in the 80s, about Fox Valley, about its sports, and how it is really a melting pot for American sports, from softball leagues to baseball leagues, ice fishing to basketball and football, bowling leagues to ten pin leagues. Wisconsin people are very outdoorsy. They've got the lakes. Deer hunting is very important. Fishing is important, and ice fishing is something that takes place every year. Snowmobiling evolved as they were created. There was delineation in sport. Baseball and then football—there wasn't a major overlapping of coverage so that it got all mixed up.

People followed the Braves. I can remember sitting on my grandfather's porch as a kid and listening to the Braves game every night on the radio. We'd drop by for a visit. He'd sit out there and smoke his pipe. That just doesn't happen as much today.

As kids, when we played football in our yards, sports wasn't marketed daily in our lives as it is today. We just played. You weren't anybody except who you were. I don't remember hearing about the university teams or their players. You heard about the Braves because they were winning. I remember going to one of the '57 World Series games with my dad.

I really do think the media today, the exposure today, and the marketing today of apparel and brand names has evolved to such a degree that parents inundate their kids, or at least the kids see it on television because they watch so many hours of television every day. That becomes a whole driving market kind of thing that didn't exist 40 years ago.

Mom and Dad had Packer tickets, but they had to work so they didn't always get to go to games. When they did go, somebody would cover the bar for them, but they would have to come right back so they could work. I can't remember my first Packer game, but I do remember *some* Packer games. Sometimes, when you are a player, you're not necessarily a fan. You may appreciate the game, but you're more involved in your own life. Given that, in high school, I was more concerned about the Xavier Hawks and how we were doing. You're playing freshman ball or playing **varsity** ball or trying to make the JV team or whatever, and then you're involved in school. All the

> **The word "varsity" is the British short form of the word "university."**

other stuff was there, but was not shoved down your throat like it is today. **Soccer** didn't exist.

When you go to college, you're still removed. You're playing Saturday games, and you have meetings on Sunday, and you have to study on Sunday. You might watch some games, but you're not really involved. You like to see the Packers win over the Bears. You watch those games. You see the Thanksgiving Day game. You see the Detroit-Packers game way back when.

I can remember thinking, and this wasn't until my junior year in college, "Could I possibly play in the NFL?" We won the national championship at Notre Dame. Winning the national championship in college only gave me a more secure position of thinking, "Maybe I can play in the pros." So I did start thinking about it then.

I went to a game and saw the Pittsburgh Steelers—what an omen. I watched the Packers play the Steelers. I would look at the roster to see if anybody was my size. I've never told anybody this, but I wanted to see if there was anybody 5'10" and 190 pounds who was playing in the pros that might give me a hope for a chance. The Steelers had a guy by the name of Jim "Cannonball" Butler, who was about 5'9 and 190 pounds. So, I identified with Jim "Cannonball" Butler. The difference between us was that he had speed—I didn't.

Eventually, I went to the biggest game of all in Packer history, to that time, which was the 1967 Ice Bowl against the Dallas Cowboys. I was a senior in college. Part of that story is that I got hurt the second to last game my senior year and had an operation on my left knee and had to miss the last game. Now, I'm home for Christmas, and dad said, "Do you want to go to the Packer game on Sunday?" I had my leg in a portable cast, on crutches, but I said, "Okay." Now this was not in the time and the era of snowsuits, or of down, lightweight warm material. It was the time of the "layered" look. When we got up that morning, it was fifteen degrees below zero. We started getting

> **More U.S. kids today play soccer than any organized sport, including youth football. The reason so many kids play soccer is so they don't have to watch it.**

dressed. I took my cast off. I wrapped my knee with an Ace bandage. I put long johns on underneath. I put a turtleneck on top of that. I put two pairs of hunting socks on over my long johns. I put a pair of lined corduroys over my long johns and then put a hooded sweatshirt over my turtleneck. I put on a pair of hunting pants with the big straps on top of my corduroys. Then, I put a hunting jacket on top of the hooded sweatshirt, a pair of gloves, stocking cap pulled down, and that was just to get to the car. We drove up to Green Bay and I was still on crutches. We walked into the stadium and found our seats at quarter till one…kickoff was at one o'clock. In Lambeau Field, there are no seats—still benches to this day. We squeezed in and everybody had 50 pounds of clothing on so we were really crammed together.

At one o'clock, I wanted to leave—that's how cold I was. I had only been there for fifteen minutes. We sat there, of course, and watched the game, freezing as we may have been, watching the Packers play. The Cowboys had scored and taken the lead the last two minutes of the game. The Packers got the ball and started to move the ball downfield. The last thing I remember was a play when the Packers threw a flare pass to Chuck Mercein down the left side to about the forty-yard line. He went out-of-bounds to stop the clock. Dad said to me, "I think maybe we should leave. You're on crutches. It might be a good opportunity." I wasn't going to argue with him because I couldn't feel *anything* at that moment. We got out and walked down, me on my crutches, and as we're walking to the parking lot, all of a sudden we hear this ROAR take place and didn't know what had happened. We were trying to get into the car. Dad's hands were freezing, and the lock was frozen—he had to breathe on it. We finally got in the car and got the radio turned on, and learned the Packers had won the game…and were the champions…but I missed it.

Who knew that a year later, I would be with the Steelers?

Five years after that, we had the "Immaculate Reception." I was on the sidelines watching that evolve. It was kind of the same thing—clock ticking down toward the end of the game. On that last throw to Frenchy Fuqua down the field that Bradshaw threw, right before that, I turned away because I could not look…I could not watch us lose that game. So I missed the "Immaculate Reception!"

Two of the greatest plays in football history…I missed them. But, I was there…both times.…

In 1968, during my rookie year—the only time I played at Lambeau Field—we *got to play Green Bay in an exhibition game.* This was the season after the Ice Bowl. Ray Nitschke was playing defense and Dave Robinson was outside linebacker. All those names were there, but it's exhibition so they're not all playing, especially by the time *I* got in there. Dave Robinson was in at the time. It was in the third quarter, and the play that was called was a sweep around the right side. There were a couple of keys—one is the defensive end and how either the tackle or the tight end is blocking down on him, and whether he spins out or not—that was my key. As I was running in the backfield, looking for the hole—was it in or was it out? I didn't know anything else that was going on. I was running. I was looking. I saw the hole—and it's in. I turned up into the hole—and it's a big hole. It shouldn't have been a big hole, but there was a big hole. These were things that you learn. If there is a big hole, it is some-body's responsibility to *fill* that hole. When you don't know that, you just say, "Hey, there's a big hole. Let me turn up in there." So I did. I turned up into that big hole. As I turned up into that big hole, who stepped in front of me but Dave Robinson. Dave Robinson, at that time, was probably one of the largest human beings I'd ever met and played against as a linebacker. He was big…a big, strong guy. He stood in front of me, and all he did was flip a forearm into me. It was like running into the side of a building—BOOM! It knocked me on my butt. The film of it, as we were watching it the following week, showed that here I was running—I saw the hole—I ducked into the hole—all of a sudden, it was like, boom, I went into the line—then you lose me. It's not real clear, the film was shot from about the 50-yard line. That's all I'm telling. That was my introduction to the NFL. It was kind of a bittersweet first experience. I got a chance to play at Lambeau, to be on the field in an exhibition game, and to actually play. Coming back to Lambeau was, "Wow, this is where the Packers play." Just to be there and to walk on Lambeau Field. I was trying to make the team, and getting to come back there was good stuff.

We didn't play the Packers that often. In 1976, when we were the Super Bowl defending champions, we went back up to play Green

Bay. We played in Milwaukee where the Packers were playing part of their home games. It was a winter day, snow packed up about four or five feet on the sidelines, but sunny and nice. For me, personally, it was the best game I ever had. I carried the ball 36 times and gained 163 yards in that game. We won the game 13-7…not a high-powered game. I ran into Mike McCoy, who had played at Notre Dame, and who was now playing defensive tackle for the Packers, during the off-season. He said, "I don't know where you came from. The Steelers had no passing game, and you were running the ball, and all we had to do was stop Franco. If we stopped Franco, you weren't a threat." And stop Franco, they did. Everything I ran worked, for some reason—all the traps. Bradshaw continued to give me the ball. It was wonderful to be able to have that performance coming off the Super Bowl, at home in front of your family and relatives and every free-loader that knew you who wanted tickets to the game.

Experts tell you, "You feel the game the next day." Let me tell you—I felt the game right away, I didn't have to wait till the next day. They beat the crap out of me. I had a difficult time walking into the locker room after the game. My appreciation for Franco rose tremen-dously…and for every other running back who has ever carried the ball more than 15 times in a game, week-in and week-out. I don't know how they could do it. I was very pleased to go back to my role, carry the ball three times—four times, that's fine, I'll block. Just win, and I'll take the recognition for whatever happens. I don't want the ball. Those were my Packer experiences.

Afterwards, I realized that playing in an exhibition season is that they're trying to determine whether or not you can play in this league, or whether they're going to keep you. The amount of playing time doesn't reflect on either how good you are or not how good you are. It's a matter of experience of whether or not you can play. There was a period of time when I was the *leading* ground-gainer for the Steelers in the exhibition season in '72, '73 and '74. It finally dawned on me that it wasn't because I was so good. How stupid can you be? Leading in the exhibition season!…

Fuzzy Thurston, who played left guard for the Packers, had a restau-rant in Neenah called the Left Guard. Ultimately, as we started to win, he expanded and built a bigger restaurant in Appleton, a big night-club called the Left Guard. It was a popular joint with all these pictures of the Packers. It was like any sports bar today, but it was really big then because it was the Packers, and they were winning…and it wasn't as if you were in New York City, you were in Appleton. And the Packers would come to it—that was even better. This would have been just after my senior year, but before I was drafted.

We went out to dinner and were sitting at the table with my girlfriend along with her sister and her husband and family. We were having dinner and some wine or cocktails. Donny Anderson was at the bar. Now, I'm a big deal because I played on a National Championship team, and I'm kind of part of the family so Helen, my girlfriend's sister, got up and went over to Donny and said, "Donny, why don't you come and join us?" He did. He walked over. He's a very affable guy, a good guy. I didn't know him then as I do today. He came over and did his PR and fan appreciation, and then sat down and had a drink. I was sitting at the other end of the table. They introduced me to him and mentioned that I had just played at Notre Dame and we had won the national championship. I had on a national championship ring. Donny said, "Oh, that's wonderful. But, he doesn't have one of these." And he showed us his Super Bowl ring. Later on, after we won our fourth Super Bowl, I reminded him of that story. "Look, Donny, I don't have one—I've got FOUR." The Packer players were a big deal, and they were in the community, and they were approachable.…

My mom said, "I don't know how we did this, but we would drive down to Notre Dame, about five hours, go to the game, go out to dinner afterward, then get back in the car and drive back to Appleton." The next day, on Sunday, they would then get up and go to the Packers game. I said, "It's called being young." Probably, on Saturday, they would leave around six in the morning and get down to South Bend about eleven o'clock. I'd see them briefly before the game. They'd tailgate with some friends. After the game, we might go out for a bite after the game. By six or seven, they were in the car driving back home and would get there around midnight. Then, get up the next morning and head out to the afternoon Packer game—true fans.

The first time I ever met a Packer player, Ron Kostelnik, was at a father-son breakfast. I was in high school. My dad and I got all dressed up and he took me. Ron Kostelnik was the Packer speaker. Dad and I went up and introduced ourselves and said "hi" to him. It was my first opportunity to meet a professional player. I think back now these many years of how important it was just to be able to say that I'd met that person. Sometimes today, we become overexposed. In subsequent times, I got a chance to meet other players at sports functions or banquets. We have a tendency to forget how important that is to the impact of the community…of getting out and being part of that community. In today's society, players are making so much money, and they wouldn't think about going to a father-son breakfast. They might have paid Ron $25, which was big money then, to do it…or not. That memory of meeting him has stayed with me all these years.

When I'm out at events, I do think about that. You never know when you're going to influence somebody—because somebody influenced you. Somebody told a story about **Mickey Mantle**, and there are many stories about him, about a kid who was waiting and waiting and waiting for Mickey to come out after a game. Finally, Mickey came out. There was only the kid there, and the kid went up to him and asked for an autograph. Mickey said, "—— you, kid." Think of how many times over many years the fan has told this story. One negative can affect somebody's life, as it did that kid, to the point he talked about it all his life. You never know how important it is to be nice to somebody, to take the time. What happens today is that people become so proprietary about their autograph and won't sign anything. Now, I'm not making my living off my autograph—some people do, and I understand that. But the majority of guys don't. You've got something else. As a player, there is a responsibility. Any time you're out in public, it really reflects on who you are, but also on the League, and on the other players, and the impact you have on people.

Sadly, I'd have to say I'm no longer a Packer fan at heart. I've been too far gone and brainwashed. I'm a Steeler. I'm a Steeler fan. You do believe me, don't you?

> **Between walks and strikeouts, Mickey Mantle went the equivalent of seven full seasons without putting the bat on the ball.**

MY ONE-HANDED CATCH FROM FAVRE WON THE SUPER BOWL. PLAY ALONG, OKAY?

DENNY MATTHEWS

*Denny Matthews has been a radio announcer with the **Kansas City Royals** since the club's first season, 1969. Matthews also has worked games for the CBS Radio Network. He is one of a few broadcasters in baseball that has broadcast exclusively for the same team, without interruption, in five different decades. Matthews was the lone induction into the Royals Hall of Fame in 2004. Matthews, a graduate of Illinois Wesleyan, lettered in baseball and football for three years. Even though he didn't intend to play football, in college he once finished eighth in the nation in the NAIA for pass receiving. Despite growing up in the Bloomington/Normal area of Illinois, Matthews somehow became a Packers fan. That allegiance still runs deep today.*

I've been to quite a few fantasy camps during my lifetime. I've skated with the Boston Bruins. I worked out with Hall of Fame quarterback Len Dawson during two or three summers to help him prepare for the upcoming season. During the 1970s, I played in exhibition games with the Kansas City Royals...but, I'll never forget working out with the Green Bay Packers.

I grew up in central Illinois, where most people were Chicago Bears fans. The Packers aren't that far away, though. A buddy of mine, Jim Bennett, who lived in the same neighborhood, and I started rooting for

In the 1979 Major League baseball draft, the Kansas City Royals drafted Dan Marino in the 4the round and John Elway in the 18th round.... Also, in the same year, the Royals hired a Missourian for their Group Sales Department. He left five years later for a job in the radio business. Say hello to Rush Limbaugh.

the Packers. They weren't very good when we started watching them, and then Vince Lombardi got there and they became really good.

During my first year of playing football at Illinois Wesleyan, I finished near the top in pass receiving in the NAIA. The Dean of Students at Illinois Wesleyan was good friends with Norb Hecker, who was the defensive backfield coach for Lombardi. The two were talking and our dean told Hecker that I was a big Green Bay Packers fan. Since I had never played football before going to Wesleyan, he wondered if it would be possible for me to go to Green Bay the next summer and watch a few practices. Norb said he didn't see any problem with it. He called back a few days later and said, "In regards to Denny coming up here to watch our practices, I'll go you one better. Tell him to bring his shoes, some sweatpants and a jersey or something, and he can work out."

My buddy and I drove up to Green Bay in August, 1964. We took a still camera and a movie camera. We stayed at the YMCA in downtown Green Bay. The next day, we got up and drove over to Lambeau. At the time, they had two or three nice practice fields across the street from Lambeau Field. We sat and watched, and my friend, Jim, ran movies of some of the regular practice. The regular practice was over around 11 a.m. The special teams guys stayed out and did extra work; that's when I worked out for 45 minutes to an hour all three days we were there.

Tom Fears, who was a great end in the National Football League, was the Packers' receivers coach. He basically was the guy that was offering me various pointers. Zeke Bratkowski was the back-up quarterback to Bart Starr, and the number-three quarterback was Dennis Claridge, who had played at **Nebraska**. I caught a few passes from Bratkowski, but I caught most of them from Claridge. One of their receivers, **Bob Long**, who was more of a track guy out of Wichita

> **Academic All-American teams have been picked every year since 1952. Nebraska leads all colleges by a wide margin in number of players selected.**

> **Bob Long was the only ex-Packer to play for Lombardi with the Redskins.**

State, was in his first year with Green Bay. He ran some patterns. He was a tall, lanky guy with very good speed. Boyd Dowler and Max McGee each ran a few patterns. They didn't stay out as long as the younger guys, but it was a great experience being out there with them.

One of those days, around two in the afternoon, Jim and I didn't have much to do, so we decided to go out to Lambeau and play some catch with a football we brought. We went into the Packers offices and talked to a few people, including Red Cochran, who was the team's head scout. After we talked to him for awhile, we said we were going to go out and play catch. He just said: "Great, have fun." (Imagine trying to do that today.) So, we walked out onto the field at Lambeau, on a nice, warm, August afternoon, without anybody around, and played catch. We did that for about 45 minutes, until we got tired and left.

During the three days, the Packer players were very professional toward me. They didn't give me a hard time about being there, or anything. Just very classy. On the third day, my last day there, Tom Fears took me into Vince Lombardi's office to introduce me and say hello. I was petrified. When we walked into Lombardi's office, he was sitting behind his desk, and Fears introduced me. Lombardi stood up, shook hands with me, and with that trademark grin that he had, said: "Dennis, it's nice having you up here. I hope you enjoyed the experience. When you play football, remember two things, the only two things I'm going to tell you—work hard and have fun because it's very short." I told him how being there was a thrill of my life. He just said: "Glad to do it. I hope you can apply it to your season." That was it. I couldn't get out of there quickly enough from being awe-struck. Good grief. Think about that. It was probably only about 20 seconds out of Vince Lombardi's day, but that's something that has stuck with me throughout my life.

It was a very cool experience. You can talk about baseball fantasy camps, which are popular these days, but those three days were my fantasy camp. To this day, I'm still a die-hard Packers fan. After those three days in 1964, how could I not be.

HE WAS ONE OF THE BEST OFFICIALS IN THE COUNTRY. THE COUNTRY WAS MONGOLIA.

BILL QUINBY

Bill Quinby, 72, Cedar Rapids, Iowa, was one of the most respected officials in the NFL until his retirement in 2002. He worked the NFL for 17 seasons and the Big Ten for 13 years. His last six years as an NFL official were spent as an observer at all Green Bay home games. Cedar Rapids is a bigger city than Green Bay.

A s an official, going to Green Bay was special. You knew of the history—especially of the Vince Lombardi and Bart Starr history of many years ago. And going way back, the Packers were one of the original NFL teams. Any new official in the league, when he was assigned his first game at Green Bay, looked forward to seeing the stadium. They've remodeled the stadium in the last three years, but the stadium that was all green with the yellow or gold letters on it gave you the feeling that you were really in the big leagues there. It was different than going to New York City or a city where you officiated a football game in a baseball stadium, such as Cleveland or Shea Stadium when the Jets played there. Another stadium I always enjoyed going to was the Coliseum in Los Angeles because of the history.

The fans are definitely different in Green Bay. They're down-to-earth. They're pretty much home-town, home-state people. You get into the bigger cities, they're still home-town, like Philadelphia, St. Louis or Dallas, but Green Bay people who attend these games are stockholders of the team. They feel an ownership, a loyalty that probably no other team in the National Football League has. A lot of the teams are now owned by big wealthy people or corporate-type people. But Green Bay still has that home-cooked feeling that "This is my team. I help buy stock here. I live here in Wisconsin."

I remember a 10-10 tie game with the Vikings in 1978, my first year in the NFL. We went overtime and didn't break the tie. Fran Tarkenton was the quarterback for the Vikings. Neither team could score a field goal or safety or touchdown in the overtime so it ended all tied up. There aren't too many ties in the NFL history, maybe 10 or 15.

Bart Starr was one of the finest coaches to work with. He was a gentleman. During his years, he didn't have that great a winning season, but you always knew, when you worked a Packer game—home or away—Bart Starr kept his composure. He'd maybe question you if you were the official on the sideline, but he was very good. Bart Starr stands out being the Packer hero and a class act.

I was assigned to their pre-season camp for three days one year when Bart was coach. The officials stayed in a motel right by their practice field, but the team stayed at the dorms at St. Norbert's College, and they ate out there. One of the evenings, Bart said, "Why don't you guys come on out and have dinner with the coaches? We have our wives tonight." It was a Saturday night after a scrimmage. Everybody was worn out. I remember he allowed a glass of wine at the table. We ate in a private room. He was just down-to-earth.

There's not a lot of conversation on the field between the players and officials. You talk with them if there's a little bit of breaking up to do. If you can see something boiling between some player and his opponent, the official will go in and say, "Let's knock it off." They respect you pretty much most of the time. They do get angry at you when they think you're wrong, or when they were penalized and didn't think they should have been. You really don't have a lot of personal chat with them. It sometimes depends on what time of the game it is. Maybe if they're winning at the end, there might be a little bit more conversation going on—friendliness and that sort of thing.

Brett Favre is one player who talks with the officials, and talks with other players, and most of it is just down-to-earth, "Good football game. Let's have fun at it." I've gotten to know Brett pretty well. When I'd be there observing in the stadium before it was remodeled three years ago, the officials' locker room was within ten—twelve yards from the Packer locker room. I used to have the privilege, as an observer, of going into the equipment room. Sometimes, we'd need to get warmer gear for the officials or maybe hot pads for the hands or feet to keep warm. Brett would always speak to you. He'd call me "Mr. Ref," even though I wasn't officiating then, because he knew I used to do that.

As an observer, I would sit in the press box, on the 50-yard line, right in front of Lee Remmel. Lee sits right behind the observer in the next row. His staff are all to his right or left. The observer always was responsible if Lee asked, "What happened?" or, "Can you get an interpretation?" We would always get that interpretation so Lee could give it to the press. When I go up there, he'll be very kind to me and welcome me back. Lee has seen almost every Packer game in the last 55 years.

The officials always stayed in one of the hotels there, and a lot of the Packer fan clubs came into that hotel from all over the country. There are about 200 per game, and they get in about noon hour on Saturday. They come to the hotel and there's a welcoming table with T-shirts, game programs and their itinerary. That evening they might have a beer party, then a picnic-type lunch at the hotel, and then on Sunday morning, school buses would come in and take them over to the stadium about 9 a.m. After the game, they would bring them back to the hotel where they'd party after the game. They never knew we were refs.

There's a Green Bay-hometown fan and there's a Green Bay-Milwaukee fan. The Milwaukee package has two home games. The police have said that when the Milwaukee fan has the ticket for the game, there is a little more confusion because they don't know the streets as well since they only get to come in twice a year. There was always a little more control needed for these fans. This crowd would come in and party in a little different way from the regular fan.

I'm nothing in the football world, but I've had the wonderful experience of being an official in the league. Also, in that six years of being an observer at Green Bay, I made a lot of warm friends there. I worked my first pro football game in Green Bay in 1978. The last game I officially worked for the NFL as an observer was at Green Bay. I started and finished there…and didn't get fired!

NICE WOMEN FINISH FIRST

MARY DUROCHER

Mary Durocher and her husband are retired and live in Peshtigo, Wisconsin. Peshtigo is famous for being destroyed by a fire the same year as the Chicago fire. She is a former employee of the Green Bay Packers. She has four sons and nine grandchildren.

I started working for the Packers in 1963. I only managed to stay for three years because of my children. When I went to work there, Vince Lombardi was the coach and general manager. I wasn't a real Packer fan before I got the job. My husband was a true fan—he had his name on the ticket list ever since he was a sophomore in high school—but I never really paid attention to them.

I saw an ad in the paper one day and it didn't say who it was for. The ad was for a keypunch operator, which today would be a computer operator. When I went for the interview, I found out it was for the Packers. My husband was quite excited about me getting that job! I got hired, and went to work for the team. My job was entering in the information from the scouts. They would bring in all the information they could get about a prospective college player and I would enter it into the computer. I remember Vince Lombardi being so excited about the system, because they had just gotten it when I got there. They had also purchased a sorter, which would take the IBM cards and sort them into any way you wanted it to. The coach would come in to my office and say, "Mary, can you get me a list of all the linebackers who are over six feet-five and weigh over two hundred pounds." In a little while, I'd hand him the printout and he'd just be so excited. He'd really be amazed today.

I still remember my first day on the job. Coach Lombardi came in and asked me to type up his itinerary. I can't remember how many copies he asked for, but he gave me the list of names he wanted the schedule given to, and his mother and father were on the list. I laughed and said something like, "Oh sure," because I thought he was kidding. He said, "No, it's true. My parents are elderly and I like them to know where I am all the time." I thought that was really nice.

The coach came across like a real rough and tough person, but he was so sensitive to others. He was a very gentle person. One day I called home and my oldest son answered the phone. I asked him where the baby-sitter was. My son said she was sleeping on the couch. I told him to wake her up. When she got on the phone, I told her what I thought of her sleeping on the job. When I hung up the phone, I was so upset that I started crying. Coach Lombardi saw me and called me into his office. He asked me what was wrong and I told him the whole story. He said, "Get your coat on and go home, and don't come back until you've got a good baby-sitter." He was so nice and so family-oriented.

One of the things he insisted on was Thanksgiving dinner at the Elks Club. You didn't have a choice about going to that. He considered the Packers his family, and he wanted us all together at Thanksgiving. Since this was the time before VCR's, Vince would have someone upstairs running a projector to show the kids movies or cartoons. All of our children would be taken up there. They'd have popcorn and snacks while they watched movies. The adults would stay downstairs and enjoy cocktail hour. After a while, he'd send someone up to get the kids and they'd come downstairs and we'd all have our dinner together.

One year, he had two of my sons, one in each arm, and he walked over to Bart Starr and said, "These are Mary's boys!" It was just like they were his own family. He just made you feel like part of the family. The dinners were so much fun. You had interaction with the players at the office, and you'd see them at the games, but the Thanksgiving dinner was the one time you really got to be with the players and coaches on more of a one-on-one. It was so much fun, and it was something you looked forward to all year. You just felt like part of the family.

Some of my favorites to be around were: Bart Starr, Jerry Kramer, Fuzzy Thurston, Herb Adderley, Elijah Pitts, Willie Davis, and Dave Robinson. Paul Hornung was kind of egotistical, but he was fun to be around too. Max McGee was fun. Henry Jordan and Ray Nitschke were really down-to-earth guys. Ray was my idea of a real family man.

When I worked there, they didn't have the **draft** like they do now. They used to go around from city to city for the draft. That first year that I worked there, Coach Lombardi came up to me and asked if I'd ever been to **Dallas**. I told him I'd never been out of Wisconsin. He asked if I'd like to go to the draft in Dallas. I said, "Oh sure!" A few days later he came up and asked if I'd like to take my husband with me. Again, I said, "Yes," because I'd never even been on an airplane before and I liked the idea of my husband being there with me. Well, a few days later he came up to me and put his arm around me and said, "I hate to do this, but my secretary is very upset with me for asking you to go. She's been here twenty years and has never gotten to go. She said she could do the things you were going to be doing, and I think I'd better let her go. Don't be upset though, someday I'll get to take you and your husband." He didn't have to do that, but that's the kind of man he was.

That's the man I got to know. But I also got to know the Vince Lombardi who yelled and screamed when things didn't go right. My office was right next to the assistant coaches, so I learned when to tread lightly. When he was on their cases for something, or when one of the players got called into his office, I knew to stay low. He was a real motivator.

One day, he came into my office and he was making small talk. Finally, he said, "Damn it, Mary, my wife is making me do this. I don't want to offend you but our oldest daughter has a beautiful coat that she's outgrown and Marie says she thinks it would fit you. Would

> **During WWII, the NFL did not refer to the teams' selections of college players as a draft. It was termed the "preferred negotiation list."**

> **When the Dallas Cowboy Cheerleaders started in 1972, each earned $15 per game-the same amount they receive today.**

you be offended if I offered you that coat?" Here we were just starting out with two small children, and I wasn't about to be offended. They ended up giving me a lot of their daughter's clothes. Coach Lombardi's wife was so good to us girls in the office. She always made sure we got really nice Christmas presents and always looked out for us. They just made you feel like family.

I worked year-round, not just when the season was going on. The offices weren't all that nice. I shouldn't say they weren't nice, but they weren't luxurious by any means. Coach Lombardi's office was very nice, it was all done in cherry wood and it had a nice desk and bookcases. They had a meeting room right off his office. The assistant coaches shared a great big room, and they each had a desk. My office was just a regular office. The other girls didn't have anything spectacular.

I remember putting in a lot of information on Boomer Esiason when he was in college, but, of course, we didn't get him. At the time that I worked there, Pat Pepler was the head of the scouting department and he was very good. Tom Miller was the personnel director and then Chuck Lane came in right before I left when Tom Miller retired.

They let me come back after I left the job. On a few occasions, I asked if I could take my boys over there to have their birthday parties. They always said yes, and I got to take the boys there, and they'd get to tour the place and play in the locker room. It was really fun for them.

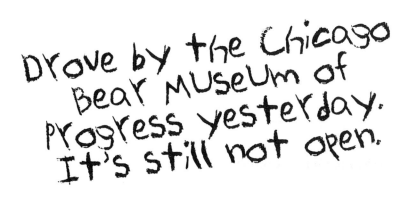

Drove by the Chicago Bear Museum of Progress yesterday. It's still not open.

WHEN THE OLD PACKERS GOT ALL THE WAY UP TO BROKE, THEY WANTED TO THROW A PARTY.

JIM JOANNES

Jim Joannes, 53, is a successful lawyer in Green Bay. His grandfather, Lee Joannes, was, at one time, both the savior of the franchise and the president of the Packers.

In 1917-18, my grandfather went to the University of Pennsylvania for college and got interested in football. But then, he went to World War I. When he came back, the bug just bit him. He played football in college but was not good enough to play pro ball. He came back to Green Bay where his father had a wholesale grocery business that was quite successful. He was able to get involved with the Packers. The Packers went broke three times over the years. The second time, my grandfather was able to go out and sell shares of stock and do fundraising for them. He was really excited about the team and enjoyed being around the players and coaches and watching a fellow like Curly Lambeau lead the team. When he was the president from 1930 to 1947, my grandmother was the secretary-treasurer. The hat used to be passed to take in money. The big game of the year was always the Bear game where they collected about $5,000. That was the big game. The small games were a lot less. You can see that everything was done on a shoestring during those days.

When I was young, there was a section for kids in the northeast corner of the end zone. Those tickets were one dollar. The kids would be sent to the end zone so their parents could enjoy the game. Because of my grandfather's involvement in the team over the years, I was lucky enough to get to go into the Packer locker room. I've seen all the Packer greats, but I really don't remember them as much as I remember they had a pool table just off the locker room. I wanted to grow up and be like Willie Wood because he was the best billiard player I'd ever seen.

My grandfather lived until 1982, and died at the age of 91. In the sixties, we would go in and shake hands with Vince Lombardi or say hi to Bart Starr or Paul Hornung or Max McGee, which was certainly a thrill but it wasn't out of the ordinary. My grandfather would walk through the locker room quite often....

Bob Harlan has done a great job and has been instrumental in getting some key people in, but Bob also knows football. It's not like he lucked out. It's hard work and perseverance on his behalf because he's been with the organization for close to thirty years now. I think the people of Brown County stepped up when they voted for the half percent sales tax, which would be charged to them for the next 16 years on virtually everything they bought in Green Bay. We had asked other surrounding counties to help us, but they said no. The Milwaukee Brewers have just faced a debacle down at their Miller Park Stadium where they received money from both the state and from a tax on surrounding communities. It was very tough at the time Bob Harlan wanted to get this sales tax through for him to do it. You've got to give him a lot of credit. People don't realize that Bob is such a goodwill ambassador for the team. When he's in his office, and he wants to take a break, he'll go down to the atrium and meet people. It's almost unheard of that a CEO would just go down and greet guests as they're coming into your store...Lee Remmel remembers every possible Packer fact known to man. He's not afraid to give his opinion on anything either. He's not just the "Green-Bay voice" so if he sees a problem, he lets people know about it. He has a great command of the English language and vocabulary. Give him credit...We weren't too fond of Ron Wolf to begin with, and then he traded away a first-round draft choice for a guy who, when he came out and threw the ball, he usually threw it thirty-feet over the receiver's head...and, too often, throwing it into someone else's arms. We thought Wolf was crazy, but what turned out to be crazy is probably one of the great trades of all time for the Packers.

Now, we have salaries around $70 million, and TV contracts are about the same or a little more. I'm sure that when my grandfather was running the team in those early years in the early thirties, they probably took in $15,000 a *year*. You didn't need a bank because at the end of the game, you'd pay the ballplayers their $30 or $40 for playing. The players all worked a full-time job then...they came to practice after work, and then they played on Sunday…with little or no equipment. There's no comparison to today. For my grandfather, being an officer or a director of the Packers was a gratuitous job. You didn't take any money—as a matter of fact, you usually pitched in money! He, along with his two brothers, was an owner of Joannes Wholesale Grocers. It was not uncommon for him to dip into his pocket at the end of the game to make sure the players got paid. In games where the pots were small, the players still had to get their money. They should have played the Bears every week, and they'd have probably done okay, but they didn't play them every week.

Then, there was a situation where there was a lady who fell while in the stands. Part of the bleachers broke, and there was a lawyer in town who sued the Packers. My grandfather had to come up with $5,000, which was a lot of money back then, to pay off the lady so the Packers could continue playing. Otherwise, they would have had to go into bankruptcy.

My grandfather used to lend a few hundred bucks to George Halas. Then, Halas would lend a few hundred dollars back to the Packers so that the team could keep going. You had teams in the league that were in small towns, and unfortunately they just didn't make it. Green Bay was the lucky one. I can remember him telling me stories about Curley Lambeau, who thought he was a Hollywood star…about George Halas who was probably the kindest man my grandfather ever met, as far as lending money and things like that. So on the inside, George was the nice, kind guy—but on the outside, he was just mean as nails.…

Vince Lombardi was one of those guys who was a workaholic. He worked day and night. You see that in a lot of the NFL coaches today. Right out of that same mold was Ron Wolf. People wondered some days if he had died in his office because his car never left the parking lot. When they'd get there in the morning, his car would be there. When they'd leave at night, his car would be there. They wondered if he ever went home.

We are very, very lucky to have the Green Bay Packers. They bring business to our community. It certainly brings recognition to the community. Even for me, in business, it gives me a leg up, when people know I'm from Green Bay. They treat you a little nicer.

DO YOU KNOW HOW PEOPLE IN WISCONSIN KEEP BEARS OUT OF THEIR YARDS? THEY INSTALL GOAL POSTS

PAUL MAZZOLENI

Paul Mazzoleni, 45, lives in Arlington Heights, Illinois. He is the Chief Financial Officer for a contracting firm in the Chicagoland area. He is the son of Palmyro Mazzoleni, a legend in Green Bay fan lore.

Palmyro "Paul" Mazzoleni

My dad was a small businessman his whole life. He owned a Standard Oil service station in Green Bay. He was a tremendous Packer fan from the time he moved to Green Bay in 1921 from St. Louis. Back then, it was just a club team, and about a half dozen players lived in his neighborhood. When practice came around, as a boy, he would go hang around and watch the practice. One day, one of the players saw him standing there and said, "Hey, why don't you run home and get us some water?" So he ran home, got a bucket of water and a ladle, and took it back to the players. From that point forward, for the next two years, he was the official water boy to the Green Bay Packers. Unfortunately, a couple of years later they moved their practice across town. He was more than willing to ride his bike across town, but his mother didn't like the idea of her 11-year old son doing that or missing school to be a water boy, so his days with the Packers came to an end.

There was the referendum to decide about moving from the East Side to what is now Lambeau Field. My dad joined in with other businessmen from all over Green Bay to work together to get this approved. The move was successful and they moved to what is now Lambeau

Field in 1957. He bought his season tickets, he bought shares of stock, and he just always supported the team. He always managed to do whatever he could to get people tickets. He had a wide group of people who came into his station. People knew that if they needed tickets he could get them for him, and if a person had tickets to get rid of they could count on him. He really prided himself on the fact that, through all those years, he never once scalped a ticket. He always sold it for face value, and in the lean years that wasn't always easy. I'm sure during the 60's he never had any problems, but there were other years that were a little tougher.

I remember coming home from college unannounced in the late 70's and asked Dad if he had any tickets. I was in college and decided I wanted to go to a game, and knew that dad would be able to take care of me. When I asked him, he reached into his coat pocket and pulled out a wad of tickets big enough to choke a horse and asked, "Which ones do you want?" Of course that was during the down years, so supply was a lot bigger than demand.

He'll be 91 on September 1st, and he's living in a nursing home now. Actually though, at this stage of his life, he's going to more games than he did when he was in his 70s. At that time, he was very content to watch the game in front of his fireplace in the comfort of his own home. This past year, my brother and I made the effort to take him to as many games as possible. He's in a wheelchair now, so we have to have special seats. We took him to a couple of games last year…we took him to this year's season opener. At 91, we realize time is important, and any game we can get him to would be great, and the sooner the better.

My father wasn't a personal friend of Vince Lombardi, but he certainly had a friendly relationship with him. That developed out of chance when Lombardi moved to the area in the late 50's. Lombardi was an Italian man, and my father was obviously Italian. Lombardi needed some work done on his car. And since my dad had the station, he helped him out and they became friendly on a business level after that.

I can remember as a boy, the early part of my life, the Packers were the dominant team in the NFL. My dad always had lots of Packer paraphernalia around the house. He would get those official "Duke" NFL footballs. In those days, they didn't have the three-sided white footballs for autographs; they just had the regular footballs that were signed by these championship teams. We didn't know any better, so my two older brothers and I would play with those footballs out on the road. Here they were, autographed by all the members of those championship teams and we're playing out in the street with them. I found one a few years ago, and you can see that there were signatures on them, but you can't make any of them out.

I'm a tremendous Packer fan, as are both of my brothers, and it's all because of our father. He was always involved in the local community, such as the Optimist Club. He sold Packer Yearbooks to raise money for the Optimist Club. As young boys, we all took our turns selling those yearbooks at Packer practices. I can remember it like it was yesterday, Ray Nitschke coming off the field after practice and putting that giant helmet of his on my head. Boy, did it stink!

After my dad retired, he'd go hang around the Packer front office and get stickers and decals from them, then go to the local grade school and give the stuff away to the kids there. He was just a tremendous guy.

I ran into a Vikings fan yesterday. Then I backed up and ran into him again.

THE DOS AND DON'TS OF BEING A PACKER FAN—DO

BEATRICE FROELICH

Bea Froelich lives in Green Bay, right across from Lambeau Field, just two blocks from where she grew up.

When I was a kid, we parked cars down at the old stadium. At half-time or the third quarter you could go inside the stadium for free and stand and watch the game. That's when I really started being a fan. I was only ten years old.

My dad was in the Packer band. He started in 1949, and stayed in it until he retired in 1974. He wasn't in good health the last year and a half, but he stuck with it to get his twenty-five years in. He played trombone, and during the Ice Bowl game his trombone froze up. The band actually wanted to play that day, but it was just too cold so they quit. They came out with a big print of The Packer Band a few years ago. My daughter looked everywhere for print number 1,949. The merchant she talked to couldn't understand why she wanted that number, since most people want low numbers. She explained that it was the year her grandfather joined the band. He had to look everywhere, but he finally found that number. She gave it to me, and I love it!

I've had season tickets since 1958. That was even before I was married. I went to the stadium with my boyfriend, who is now my husband, and got to pick out which seats we wanted. After we were married and our kids turned eight years old, they could get student tickets for two dollars. All three of my kids went to the games starting at eight, and then when the kids turned sixteen, they had to turn in the student tickets for adult ones. Way back when they were starting a waiting list for tickets, we thought it might be a good idea to get four tickets together. We finally got them, so now all of our kids have tickets too.

My two favorite players of all time were Ray Nitschke and Tony Canadeo. I didn't really see Tony play that much, but he used to come in to my father's hardware store, so that's how I got to know him. One year, my son only wanted one autograph, and it was Tony's. I hated to impose, but I knew where he lived, so I took my son out there. Tony didn't even know me, but he invited us in to his house and my son got his autograph. I thought that was really nice.

Ray Nitschke's wife was on my bowling team, and he took the time to get his picture taken with one of my sons. He was a really nice guy off the field. The players are more accessible here than in other towns. One of my sons has pictures with a lot of the players. One time, my two young grandsons, probably four and five years old at the time, went to Brett Favre's TV show. They had a little rubber football with them, and for about five minutes Brett Favre was out there playing catch with these two boys. I had my camera, snapping pictures left and right, and I know they'll cherish those some day. They really treat the kids right.

When they were voting for the new stadium, Bob Harlan called me and asked if I would get up and do a speech in front of the crowd. I told him I couldn't talk in front of a crowd, but my grandson said he'd go with me. So my five grandkids and me were all up on the stage with Bob Harlan, trying to sway people to vote "yes" on the new stadium.

From my rocking chair, I can see the players going into the stadium. My grandkids go over there and carry the players' helmets, and of course I've got pictures of that.

Flush twice...it's a long way to Soldier Field.

BACK HOME AGAIN IN INDIANA... NEVER MIND.

BILL HAMMANN

Bill Hammann, 43, lives in Evansville, Wisconsin, twenty miles south of Madison, where he is an alderman. Hammann is originally from Superior, Wisconsin. He attended the University of Wisconsin-Madison.

When I was in college in 1982, the Brewers were in the World Series playing the Cardinals. We went to a game, and as I was walking around County Stadium, I noticed there was a Packers ticket office. I walked in, not thinking I could get tickets, and said, "Can I get Packer tickets?" She said, "We can sign you up on a waiting list." I signed up to be on the waiting list, and they gave me a 3 x 5 card with a number on it. The year before we got Brett Favre and some other good players, my number went from about a thousand on the wait list down to finally getting season tickets. That year was a bad, lean year. Then I was able to retain those tickets on the Gold Pack for one pre-season game and two home games.

We have done some tailgating. I consider the atmosphere completely different in the day games from the night games. For the most part, we park in a residential area and walk to the stadium. We like to go in early and watch the team practice. We go on in to the 50-yard line, first row, sit down and watch the players warm up and practice.

The last time the Packers played in County Stadium, the last game of the season, we were playing the Atlanta Falcons. A bunch of us decided we were going to rush the field and pull down the goalposts after the game. We weren't the only ones who had that idea. We were all down by the end zone ready to jump on the field. At the end of the game, the Packers were down on that end. If they kicked a field goal, they would tie the score. There were less than ten seconds left. We hiked the ball and we were going to do a quick pass play out to the side. So if we scored, we'd win. But if we didn't score, we'd kick a field goal. Favre scrambled—signature play of Brett Favre—around one end and dove for the touchdown. If he wouldn't have gotten the touchdown, the game would have been over, and we would have lost. We won the game when they kicked the extra point—and we rushed the field. It was pandemonium. We tore down the goalposts. We made the playoffs with that game—a memorable moment.

When I worked in Ohio, I used to go to **Bengals** games and Browns games when they played the Packers. While I was there, I bought Bengal season tickets one year because the Packers were going to play in Cincinnati. We had nice seats, and that year the Bengals, with Boomer Esiason, were quite good. At the stadium there, they had TV monitors all over the place underneath. Every section had a TV set. At the Browns game, the fans were just rude in general. And the old Municipal Stadium was just a dump. The Packers won that game, and it was a very subdued crowd.

I'm a part owner of the Packer team. I own a share of stock. Many people do. If you're going to own a share of the team, you're going to be a Packer fan because you're a part-owner. They don't screw around with that. They send out their income statement, just like any corporation would. You can see all their bottom line. It's cool to look at their profit-and-loss statement. The Packers are a not-for-profit corporation. In order for them to qualify for that, they have to pour a ton of their profits into all these charities all over the place. I don't live there, but I can see they pour so much back into the community.

Our seats used to be two from the top in the corner of the end zone. When they built on, our seats stayed the same, but we have rows of seats in back of us now. A lot of the same fans are there for every game we go to except for the two in front of us. I swear whoever owns those seats must sell them on eBay because there are different people there for every game.

> **The Bengals, owned by the Paul Brown family, were named after the Massillon (Ohio) High School Tigers, where Brown coached before he became head coach of Ohio State and the Cleveland Browns**

They've done this massive renovation of the stadium. But nothing's changed for me. We spent $1200 a seat for the personal seat license. I still sit on the same old metal bench in the same location. The renovation was nice, and it's beautiful, but it did cost a lot of money for me. What did it buy me? A new stadium, I guess. The new seats they added are all chair-back, but for all of us old ticket holders, it's the same old bench. My ticket costs $50 a game. I was on the second row from the top before the renovation. Up three rows from me, they have the seats with the cup holders. They're $100 a game. They made the stadium into a legend. They added the Hall of Fame, and added other activities that reinforce that. They have black and white murals all around the whole stadium, and they're all old shots from the Packers' storied past. They really reinforce the fact that this team has been here a hundred years and has a storied history. When you walk in there, you think it's pure football, unlike when I saw the Riverfront Stadium for the first time. You walked in there and thought, "Sterile field." Right? You walk in Lambeau Field, you're thinking, "This is the NFL."

Bears' fans give it the old college try. They get drunk, pass out and say they'll finish it tomorrow.

HEAR ME NOW,
LISTEN TO ME LATER

I go to the Vince Lombardi Golf Classic every year, and take pictures of players golfing, and then go back the next year and try to get them to autograph their picture. I have a ball that is signed by Packers who played in Super Bowl I and Super Bowl II and I have footballs signed now by the present players. The players have been pretty receptive when I've gotten these signatures, but I do notice a difference between the older players versus the newer players. The older ones appreciate giving out autographs more than the younger ones do. Nowadays, they are after money. Ray Nitschke and Fuzzy Thurston were probably two of the nicest and easiest players to get autographs from. Ray Nitschke would sit down and just sign and sign and sign. Bart Starr likes to personalize everything now. He doesn't want to just sign something, "Bart Starr." He'll sign it, "To Mike, from Bart Starr."

———MIKE DICKERSON, 52, Ripon, Wisconsin

 In 1943, I got a job on the Green Bay police department, and from that time on, it was my job to work traffic at all the games. I took care of the special reserved section for people who had yearly passes. With the exception of a year and a half that I was in the service, I never missed a game. That was from 1943 to 1980. I had to work the traffic before and after the game, but during the game we got to go inside to try to keep things under control…. If the Packers won the game, we had very few problems after the game. If they lost, however, you had to be on your toes or they'd run right over you. The way the Packers played had a big difference on the temperament of the fans. It wasn't so much winning or losing, because the fans could take a loss if they thought the team had played its best. The Packers moved into the new stadium in 1957. The traffic was so bad that I devised a plan to create a couple of one-way streets leading to the ballpark, and reversing them to outbound after the game. I came up with that and they're still using that system today.

———RAY SLOAN, 85, Green Bay

The company I work for is headquartered in Neenah. We went up for the company picnic one time on a Saturday, so we said, "Let's go up to Green Bay and stay overnight and see if there's anything to do at the stadium." We just wanted to see the stadium. On Sunday, we got up, went to the stadium and ended up spending most of the day there. We took a tour of the stadium and got to walk out the tunnel where the players come out. My wife even got a little choked up at that point. They had the original bricks from the old stadium there, with a sign that said, "You're walking across bricks where champions have walked a record twelve times before." It was kind of an eerie…a hallowed-ground kind of thing. We got a little choked up just walking over that, even though there wasn't even a game, and the players weren't practicing yet—it was still July.

———DAVE HENKE, 34, Janesville

Before the renovation, Lambeau Field had very basic amenities. The men's toilets were nothing more than a large open room with a metal trough that ran the length of the room on the back wall. I had taken my son, Scott, to his first game in 1992 when he was eight years old. This was a cold weather game and of course we were very bundled up and had many layers of clothes on. We waited and waited in line and finally cleared the doorway of the toilet and he saw the trough. There was no privacy in the men's toilet at Lambeau at that time. Men were side-by-side for 30-some feet in front of that trough. I had gotten the necessary clothes off so he could go, and when he saw that trough he wheeled around and dragged me right out of the bathroom. He decided it was better to be miserable the rest of that game than to be subjected to that kind of "exposure."

———JERE JOHNSON, 49, Wisconsin Rapids, Wisconsin

A buddy of mine who works for a local paint company sold paint to the Packers for Lambeau Field, and I've been fortunate enough to help him administer the paint for the field. I spent a wonderful October afternoon on Lambeau Field. It's an amazing environment. People talk about the frozen tundra—it's too bad the NFL doesn't wake up and say, "Let's play all Super Bowls in January at Lambeau Field." With the remodeling they've just done, it's just beautiful. That day I was on the field helping paint, I was actually able to walk up the tunnel that Ray Nitschke and Vince Lombardi came out of. I was just overwhelmed by the amount of litter. I said, "Wait a minute. This is where these greats came out." The next thing you know, I found myself cleaning up the tunnel. It's all about respect!

I work in the restaurant business and we're open seven days a week, and for that four hours of sitting at Lambeau, there's nothing else that matters—just football. Some people may do heroin. Some people may needlepoint. I watch football. No, I take that back—I watch Packer football. It's like fishing. I don't care if I catch fish, as long as I'm fishing. I don't care if they win, as long as I'm watching Packer football. That's how it is here.

——JEFF MEINHARDT, 42

I used to work for a company that made golf carts. I had a golf cart dealer in Appleton that worked the area around Green Bay, and I got this great idea. We had an ambulance vehicle that we made. I met with our dealer and told him we had to talk to someone at the Packers about using one of our ambulances. The week before some player had been injured and they had to carry him off on a  stretcher, so I thought this was a perfect opportunity. I walked up to the gate with my dealer, and he said, "Bob, they're having a game here on Sunday. We're never going to get in." But I wasn't about to stop. We walked up to the gate and there was this young female security guard who was very good at her job. I handed her my business card and told her we were there to see "so and so" about the ambulance for Sunday's game. She said, "OK," and let us in! We walked in and found this guy's office and just walked up to him. He was talking to some official about the field and he looked up and said, "Who are you and how did you get in here?" I told him who I was and what I was doing, and that the guard had let me in. He told me he appreciated it, but that the trainer was the guy I had to talk to. I left a message and this guy actually called me back. Here he is the trainer for the Packers, and he took the time to call me back. They couldn't use my idea because they had a deal with John Deere and they couldn't use ours, but I was just blown away that they took the time to even call me back.

——BOB BACON,

The first Packer game I ever went to was back in the 20's. We parked in the end zone and they passed a hat. The players got paid fifty dollars a game and they played with a round ball. I don't know how the heck they played like that. I ended up going into the service and stayed in. It was hard making it to games as much as I could, but I followed them religiously wherever I was. I listened to Armed Forces Radio, and read whatever I could to get my hands on about them—even when I was overseas.

My nephew graduated from Notre Dame, so I go to a few games there. To me, there are two great places to see football games, Lambeau Field and Notre Dame. Those Notre Dame fans are a lot like Packer fans, just uglier. You know that's where the Packers got their team colors—Notre Dame! That's where the green and gold came from. Curly Lambeau played at Notre Dame and he wanted the same colors. My mother-in-law was a Missouri Lutheran. All you had to do was say the word "Catholic" to her and her hair would stand on end. She found out the Packers colors were copies of Notre Dame and she refused to be a Packer fan, so she became a Bear fan instead.

There are quite a few Packer fans here in Atlanta. I've gone to a couple of Packer bars down here, but I don't like it. It's too damned noisy. I like to be able to hear the game, so I usually have a couple of guys over and we watch it on TV.

——**HERBERT T. BARNES**, 83, Atlanta

I was 16 years old when I went to my first Packer game in December of 1966. We were playing the 49ers at Milwaukee County Stadium. There was freezing rain all day long. Of course, the Packers won. I had a broken foot from playing offensive and defensive line in high school football. I remember trying to climb the steps with a walking cast on and almost took a header down the steps every time because the steps were ice-covered. Also, anybody who was wearing a waterproof parka ended up with a sheet of ice covering the parka by the end of the game. After the game, I got Jerry Kramer's and another player's autographs on my Packer program. We were able to see the players in an open area where they would come up the ramp out of their locker room before walking out to their buses. This same open area led to the general parking area of County Stadium...I haven't gone out and hunted down players for autographs. I feel that's for kids to get for free rather than paying athletes money to get their autographs. I just don't believe in doing that. I just think it's wrong. These people make enough money. The rest of us don't even come close to their income, and they want to *charge* us for their signature....

——DAN DUNN, 54, Hartford, Wisconsin

My first year was 1975, and I was 13 years old. I was not supposed to be a ball boy until I was 14. A guy named Paul Roach coached the running backs. Paul had been head coach at Wyoming and had also been on the Raider staff with John Madden. Paul Roach saw me watching practice one day and called me out there and told me he wanted me to be his ball boy. I started out with the running backs—every ball boy was assigned a group. That was my group, and I was his guy.... We only got paid thirty bucks a week. If we had two years of experience, we got 35 dollars a week, so none of us were in it for the money. We got three meals a day, which was nice. We ate at the training table. We stayed in the dorm. A lot of us were playing high school football, and we were able to work out. It was a good experience. The hours were long, and the work was hard. At that time, things were a lot different. A lot more things were done by hand—no computers and things like that. We had to do the laundry by hand. We did have the big washing machines, but there was all that folding. Everything was done without the modern-day machinery. We had to take care of the equipment and tighten up helmets and cleats....The Packers weren't very good, but while you work for them in the summer, everyone is still optimistic about things. I wasn't around the team during the season when things would go bad. Everybody feels good about their team in training camp—you haven't lost your first game yet, so it was a different environment.

——BRYAN HARLAN, 42, Chicago

*Name the Raiders coach—
Win valuable prizes*

Subject: Chicago Bears Trivia...

The Chicago Bears have a new stadium, and some new stadium firsts:

1. 1st touchdown ever in new Soldier Field: Green Bay Packers

2. 1st field goal ever in new Soldier Field: Green Bay Packers

3. 1st sack ever in new Soldier Field: Green Bay Packers

4. 1st blocked punt ever in new Soldier Field: Green Bay Packers

5. 1st 100-yard rusher ever in new Soldier Field: Ahman Green, Green Bay Packers

6. 1st Bears interception ever in new Soldier Field: Green Bay Packers

7. Most touchdowns ever thrown in new Soldier Field: Three. Record held by Brett Favre, Green Bay Packers

8. Most rushing yards ever in a game in new Soldier Field: 176 yards. Record held by Ahman Green, Green Bay Packers

9. Most rushing touchdowns in a game in new Soldier Field: Two. Record held by Ahman Green, Green Bay Packers

More Bears trivia...that most Bears fans do not know what quarterback holds the following records in "old" Soldier Field?

1. Most passing yards
2. Most completions
3. Most starts
4. Most touchdowns — 47

It's a Bears quarterback right? After all, they play 8 home games there a year, right? Is it the famous Jim McMahon? Erik Kramer? Cade McNown? How about Bob Avelini? No, Bears fans, it can only be the greatest quarterback to ever set foot in Soldier Field —new or old.

You know who it is, right? Give up? Let me give you a hint...he wears No. 4. Records held by Brett Favre, Green Bay Packers Go Pack!!!

Chapter 2

Fandemonium

Packer Backers

A DIAPER DANDY

Bart Starr and Larry Primeau

LARRY PRIMEAU

Larry Primeau works for Kimberly-Clark in Neenah, Wisconsin. He is a mechanical engineer who designs equipment for Huggies Pull-Ups, the disposable diapers. He was born in Wisconsin Rapids, moved to Washington state at age six and moved back to central Wisconsin ten years later. He is known to Packer fans as the Packalope. He is a member of the Fans' Wing at the Pro Football Hall of Fame.

In 1990, I took an old, vintage Packer helmet which was too small for my head, took the liner out of it and was able to get it over my head. I mounted a six-point deer rack to the helmet with a couple of lag bolts. I took it to a few of the Packer games and just threw it on, basically, as a joke. Fan would come up asking, "Can I get a picture?" It seemed to be a big hit with the fans, and they all seemed to enjoy it. At that point, we were tailgating out of the back of my car.

As years progressed, we were able to get a van and brush painted it green and gold. My brother-in-law does painting so we took the same van, and he did a nice paint job on it. It took us weekend-after-weekend-after-weekend to do it, but we put on a base coat and sanded it and painted. We finally got it done and it was our tailgate machine to go back and forth to Lambeau. It worked out great for us because we put Packer flags up and put a stereo in it with a nice five-disk CD player that we could power off a portable generator.

All of this just evolved. It didn't happen at one time. In 1996, when the Packers were on their way to the Super Bowl, I took a second helmet, very similar to the first one, and mounted a ten-point deer rack on it. One of the horns had a bullet hole through it. I put some green and gold Mardi Gras beads on it and put a little cheese wedge on the front. That's what I wear to games now. For a while, I kept the smaller helmet at my tailgate just for when kids come by. They like to wear it, and we pose together in the helmets for pictures. I've since donated the small helmet to the Pro Football Hall of Fame where it was on display for a few years. Then the State Historical Society in Madison did a tailgate exhibit there, which was supposed to be temporary. They wanted to know if they could have the helmet, but I told them I didn't have it anymore-that I had donated it to the Hall of Fame. They contacted them and managed to get this helmet to Madison where they now have it on display there....

We used to do a Bishop Charities game, which is for all the Catholic Dioceses here. I'm able to get a bunch of tickets for that. Sometimes, we would have as many as seventy to ninety people at the tailgate for that game. The problem is that we have friends we like to have come and tailgate with us because they have parking passes, too. It's hard to put 75 people into the area of one parking space. We usually work it out where all of us get there at the same time so we can have five or six vehicles together. That gives us room for a huge tailgate party. For regular games, the number varies, up to twelve people. It seems like the same people always come by and tailgate with us. We have friends and neighbors who stop by. My dad always liked to do things where he could meet different people, and I'm kind of the same way. That's one of the reasons I like doing the Packalope thing. You meet some fantastic people from all over the country. I've made so many friends. I tell people, "I never thought doing anything so stupid could give you so much notoriety." I've done so many unbelievable things as a Packalope....

I'm an autograph collector. I always knew that someday I wanted to have some sort of a Packer shrine or Packer-decorated basement. We moved into a house and my father-in-law and I started working on it. We started on one end and fixed up that end as a place for my wife to do craft work. I knew if I started on my end with the Packer part first, I'd never get around to doing her room. We dry-walled my end and did it all up in green and gold, and it turned out awesome. I've had people tell me it's the best looking sports room they've ever seen.

I have collected stuff all through the years. The first thing I got and that I still cherish the most is a book my dad had gotten at one of the Packer games. It was an autographed copy of the book *Run to Daylight* by Vince Lombardi. I have it on display here in the room.

I have thousands of Packer pictures and autographs. They have local radio talk shows and a player will come in as a guest. You can go meet him and get his autograph. I have gone to these for years and have gotten these autographs in person: Brett Favre, Reggie White, Ray Nitschke, Paul Hornung, Bart Starr. I have jerseys on display down here. Everything I've gotten in person so I know it's all legit. I've used up all the room to display things so I don't get as many anymore.

I've met hundreds of the players. About seven years ago, we were tailgating at Lambeau Field. My wife and I had parked the van there, and I had my helmet sitting on the table. I was sitting in my lawn chair with my back to the table. I heard somebody come up and say, "Nice deer rack. Did you shoot it?" My wife said, "Oh, hi Lynn." I thought it was this friend that we have from Milwaukee, but it was Lynn Dickey, ex-quarterback of the Packers. He was standing there at our table looking at this deer rack—I didn't even know what to say. What were the chances of him walking through the parking lot and coming up on my van and actually talking about the deer rack. It was cool. We talked and he signed a couple of things for me. We got a picture together by my van. I have that here in my basement, too....

In the early nineties, on Mondays, we used to go to a small bar named Nicky's Bar in De Pere. A lot of the players in the Eighties used to hang out there: Larry McCarren, Lynn Dickey, Paul Coffman. It was cool to see the players there and sometimes we got to talk to them while we watched Monday Night Football. One Monday, we were talking with a friend and she said, "Have you ever met Tootie Robbins? I'll introduce you to him." I look down and see this big, black guy down at the end of the bar. We met him and talked to him for a little bit. He was really a nice guy. He asked if we'd ever been down to Nights on Main in downtown Green Bay. We said, "No." He said, "What do you do, live under a rock? Follow me down there and I'll buy you a beer."

We followed him down to this little hole-in-the-wall bar. He opened this door at the back, and it was like *Animal House*. You couldn't believe the players in this little dinky bar—Sterling Sharpe, Brett Favre, Edgar Bennett, Frank Winters, Chmura—unbelievable the number of players there. I just could not get over that. Then, for the next couple of years, every Monday, we'd go down there and hang out. There would be so many players down there, and it was so cool to be around them. We shook dice with a lot of the players. You'd think they'd hang out at some big fancy nightclubs, but there they were. As long as you didn't really talk football—'cause that's the last thing these guys want to do—we could talk to them. They liked it when you talked about other things they were interested in. One guy liked old Chevy's, and I've got an old '62 SS Chevy. Once we found out we had that in common, we'd always talk cars. Tuesday was their day off, so on Monday nights they could do whatever they wanted. They liked it because it was a small place. The guy who owned the bar just let them do what they wanted. They just loved this place....

The Packer fans treat everybody here so decent. People come by my tailgate party, even if they're for the opposing team, and we treat them really decent. I rib them a little bit, but it's all in good fun. I hear stories about fans who go to other stadiums, particularly Minnesota and Philadelphia, and if you come out alive, you're lucky. Packer fans treat the opposing team's fans really great. They come up and we show them respect. Of course, you're going to have the obnoxious drunk once in a while. We've been to Kansas City—great fans there.

I was one of the first Packer fans picked to be in the Visa Hall of Fans down in Canton, Ohio. I got picked by Visa, The Pro Football Hall of Fame, and the NFL as one of the ultimate fans. I didn't know what it was going to be like. We met fans like the Hogettes, Arrow Man from Kansas City, Fireman Ed from the Jets. They flew us out there, and wined and dined us the whole weekend. We have a permanent enshrinement in the Pro Football Hall of Fame as fans. After that, Monty Short, the Arrow Man, said, "Do we want to just leave here and never see each other again, or do we want to make this an annual event?" We had just gotten along so well that we decided to go back every year for our Hall of Fame Fan Reunion. It coincides with the player enshrinement, too, so we made some really good contacts down there. We go through their parade in Canton, which is really huge. It's the fifth biggest parade in the country. We have a float sponsor, Home-Bound Health Network, that sponsors our float for us. We have so many fans now who come. Some of them are on the float while some walk next to it. Every year when we have the reunion, we have a big tailgate party there. It just keeps getting bigger and bigger. We have a United Way event that we put on at the Community Center and this year, our third year, we had over two thousand kids attend. We had Red Baron pizza agree to cook personal pan pizzas for the kids. They cooked 9,600 pizzas. We signed autographs for about four hours nonstop. Every year, Red Baron brings all kinds of things—blow-up airplanes and trinkets like that. The kids really go crazy. We handed out football cards. Next year, we may have to cut the quantity of the kids down just because it has gotten so big—it doubled in size in one year. I'm vice-president of the association, our Giant fan is the president, and we have a treasurer and secretary and are trying to get better organized. It's a great weekend.

The History Channel wanted to do a program on NFL rivalries. They contacted me and they contacted Roy Taylor, a legendary Bears fan. The History Channel was riding in their RV to Lambeau and were going to park next to us, and we were going to do a big tailgate together. That was in December, so we had our Packer Christmas tree set up. It has been running for six months on the History Channel, off and on.

My whole life, my allegiance has been with the Packers. I couldn't really, truly in my heart, root for another football team besides Green Bay. I don't care how bad they play and I don't care what goes on. The Packers are my life. I'll die a Green Bay Packer fan. It's just been in my blood since I was old enough to know.

WHAT'S THE DEFINITION OF GROSS SPORTS IGNORANCE? 144 VIKING FANS

DR. HAROLD GROSS

Dr. Gross is a retired physician from Appleton, Wisconsin. He is 90 years old.

I became a Packer fan when I moved to Appleton from Ohio. I did my residency work in Columbus, Ohio, then I went in the Navy during World War II. After I left the Navy in 1948, I moved to Appleton to join two other physicians in a practice. From that point forward, I heard nothing but the Green Bay Packers. Prior to that I'd lived in Chicago, and was a big Bear and Cub fan. I actually lived close enough to **Wrigley Field** that I was able to walk to games. But once I got here, it was all Packers.

When I lived in Chicago I worked at the World's Fair. My job was pushing people around in a wheelchair when they couldn't go on for one reason or another. One day I got called to the office and they told me I needed to push this gentleman to his car. Well, it turned out to be Dizzy Dean! Dizzy had had a little too much to drink that afternoon and couldn't walk, so I was supposed to take him to his car, but he wasn't ready to leave. I ended up pushing him around the Fair, and we eventually ended up at a booth where this man was in a cage over a tank of water. You could pay to throw a baseball at a bulls-eye, and if you hit it you would dump this fellow into the water. Well, when people saw that it was Dizzy Dean there, they all started paying for

> Until 2003, Wrigley Field had hosted more NFL games than any other stadium even though the Bears' last game there was in 1971. The Meadowlands passed Wrigley Field midway through the 2003 season.

him to throw the baseball. Even though he was drunk, he hit the target thirty-four straight times. The fellow in the cage finally quit because he got so tired of climbing up that ladder. Dizzy Dean was on the radio in Chicago in later years, and I almost called in to see if he remembered that, but I'm not sure he would have.

I was also at the famed "Snow Bowl" game against Tampa Bay. Tampa was an expansion team, and John McKay was their coach. Since he'd been in southern California, and then in Tampa, he'd never been in a real snow game. When he brought his team down the runway to go onto the field, he looked out at the snow piled six feet deep on the turf. He told his team, "OK the game's gonna be cancelled, so let's go home." One of the officials asked him what he was doing, and told McKay that we played like this all the time. At first, he was in shock, then he just got mad. Of course the Packers loved it, and they really walloped Tampa Bay that day. After the game John McKay said he'd never play another game there, and I don't think he ever did.

If you talk to any real long-term Packer fans they'll all agree that the Lombardi era was special. The secret was that the same team played every year for nine or ten years and you could relate to them. They were all great players too, so every year you knew what Bart Starr was going to do, you knew what Hornung was going to do, you knew what Taylor was going to do, what Fuzzy was going to do, what Kramer was going to do. You just loved that whole era.

Of course it was a little different football back then. Some of those guys had a little bit of a bottle problem. I remember a story about Paul Hornung staying out all night drinking one night, and he has admitted this. Anyway, he drank all night and then played the next day and won the MVP award without even remembering any of the plays he ran. Paul Hornung and Max McGee were great pals who ran around together, and they broke all the dormitory rules. They might stay up all night and have a giant headache on game day, but they played great. People used to say, "Keep 'em out on Saturday night!" because they seemed to play better when they were hungover.

It was an odd mix of a team. You had Bart Starr who was very straight-laced. Bart was such a nice guy, and a great example to prove that nice guys *can* finish first. Nowadays you have Brett Favre, who all of us old timers have shifted to. I have a little Packer display here in my house. I have a very nice caricature that has Brett Favre on one side and Bart Starr on the other. The drawing is really good, where you can actually tell who it is. I think it's by the Franklin Mint.

I'm also a stockholder. I have a $200 stock certificate that's non-negotiable, pays no dividends, and cannot be transferred! I'm a stockholder and I've got a brick up there at the Hall of Fame too.

GREEN BAY PACKERS GREEN BAY PACKERS GREEN BAY GREEN BAY PACKERS GREEN BAY

THESE SEVEN THINGS
ARE THE TEN REASONS
HE'S HOOKED ON THE PACKERS

KEN RAMMER

*Ken Rammer, 73, is a semi-retired accountant. He'
has lived in Appleton for the past 36 years.*

In 44 years, since 1960, I've only missed one regular season game in Green Bay. That was on December 17th, 1978 when my oldest son got married. The Packers lost to the Raiders 28-3 anyway, so I didn't miss too much. I tried to get him to change the date of the wedding. He was getting married in Milwaukee and wouldn't change it. I couldn't get back to the game in time. So that's the only game I've ever missed in 44 years. I went to every game in the strike years, through the bad years, which was about 24 years of bad teams. That lasted until Wolf and Holmgren came. Back in 1996, I had to have surgery. In November, the Packers were on the road for three straight weeks and I scheduled my surgery around that road trip. I had my surgery on November 12th, and their next home game was on December 8th. The doctor gave me my clearance and I made it to the game on December 8.

I've seen a lot of games in Green Bay. When people ask me which was the most memorable game I'd ever been to, its kind of hard to pick just one. Of course, the Ice Bowl always comes up. I was there with the other 500,000 people who claim they were there. We were living in Appleton at the time and were smart enough to dress for it. Another memorable game was the Redskin game on a Monday night. **Joe Theisman** was the Redskin quarterback and Lynn Dickey was

> **Joe Theismann holds the NFL record for the shortest punt that wasn't blocked—one yard.**

the Packer quarterback. It was a shoot-out, and we kept saying that whichever team had the ball at the end of the game would win, and it turned out to be true. The Packers won 48-47.

Another game I'll never forget was Brett Favre's first game. Don Majkowski got hurt against Cincinnati and they put Brett in. He threw a touchdown pass, probably about 50 or so yards into the far corner at the end of the game and the Packers won 24-23. It was hard to understand the trade they made for Brett Favre. We'd never heard of the guy. As it turns out, all the Packer fans are going to miss him. We've gotten spoiled having him in the lineup. We went through many years of bad quarterbacking. Ever since Lynn Dickey left, we went through a lot of quarterbacks and never found a good one. Dan Devine traded away seven draft choices to get Lynn Dickey, and everything went downhill after that. It's a shame, because if Lynn Dickey had an offensive line in front of him there's no telling how good he could have been. He was always hurt, and always limping because he got roughed up so much.

To me, what makes the Packers so special to fans everywhere is the fact that they come from a small town. That and the fact that they don't have an owner who can do what he wants with the team. The fans are actually the owners. The fact that we're sold out year after year for the entire season instills something into fans everywhere. You have all these Wisconsinites who have fanned out all across the country, and they follow the team religiously no matter where they are. I have a son in Austin, Texas who flies up here for three or four games a year. The people in Austin talk more about the Packers than they do about the Dallas Cowboys.

I have always been amazed at players we've gotten from other teams who have excelled here. Fuzzy Thurston was not a front-line player, and Willie Davis was a castoff from Cleveland, just to name a few. Lombardi got them and put an attitude in them, and made them into winners. There's just something magical about playing for Green Bay. Players come here and never want to leave.

I only have one grandchild. She hasn't been that interested in foot-ball. She used to go with me sometimes, but she enjoyed the crowd more than the game. She liked watching everyone tailgating. There's this one guy that dresses like the Pope with the whole outfit and a ring with a Packer emblem on it. She really enjoyed watching him more than the game.

GREEN BAY PACKERS GREEN BAY PACKERS GREEN BAY GREEN BAY PACKERS GREEN BAY

AS GOD IS MY WITNESS, I THOUGHT TURKEYS COULD FLY

BARB LUDLOW

Barb Ludlow, 62, lives in Kewaunee, Wisconsin, where she is a news reporter for Gannett. When she returned to the Green Bay area in 1968 from California, she put her name on the season ticket waiting list. In 2001, she made the top of the list.

I've had a lot of good times going to Packer games. I remember a game back in November in the eighties, when the most exciting thing in the game was the skydivers hitting the 50-yard line at the beginning of the game. Then, somebody let a turkey loose in the middle of the game and it ran down the sidelines…. I used to always take a rubber chicken to the games. I stuffed it full of plastic bags so he was poofy—kind of puffy. I always put some article of clothing on him that was the colors of the opposing quarterback, with a number on it. I had him attached to a stick, and we would wave it up in the air every time we got a sack or scored a touchdown. Since 9/11, we haven't been able to take anything in. There was a game in 1989, we were playing the Chicago Bears. Majkowski threw a touchdown pass. They had instant replay. At first, the touchdown didn't count. They reviewed it and reviewed it and reviewed it, and finally they decided the touchdown did count. Ditka went crazy! There had been some question about Majkowski being over the line of scrimmage. We won that game. I was waving that chicken, which had a navy blue shirt with orange trim that said, "Crybaby Ditka." We had taken a school bus to the game. We were all excited after the game, and were on the bus. I was sticking my chicken out the window, waving it around. This guy came around—had to have been a Bear fan—grabbed my chicken off the stick and went running down through that line of buses. I could see those rubber legs just flapping under his arm, but I was helpless…I couldn't rescue my chicken. I had to find another chicken, and probably had four or five of them over the years.

I've been to quite a few away games. In the early eighties, we would go to Minnesota to the Packers games. At that time, the fans there weren't too bad, but I don't think I'd want to go there anymore—they've gotten really ugly. I've been at the old Soldier Field, which was the worst stadium I've ever been in…and most Bear fans have always been awful…. We were at Detroit one time, and the fans were just terrible to us. One of my friends—a little older gal who was with us—looked at this guy and said, "If you came to Lambeau Field, you would never be treated like you're treating us." That's just the way they are.

We were at a game against Tampa Bay on December 1, 1985. We had 13-inches of snow in the stadium. I'd been to a bowling tournament on Saturday, and we drove up to Green Bay on Sunday. It was so bad coming up on the freeway that the minute we got to Green Bay, we got a room and stayed at the Midway Motor Lodge, about a block from the stadium. We were able to walk over to the game. Nobody was prepared for any snow. We didn't have any long underwear or warm clothing. It snowed like crazy. At half time, we watched them plow the snow off the field. We watched people in the south end zone who were sliding down the aisle steps, on pieces of cardboard. We left at the beginning of the fourth quarter, went back to the motel, dried off and watched the rest of it on TV.

We've tailgated for years. Back in 1970-71, we went to a game and were in the northwest corner of the end zone. We took sleeping bags to the game to crawl into and keep warm. A guy told us we should take hot Southern Comfort to the games, and make hot Southern Comfort Manhattans. We took this thermos of Southern Comfort into the game. We each crawled into our sleeping bag and zipped it up. We're sitting there sipping on our hot drink during the game. By the time the game got over, we couldn't get out of our sleeping bags. We were sitting there, probably the last few people left in the stadium. There was a guy down in front of us who was totally drunk, and we were sitting there laughing at *him*, "Look at him. He's totally drunk." You can't get that kind of clarity when you're sober.

TURN YOUR RADIO ON

MIKE ZURFLUH

Mike Zurfluh, 43, is known as "Mr. Packer" in Wisconsin Rapids. He is the broker/owner of Zurfluh Realty and Rentals. His office, 99 miles west of Lambeau Field, is sometimes referred to as Packer Hall of Fame-West with over 400 Packer items. His confirmation name is Vincent, after you-know-who!

My dad was a Packer fan, and he died when I was eight years old. He'd keep track of every play, and I still have those notes somewhere. I remember being by him while he was writing that stuff down. I became a fanatic after he died. Since nine or ten years of age, I don't think I've ever missed watching, listening to, or being at a game. They lost a lot of games back then. I remember sometimes, after a close game, crying when they'd lose.

The first actual game I got to go to was with a Big Brother through the Big Brother Organization. He took me to a pre-season game against the San Francisco 49ers. I can still remember going through the tunnel to actually see the field. It was so green. I didn't cry, but almost did—just the beauty of seeing that. Of course, back then we didn't have sprinkling systems so our lawns were never that green. If we had a color TV, we certainly didn't have cable so it wouldn't have shown up clearly on our TV either. To me, it was just beautiful.

When I was ten, my uncles took me to a game. It was at the time in the fall when they pushed the clocks back. I was ready an hour before they were supposed to pick me up, but they forgot to set their clocks ahead. I was going crazy. My mom kept saying, "They'll be here. They'll be here." Finally, they were about a half hour late, and I had been ready for 90 minutes. They only lived about half a mile from my house. My mom called and they told her, "It's only such and such time." She told them, "No, daylight savings time is over." They got over there real quick after that.

I've been fortunate in getting to meet some of the players. The year we won the Super Bowl, we had tickets to go down to New Orleans for the game. We left on the Tuesday before. I had called up our local newspaper, the Daily Tribune, and asked if they would be interested in doing an article on our going to the Super Bowl. They said, "We'd love to. Do you have tickets?" They invited us to come to their office so they could take our picture with the tickets. I had, by this time, sold a bar and restaurant that we had owned. I had an area in my house that held a lot of my Packer items. They came over and did an article on us. At that time, I offered to call back and give reports from New Orleans during the week before the game. It was on the front page of the paper.

I knew a sports guy at the local FM radio station and called him and told him what I was doing for the Tribune and offered to call in and do spots for the radio. So I ended up doing two live call-ins for the radio station every day. After the season was over, they decided they'd like to do an armchair quarterback type call-in show after each game. I called up and met with the station manager and the sports director. Ever since 1997, we've done Monday Morning Quarterback.

Through that, I get a press pass to go down to the games occasionally. I've had four or five press passes and can be down on the field before the game starts and be in the locker room after the game and in the interview room. I've gotten more and more involved. I've met Bob Harlan on a couple of occasions and have met Ron Wolf. Mr. Harlan is an amazing class act to me. I know how busy I am in my business, and I'm sure he's busier and more sought after for his time than anyone in Green Bay. The first time I called him was after the '96 Super Bowl. I called up the Packer office and said, "Is Bob Harlan in?" They said, "Just a minute. Mr. Harlan's not in, but you'll get his voice mail." I said, "Mr. Harlan, this is Mike Zurfluh. I do a local radio program and wanted to see if you or someone else could be on our call-in radio program." I got a call back, "Mike, this is Bob Harlan." I thought, "You've got to be kidding me." He agreed to do it, and we had him on a couple of weeks later. The program's normally an hour-long program, and that one ran an hour and a half. He was gracious enough to stay, as long as we had fans calling in....

My wife and I always go to Door County the first week of October. We usually go down on a Thursday and spend four nights. I found out about the Packer Hall of Fame auction held the first Sunday in October. That was the weekend we were going to be in Door County. I told my wife about the auction. She wasn't too happy about that since our usual Sunday routine was to sleep late. But the auction started at eight o'clock on Sunday in Appleton, which meant we had to leave by 6:00 a.m. When we were driving there, she said, "You're not going to buy anything. That stuff's going to go so high." When we got there, I don't know how many items there were, but I probably ended up buying about a third of them. We bought so many items that my wife went and rented a U-Haul truck. There were several big murals, probably seven to nine feet high by fourteen feet long. Nobody had spots for these. Well, my office, where we were doing a Packer theme anyway, had this long hallway which was just perfect for them. I bought four or five murals, a set of lockers. I have Vince Lombardi's locker. I have Ray Nitschke's locker from the Hall of Fame. There is a "Big Receiver" outside of the Hall of Fame—well, I bought a life-size one that had been inside the Hall of Fame. That's in our lobby. I also bought numerous other items.

I was amazed that the Hall of Fame sold off the "Receiver." I was glad the Packers decided to keep Lambeau Field. They've done a spectacular job with Lambeau Field and the Atrium. Initially, I hadn't been too excited about making changes at Lambeau. That "Receiver" certainly would have stood out, and maybe that's what they didn't want it to do inside the Atrium, with the statues of Curly Lambeau and Vince Lombardi. I was really surprised they didn't want the life-size statue from the Hall of Fame just to say "This is a replica of the one outside the Hall of Fame." I'm certainly glad they didn't because we have it, and it's quite the conversation piece....

As a kid growing up, there was a local guy who'd buy a bar, fix it up and sell it. He owned one that was called Early America. He had some tie-in with the Packers so he would have players down. I remember as a kid getting to meet Ray Nitschke and Chester Marcol and Jerry Tagge. Every year, he'd have a couple of guys there, and you could come in and get autographs.

I'm not a fanatic fan. I don't paint my face up and stuff like that. I love the Packers, and I always will. There's so much tradition there. My kids are six and eight right now and are both on the season ticket waiting list and are already starting to watch the games with me. It's kind of a family tradition. I can't think of a better franchise in all of sports with the tradition. It's hard today with the salaries these players are getting. It's changed so much. It would be interesting to see how Lombardi would coach today's athlete.

My mother was also a huge Packer fan. My mother was my hero, without a doubt. She raised eight kids and did an outstanding job with all eight of us. I was the youngest and was eight years old when my father died. My mother passed away seven years ago so she did get to watch the Super Bowl even though she was very sick with Parkinson's disease. We were able to keep her at home the last year of her life with around-the-clock caregivers. One of these caregivers was Janet King. She and her husband, Rich, used to run a place called Rawhide with me. She got to know Bart Starr real well. Bart Starr is, to me, a huge part of the Packer lore. He's a class act from everything I've read. I got to meet him once as a young kid.

I'm not big on autographs either, but I said to Janet, "I'd just love to get Bart's autograph. I've got a helmet. Could you possibly get him to do that?" She said, "He doesn't like to because people will sell them then." I said, "I'd want it to say, 'To Zurph, best wishes, Bart Starr.'" She said, "I'm sure we could get him to do that." She took a picture of him holding it so he did sign one of my helmets and I have the picture of him doing it. That's one of the things I'd like to do is buy him lunch or dinner. He's such a class act. My mother really respected him, and it meant a lot to me to have him sign that helmet.

I am trying to get on the Board of Directors for the Packers. I've been announced at the last three or four shareholders' meetings. A lot of people want to be on that board, and they're just fans. There's no argument I'm a huge Packer fan, but the thing they're looking for is the business end of it. I have a pretty good history and good success with a bar and restaurant business, and my real estate business is the number one company in town. That's a goal of mine, and I believe that's going to happen someday. I believe I'll be an asset to the Green Bay Packers. They have over 50 on their board, and I believe there's a mandatory age of retirement. I've been a shareholder since 1990.

SHE SAYS SHE'S A NUN, YET SHE DOESN'T HAVE A GUITAR

SISTER ROUSSEAU

Sister Rousseau, 83, was born Marjorie Rousseau in Green Bay in 1921—the same year the Packers were admitted to the NFL.

The Packers and I have traveled a long time, together. At age 17, I left Green Bay in order to go to the convent in Milwaukee. At that time, convent life and football games were really not very compatible. I always kept an interest in the Packers and found out where and when they played, but I did not have the opportunity to go to a game. When I was a kid of eight or ten in Green Bay—before I left for the convent—my father used to take the tickets. I'd stand next to him, and as soon as I could, I'd sneak in to see what had happened. I remember watching the Packers triumphantly walk away after the game, and that was about it.

I knew about the Bears because the Bears and Packers had the longest rivalry of any team. The Bears would sometimes come to Green Bay, and of course, we would all growl like bears and pull for the Packers.

I was in Milwaukee for several years and then went to Chicago, the home of the Bears. I taught there for six years, but I never deserted the Packers. I saw them play once in Chicago. At that time, we were wearing the old habits, real starched things—and it wasn't that easy to get permission to go. We just didn't do those things, even though we stayed in the background and said, "Oh, God. Let the Packers win." After six years in Chicago, I went to the Catholic University of America and was there for six years studying. There, when there was a Packer victory, I would have the whole Classics Department join in with me in celebrating the Packers. After I left Catholic University in 1958, I went back to Milwaukee. Of course, Milwaukee doesn't have a football team. For a while, the Packers came to play in Milwaukee, but it was never *their* team.

In 1996, I had that hopeful feeling all year that this was the year. I think somehow one gets that feeling and keeps it….That game Favre played right after his father passed away was a marvelous game. That Brett Favre had that courage and that energy somehow, to me heaven seemed very near, and I felt the presence of heaven during that game when Brett Favre ran and won. Heaven isn't really that far away.

I read a very good article in the *U. S. Catholic* on the connection between sports and spirituality. The author of that article explained that both religion and sports depend upon community. That is true. We have the people going to church services on Sunday morning, then, in the afternoon, going to football…in almost the same numbers. So first you pray, and then you play. Most communities then join together.

Recently Marco Rivera was in Qatar entertaining the troops. One of our Mt. Berry students was at the place when Rivera came and told him about me and got an autographed picture from Rivera, plus a Packer shirt. Imagine my surprise to get a big package from the Middle East containing Packer stuff. That really was a surprise. I do want to write to Rivera and tell him how happy I am. There are Packer Backers everywhere. Somewhere, I wrote, "A Packer is never alone."

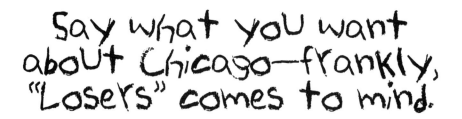

Say what you want about Chicago—frankly, "Losers" comes to mind.

A COOL GUY IN HOTLANTA

HERBERT T. BARNES, JR.

Herb Barnes is a retired Lt. Colonel in the United States Army. He was born in Delafield, Wisconsin the same year as the Packers, 1921. He's been a Packer fan ever since. He lives in Atlanta.

I always tried to get to the games when they played the Rams. I always loved seeing them trying to get Crazy Legs Hirsch. I've gotten to know some of the Packer front-office people, and I've contributed to the Packer Hall of Fame and now have a lifetime pass. I'm good friends with Lee Remmel. When I lived in Denver and the Packers played the **Broncos**, Lee would always come out and have dinner with me. When I used to go to Bronco games, I'd always wear all of my Packer gear. I'd try to get tickets to the south end zone, which was a rough place. It was loaded with Bronco fans. They'd start teasing me, and I'd tell them, "When you win twelve championships, I'll talk football with you. Otherwise, shut-up!" We had a lot of fun, because they were great fans.

Now that I live in Atlanta, I make sure I go to all the Packers-Falcons games. The Falcon fans are funny folks. They didn't really have die-hard fans until this new owner took over. They were very fickle. They would back the team when they were winning, which wasn't very often, but they stayed away when they were losing. I remember one game back in the 70's when I was stationed here. It was raining really hard, and when the TV camera showed the stadium it didn't look like there were any fans there. All the fans that showed up that day were huddled up under the roof, and the seats were almost empty.

> **Superstitious ex-Denver Bronco Terrell Davis demanded that the name tag above his locker always read "Joe Abdullah," and Bronco center Tom Maler won't wash his practice gear during the year because he feels that he's giving the equipment "natural seasoning" to shield "evil spirits."**

One of the saddest things in sports is when a team moves. When the Baltimore Colts left town in the middle of the night that was just terrible. The Colts had true fans. They were second to the Packers in fan strength, and then you leave town like that. It's like when the Braves were pulled out of Milwaukee. They had more attendance at that time than any team in the National League. But these two owners bought the team with Coca-Cola money to bring the Braves to Atlanta. You go up to Milwaukee now, and you don't see that many Coke machines. Those old Germans don't forget!

I hated to see the St. Louis football Cardinals leave. In fact, Curly Lambeau at one time coached the Cardinals. That's when they were still in Chicago. He'd gotten in trouble with the Packer fans with his shenanigans, so the Cards hired him. He finally left football altogether after that. I always thought the Cardinals and the Packers was a good rivalry. It's not the same now.

The Chicago Bears used to practice in Delafield, where I grew up. My father was the doctor for the team during spring training. Twice a year, George Halas would invite us to games in Chicago. We'd actually sit on the bench with the Bears. They were the worst seats in the house, because with the slope of the field, you couldn't see anything unless it was happening right in front of you. I was just a little bitty kid at the time, and the Bear players used to toss me back and forth. They'd literally pick me up and throw me to one another. They knew I was a Packer fan, and they really kidded me. I've got pictures of them practicing up there. In those days, they were still the Monsters of the Midway. Those were the days of Bronko Nagurski, Bulldog Turner, and guys like that.

The whole Packer organization is wonderful. My daughter, Sandy, is a physical therapist. We drove up to Green Bay in 1975 and met Lee Remmel. He took Sandy down to meet the Packer trainer, Dominic Gentile, and he got her enrolled in a school in Vail, Colorado. She learned a helluva lot there and had a marvelous time. But that's just the way that whole organization is...they look out for their fans. They understand business: if you take care of your customers they'll keep coming back. Just imagine in the lean years, they were still selling out.

Before Lombardi came to town, some of the local merchants would say, "Why do you bother going to games, when you can see the players walking down the street?" That all changed with Lombardi. Curly Lambeau may have started the team, but he allowed the players to do too much. He didn't have good discipline on the team. But now, the Packers are owned by the stockholders, and the team will never leave Green Bay. I'll never forget the first Green Bay Monday Night Football game. Howard Cosell said, "I'm looking out over the skyline of Green Bay and I can't find one building over five stories high." That's what is so unbelievable about the Packers, people can't imagine a town that size supporting a professional football team, but they do.

Once a Packer, always a Packer. I'm not the fan I used to be, because of the salaries these guys are getting. We take our children and we put them in the hands of teachers eight hours a day, and what do we pay them? Nothing. Our priorities seem a little out of line, but I'm still a fan, so I guess I'm contributing to the problem.

Being a fan gives you a sense of belonging to a family. I ran into a guy the other day and I had my Green Bay shirt on. He told me he was from Pittsburgh, and I told him they had a helluva team. I told him whenever I think of Pittsburgh, I think of Rocky Bleier. His parents owned a tavern in Wisconsin, not far from Green Bay. He went to Vietnam and got his foot shot up. He came back and went through rehab and the owner of the Steelers worked with him and he ended up being a great player.

You should see my den. It is absolutely full of Packer memorabilia. I've got my stock, a letter from Bob Harlan, my Super Bowl ticket stubs—it's a shrine. My wife passed away in 1996, the year the Packers won the championship. Years before, she bought me a mug that had the front page of the Green Bay paper on it. It was the picture of Max McGee catching a ball and it was titled, "Max McGee's Swan Song." When she passed away, Lee asked me if my wife had given me anything that I'd like to give to the Packer Hall of Fame, and I gave them that cup. Now it's in the Hall, in memory of my wife. She was a great lady and a real fan.

HE COULD HAVE BEEN A VIKING FAN, BUT THE DOG BEAT HIM OVER THE FENCE.

CARL NELSON

Carl Nelson, 50, just recently moved to Duluth after living his whole life in Superior, Wisconsin. He is a registered nurse and works in the operating room in St. Luke's Hospital in Duluth. He's been a registered nurse for the past twenty years.

I have a brother who is ten years younger than me who is a real avid Vikings fan—I think it has something to do with that rock to the head when he was a kid. He and I managed to make it to twelve Packer-Viking games in the Metrodome in a row. Through the 80s and 90s, he could always get tickets, but when they started playing better it got a little tougher. Seeing a game indoors is not a natural way to see a football game. It's not like seeing it in the snow and the cold.

My daughter goes to college in Green Bay and I know that it's 352 miles from my door to Lambeau Field. Superior is located on the westernmost tip of Lake Superior, right across the bridge from Duluth. It's only 150 miles to Minneapolis, so we're in die-hard Viking country, although us Wisconsin natives manage to hold our own.

When I was a child, there was only the Packers. When I was six or seven, the Vikings came into being, and suddenly, the Packers weren't on TV every weekend. As a kid, I just knew that I didn't like that. Pretty much from the time I remember watching football, I can remember my dad watching the Packers. I've managed to instill it in all my children as well.

I went to my first game at Lambeau in December of 2000. I got goose bumps, and was almost moved to tears walking into that stadium for the first time. It was in December—it snowed the previous night. Of course, I couldn't sleep that night. The next morning, it was like a prototype day. The sun was shining, the snow was bright and you could see the swirls of snow flying in the air. I was almost moved to tears because it was something like I'd never experienced before or since. They won too, so it was one of the few experiences of my adult life that I could say was everything I wanted it to be. It was a close game and, for a Christmas present, the family had upgraded my tickets to about fifteen rows above the Packer bench. I could hear the players talking, I watched one of the players catch his glove on fire with the heater—it was great!

My wife, Deb, and I got married in March. We moved into her house here in Duluth. To make me feel welcome, she took all my Packer memorabilia, which I'd never had a place for, and created a Packer room in the basement. Now I have this great room and it is just covered with Packer material. It got picked up by the local newspaper with photos. I have about 40 Packer hats in my Hall of Fame on the way to the den. I've also got my 1940 program that someone gave me. It was quite a treat—this lady saw the story and brought me this program. She said she'd always meant to throw it away, but thought someday, someone would come along that would appreciate it. Her brother had given it to her after he'd gone to the game. She saw the article in the paper and wanted me to have it.... I just bought a pretty, new pickup truck, and, as part of my birthday present this year, my boy arranged for a graphics guy to put a big "G" on it. It's pretty cool.... I've written Packer poems since about 1990. I got to read them on a local radio station for a couple of years and that was fun. It keeps me involved with the team. I always hope they draft players with challenging names. Favre has always been a tough one to rhyme. Gbaja-Biamila would be a real challenge although, I guess, I should try.

It was neat when the Packers won the 1996-97 Super Bowl, because my middle boy was the exact same age that I was when they won the first Super Bowl. I've got an autographed picture of Brett Favre running and holding his helmet after that Super Bowl. My wife got it for me as a wedding present. She actually wrote to the team and asked if he could come to our wedding and jump out of the cake, but they sent the picture instead. That was good enough for me.

Growing up where I did, we only got about two Packer games a year on TV, and that was just when they were playing the Vikings. So I always listened to the games on the radio. The Packers have always had such great announcers: Ray Scott, Max McGee, Jim Irwin—I mean my whole adult life had been listening to the Packers through those guys. That's what was so cool about going to that first game, that it was exactly like I had pictured it.

When my kids were born, all three came home from the hospital in a Packer sweatshirt. I think it's genetic.

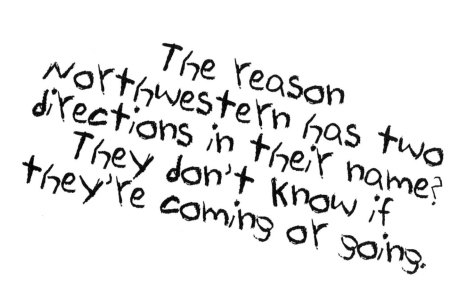

The reason Northwestern has two directions in their name? They don't know if they're coming or going.

Bury Mike Ditka 10 feet under...deep down, he's a good guy.

CLASS-Y LADY

WANDA BOGGS

Wanda Boggs, 39, is a first-grade teacher at Brookfield Elementary in Brookfield, Wisconsin. She was honored as the Packer Fan of the Year in 2002. Her cat is named after Reggie White.

I became a Packers fan when I was about three or four years old. My dad was a big fan and we had a tradition as far back as I can remember. We would go to church, then pick up ham and rolls and sweet rolls, then get home to watch the game. We never had season tickets but we managed to get to a few games a year, especially when they played in County Stadium. We never got season tickets, but we're wannabees.

I use a lot of Packer material in my class. I use graphs with Packer information as the examples. On Mondays we always talk about the Packer game the day before. We'll compare what went right in the game and what went wrong with things that were going on in class at the time. We use a lot of math that's Packer related.

One of the students in my third grade class saw the Packer Fan of the Year contest advertisement in the paper and told her mom that it reminded her of me. Her mom agreed and said they should send it in. A few days later, the mother saw the paper in the recycling bin, and turned around and retrieved it so they could enter me. She brought it in to me and told me that she knew how much I used Packer stuff in class. She asked if I thought the kids could write something about me to enter in the contest. She said she was going to do it, but didn't know how to gather the kids together and how to go about it. I didn't want them to have to sign their names to something, or to write something they didn't want to, but they were all really excited about it.

We had been working on these things called, bio-poems where you take your name and write something about it. One of the kids came up with the idea of calling it "Go Packers" and they each wrote a mini-paragraph to go with it. After that, they had to cut it down to five hundred words, so we had to keep working on it to get it down. One of the kids had the idea to put it on a piece of paper that would look like the field, so we put it on a sheet of green and yellow paper and another kid made a goal post. Abby, the girl who wrote the nomination wrote a funny paragraph to get their attention. So we were able to apply everything we'd been talking about in class, and I thought that's where it would end. The little girl who nominated me was originally from Chicago. At the ceremony, they interviewed her and asked her if she was a Packer fan. She said, "No, I hate the Packers, I'm a Bears fan, but my teacher loves the Packers!" Her mother looked like she wanted to crawl in a hole, but it was cute.

About four or five weeks later I got a call informing me I'd been picked as one of the ten finalists. The whole thing went on for three months before they even picked the finalists. For the rest of the school year there were ancillary programs going on around the contest, so the same class was involved almost their whole year. The voting was done over the Internet, and when my students and parents found out I was in the final ten, they all started contacting former students, the teachers' association got involved, and all of them e-mailed their friends, and the whole thing just networked. It was pretty amazing seeing how many people you'd touched in your life.

The students writing my nomination helped me a lot. The fact that it was unique and not so much emotional as a lot of other letters were may have put me over the top. Once the finalists were chosen, it became a pure vote count.

At the induction ceremony, I really met a lot of people: Mike Sherman was there, Max McGee, Lee Remmel, Fuzzy Thurston, Lynn Dickey, James Lofton, and Dave Robinson. There weren't as many current Packer players there, but it was kind of neat because there was such a generational thing. Meeting most of them was kind of a quick "hello" but a few were really nice. Lee Remmel was really nice and I got to talk to him. Donald Driver was there. I had to make a speech. I got up and did my thing about the kids in the class and what this meant to the community and me. Afterwards, Donald Driver got up and said, "Thanks a lot Boggs, you stole the show and now I have to follow you." So, he did his talk and then sort of made a beeline to get out. Somebody yelled and asked if he could do one more picture, and he yelled, "No, I'm done, I'm done." Then, they said, "Come on Donald. It's with Wanda Boggs." He stopped and turned around and said he'd take one with me. He put his arm around me and I got the picture. I felt like a queen for a night.

The actual announcement that I had won was made on the last day of December before Christmas vacation. When the announcement was made, a lot of people were at home watching the internet to see who won. As soon as it broke, all these people started calling the school saying, "She won! She won!" They made the announcement and everyone went crazy, jumping up and down, yelling, and screaming. It was something we had talked about so much, but we'd always said we weren't going to win. It was just so amazing when the news finally came that I had. For winning, we got tickets and airfare to a game in Florida. We didn't have any choice in which game it would be, but they did promise it would be some place warm. We really enjoyed it.

The Super Bowl... or as they say in Minneapolis...Passover.

A TITLETOWN FAN IN TITANTOWN

JOHN PAGEL

John Pagel was born in 1943 in Green Bay, Wisconsin. He attended Wisconsin State and received his Masters degree at Vanderbilt University in Nashville, Tennessee. After graduation he worked for Vanderbilt University for 26 years, retired for two years, then returned to Nashville to work for a private company in the radiation safety industry.

Growing up in Green Bay you almost had to be a Packer fan. My father was a reporter for the Green Bay paper, so that helped make me even more of a fan. As a young boy the Packers were still playing games at the old City Stadium, so we used to sneak into games there. We used to get into the stadium in the summertime too, I remember once my younger brother and I got inside and brought a baseball bat and a variety of balls with us. We had a rubber ball that didn't go too far, then we hit a few baseballs that traveled pretty good, then I hit a golf ball that went all the way out of the stadium. It's lucky the golf ball didn't go back at the pitcher, because he never could have reacted fast enough to get out of the way!

We lived on Cherry Street in Green Bay and there were several players and ex-players living on the street with us. Arnie Herber, a retired quarterback lived just down the street, Paul Hornung and Max McGee lived on the street during the season, and the house that Curly Lambeau lived in was just a few houses down from us. He actually didn't live there at the time, he had moved before we got there. I can remember waving to Paul Hornung and Max McGee as a kid, which was kind of neat.

I went to the Ice Bowl with my father. I was in school at Vanderbilt at the time and drove home to go to the game. The temperature dropped so fast that there was talk that the game wouldn't even be played, but of course it was. Usually when you went to a game you had room between you and the person next to you, but at that game everyone was so bundled up that you practically had to sit sideways to fit into your seat. I remember the Packers started off so well in that game that it didn't even seem cold during the first half. At halftime, it seemed to get a lot colder, then when the game came down to the wire it felt like summer time in that stadium. I don't remember it feeling cold at all.

I also went to the Snow Bowl against Tampa Bay. We lived on the other side of Green Bay at the time, so I got out to go to the game and spent some time shoveling out the driveway, then got my car stuck in the street. A couple of neighbors pushed me back into the driveway and I went in and called a cab, so I made it finally. I bet the stadium was only twenty percent full, so I had my tickets up in the sixtieth row and I kept moving around trying out better seats. It wasn't that cold, but it was snowing so hard that if you stood up to cheer for a play, you had to sweep your seat off because the snow would have already started piling up in that short of a time. After the game, I called the taxi to come get me and they told me they had shut down for the day because of the snow. Two guys standing next to me overheard my conversation and offered to give me a ride. They were staying at a hotel across town, so we made it that far and went inside to a restaurant and had a few drinks, after that I just walked the last mile or so home.

There used to be a restaurant in Nashville that televised all the Packer games, but once the Titans came to town I think they closed down. I was surprised though at how many Packer fans there are in Nashville. I think the Packers attract a lot of out-of-town fans because they come from such a small city. Even fans that have their hometown favorites like the Packers too. There's something about the history, about the championships, about the city, that makes the Packers special.

Even though I live in Nashville I still make it home to see the Packers. That's what being a Packer fan is all about!

SO SAY YOU ONE, SO SAY YOU ALL

 What used to bother me was that back in the bad days of the Packers, any time you watched highlighted films, the Packers were always the team they showed as the "other" team. It's been kind of nice to be on the other side of the highlight reel for a while. Of course, you know it will turn some day and we'll have to eat crow again, but I guarantee that there will be very few Packer fans jump ship.

You wonder sometimes what's going on. These are overpaid athletes, and it's like the games of the Roman Empire, but you just identify with the team. My wife laughs at me because I'll be watching the game and they'll be in a running play and I'm raising my leg trying to help them get through. There's just something about America that makes us identify with the athletes. It's good to have a team that's popular and a team that's good. We have both with the Packers!

——REX BECKER, 49, Janesville

The way the Packer fans dress up is amazing. Like St. Vince, the guy who dresses up like the Pope, except he's Vince Lombardi in the cheesehead. My parents didn't quite understand my move from the Bears to the Packers. The first year I was doing the Packers was 1999. My folks happened to be on a trip out west when we were playing San Diego. They spent the weekend there and went to the game. My mother could not believe the green and gold all over **San Diego** that weekend, and the stadium filled with Packers fans. It was almost like a Lambeau Field-West effect. It was incredible. She said, "I had no idea it was like this—that they were such a national story." The fans of this team travel better than any team in the NFL. It's a testament to their loyalty. They plan their vacations in the summer around

> The Chargers were originally the Los Angeles Chargers in 1960, the first year of the AFL. They were owned by Baron Hilton of the Hilton Hotel chain. Hilton owned the Carte Blanche credit card company and named the team, the Chargers, to promote the card.

training camp. They line up around that fence on the practice field. It's not an easy see. It's not an easy view. But they do it every year. When we're on the road, wherever we go, the stadium is almost always sold out. One thing you can count on, the Yankees and the Packers will sell out wherever they play. We were in Tennessee, and they have trouble selling pre-season games. That was the one game they sold out.

—WAYNE LARRIVEE, radio voice of the Packers

My Dad was stationed in Virginia back in the late 50's He says that on the weekend he could always get a football game on the radio and it was usually the Packers. They seemed to always lose so he started rooting for the underdog Packers. I was raised on the Packers-didn't know any different. I didn't know the Browns were the hometown team until I was 14. A reporter at one of the local TV stations, did a story about my Packer collection. In the piece, he asked if I got beat up a lot when I was young? I told him no because a lot of the kids thought my dad was a coach for the Packers. A girl that I went to school with married Mark Murphy, who had a long career with the Packers. I wish that I would have made friends with her. A girl that I had dated for about a year and a half told me it was either her or the Packers! She shouldn't have done that…. I have made many trips from Ohio to Green Bay for training camp. I signed my niece up for Junior Power Pack, which is a great Packer fan club for kids under 14. Her highlight was meeting KGB. I have been there for a few shareholder meetings. The Packers Partners Club of Champions is a club that started three years ago which I am a charter member.

I have converted several Browns fans to the Packers when Cleveland lost the Browns. I showed them what a real team was, and they didn't want to go back when the Browns returned.

—RICK NELSON, 44, life-long resident of northwest Ohio

The greatest pride I get out of being a Green Bay Packer fan is when I see letters in the Green Bay paper and the *Milwaukee Sentinel-Journal* about peoples' experiences after they've been to a game here. I get goose bumps reading them because they talk about the Green Bay fans being so friendly to them. If any of the young guys get on somebody like that or throw something at them, the old guys really let them have it—you don't treat people like that. Sometimes the people are overwhelmed because they'll be walking by and don't expect that someone will say, "Come on over. Have a beer. Have a brat." Once you get them in, everybody starts asking, "Where'd you eat? Have you gone to Chili Johnson's? Have you gone to Kroll's? Is this your first time to Lambeau? Wait till you walk in. Where are you staying tonight?" Sometimes they just get this look on their faces like "Who are these people?" We just love hearing what they have to say so much.

Bob Harlan had only two professional jobs, the Packers and the Cardinals. He tells people the fan support was very similar between the two teams. I played hockey with his older son, and I used to do spotting for his son when he was up in our booth doing our high school games. Now, of course, he's Kevin Harlan, the famous FOX announcer.

———BILL ANDERS, Atlanta, Georgia

Green Bay has very avid fans, there's no question about that. I would put our fans up against any fans of any team in any sport as far as loyalty and perseverance are concerned. In 1967, the Packers won their last championship of the sixties under Vince Lombardi. We had won a division championship in '72. That was the only championship we had from '67 until the nineties. That is, except for the year of the strike in 1982, when we were at 5-3-1, and we were declared division champions. Actually, that was kind of a manufactured situation, to be honest about it. So, for over 20 years, we had one division championship to hang our hats on…that's a long time.

The Green Bay Packers have a "David vs. Goliath" scenario. That's certainly a factor in attracting so many fans. The Lombardi era brought a great deal of attention to Green Bay and the Packers. That developed a great many fans who had never followed the Packers before. Over the history of the NFL, the Packers are the most successful team having won 12 championships. No other team has been able to do that. The Bears are second with nine. I don't know if the uniforms have anything to do with it or not, but I do know this, the uniforms are incredibly popular.

I remember a few years ago we were playing a game in Seattle, and there were over 30,000 Packers fans in the stands—2,000 miles from Green Bay! The Packers were playing at the Pontiac Silverdome six or seven years ago, and there were more Packers fans in the stands than there were Lions fans. William Clay Ford reportedly was exceedingly upset about that and ordered his ticket office to make sure that never happened again. Now, if Packer fans want to buy tickets to a Packers game in Minnesota, they are required to take one pre-season game, along with the regular season game. That's a tribute to the Packers fans loyalty.

——LEE REMMEL, member, Packer Hall of Fame

I love the Bears, but I have to say that the Bears are not friendly to their main fan base, the fans who have been the most supportive of them. In 2001, I had tickets that I bought to a game, and they were fifty dollar tickets. They were on the thirty-five yard line, but the next year, the people that owned them just got priced right out of their season tickets. With the advent of the PSL, the right to own the seat, just ran people out of the park. These were people who had been coming to the games for upwards of thirty years, and now they couldn't afford the tickets. On top of that, they built an underground parking lot where they raffle off spots. Even if you're a season ticket holder you're not guaranteed a parking spot. Even if you do get it one year, there's no guarantee you'll get the spot the next year. On top of that, even if a person wanted to tailgate they can't very well tailgate in a parking garage. They're just not fan friendly. I mean why not put out port-a-potties?

I went up to a game in Green Bay and I was just amazed. The fans there were just great, they couldn't have been nicer. We were Bear fans and we didn't hide it. We were just walking down the street and people were there with coolers and barbeques and everyone was just super nice. I was also shocked at the stadium. They had entrances to the bathrooms from outside the stadium, so even before the game you could go to the bathroom. I thought that was really nice. It's like you're driving through a residential neighborhood and suddenly, "Bang" there's the stadium.

I learned a lot when I went to Green Bay. They didn't seem to care that I was from Chicago, they were just glad I wasn't from Milwaukee! I got the impression that the Green Bay fans don't like the people from Milwaukee. You talk about people being prejudiced against people of different races or whatever, just don't tell a person from Green Bay that you're from Milwaukee!

——CHRIS BIELFELDT, 30, Police Officer, Chicago

I am a Vikings fan! I was born and raised in Minnesota, was born and raised a Vikings fan. I actually only went to one Viking game though. The game I went to was in 1987, the night after the Twins won the World Series. It was supposed to be a Monday night game, but they moved it to Tuesday because of the World Series. I just remember it being the most quiet football game ever. I think everyone was so tired of yelling for the Twins that they were just worn out. My involvement with the Packers comes through my church. Every year for one of the Packer/Viking games, our church holds an event for the WAFER program. WAFER is the local food pantry. We have skits for three weeks leading up to the game, and we have two food boxes, one labeled "Packers" and another labeled "Vikings". People come to church with food items to donate and drop them in the box of their favorite team. It is a competition to see which team can bring in the most food. The first two years, the Packer box won easily. Last year, we added a "I Don't Care" box for the people who either didn't follow football or didn't have a preference. That box actually won this past year!

——JAN STOWERS, LaCrosse, Wisconsin

I can honestly say I've been a Packer fan since the day I was born, since we have the same birthday. When I was a kid, before I was old enough to go watch them, my folks had a radio, which in those days not everyone had one. We used to listen to the Packer games on Sundays, that was a ritual. When I got older, about twelve years old, my buddies and I would walk from the West Side over to the East Side where the stadium was, and try to get into games. We'd hang around the entrance, and catch the Packer players and ask them if we could carry their helmets in, that way we could walk in when they did. If that didn't work, we had a way of going around the back and sneaking in. The stadium used to sit near the East River, and one side of the stadium was actually right up against it with a fence to keep people out. We used to have a place where we could sneak under the fence and get inside the stadium. We never got caught.

I knew a lot of the players because I lived here on the northwest side my whole life, and for some reason a lot of players lived over here, too. When I got out of high school, I got a job at a soda fountain just a few doors down from the Astor Hotel, which is where a lot of the players lived during the season. The players would always end up at my soda fountain for their malted milks. One player that always stopped in was Smiley Johnson. He played down in Georgia and was drafted by the Packers. He was the most likable fellow you'd ever meet. He used to come in all the time, and then one day he stopped coming in. I found out he'd been drafted into the army during the war. He ended up getting killed in the Pacific, Okinawa.

——RAY SLOAN, 85, born August 11, 1918, in Green Bay, the exact same day the Packers were formed.

What makes the Packers "America's Team" is the mystique of a small town. I mean a town the size of Green Bay being able to support a professional football team is really unique. Then Lambeau Field has become an international theme with the Lambeau Leap. LeRoy Butler invented the Lambeau Leap. So you have the new Lambeau Field, which has just ballooned in the past few years. There was a big controversy about tearing down Lambeau Field, and the old timers just threw a fit to keep the old stadium. Bob Harlan, who was just inducted into the Packer Hall of Fame, managed to get a tax through to keep the stadium. Now the place is open all year long, and it is just a tourist magnet. There's a pro-shop in there, the Hall of Fame, restaurants… it's not closed up ten months of the year. Now you can go in there and eat anytime you want, not just on football days. Curly's is a great restaurant and Brett Favre has a restaurant there. The pro shop is just selling stuff like you wouldn't believe. The atrium has thousands of seats, and they just had the Hall of Fame induction ceremony there.

——DR. HAROLD GROSS, 90, Appleton

The success the Packers have had over the years I think has helped make them so popular. The fact that they're a small town team means a lot. At one time a lot of teams were based in small towns. The Pistons actually started out in Fort Wayne, Indiana. I think it's funny that Green Bay has a team and Los Angeles doesn't!

——VINCE PRYGOSKI, 40, Gaines, Michigan

When I hear someone call the Dallas Cowboys "America's Team," I get all riled up. There is no question that the Packers are the true "America's Team." I think the reason is simple: we're a small town, and we own the team. There's real pride in this town around that. We know that they're not gonna up and leave Green Bay for a better offer.

Even if everyone in town decided to sell their stock, the charter is written so that the American Legion would take over the ownership. The Legion would never let them go. Bless the Green Bay Packers. I just hope they're around till the end of time.

——WALTER RILEY, JR, Sparta, Wisconsin

What makes the Packers "America's Team" is being part of the Black and Blue Division. I think the Pittsburgh Steelers are the same way in the AFC. I think with blue-collar teams, the fans can relate to the players on the field. Teams like the Cowboys are all show, all glamour. I hate to say it, but the Bears are like the Packers in that way. The Cleveland Browns are a lot like that, too. I'd like to encourage Packer fans to stay true to the team. Even when they have a bad year or game, with their management you know they're gonna come back. It's so amazing in Green Bay. When you drive around you see houses painted green and gold, you see people with Volkswagens painted with the Packer colors, they're just real die-hard fans. That's what makes the Packers so special—the loyalty of the fans!

——DAVID MELLINTHIN, 37

The fans of the Packers are a little bit like the fans of Notre Dame and the Chicago Cubs and the Dallas Cowboys. The Packers are really America's team. They've got season ticket holders from every state. At summer, in training camp, you look at the license plates in the parking lot, and the vehicles are from all over the country. A lot of people planned their summer vacations, and still do, around the Packer training camp. It's unique to have the kind of following they do, and to have the sell-outs they do every year regardless of how good the team is. The passion of the fans and how big the team is in the community and how it really is the face of the community…no one would know about Green Bay if it wasn't for the Packers.

——BRYAN HARLAN, Harlan Sports Management

The video director of the Packers, Al Treml, was the last guy in the organization who was actually hired by Vince Lombardi. In late December of 1997, at Soldier Field, he asked me if I'd like to help him out. The guy that was supposed to run the pictures out to the offensive, defensive and specialty teams coordinators after every series was on vacation. He called me and asked me if I wanted to go on the field and run these pictures out. The pictures come out on a little printer that is on the sideline at midfield. I would pick up these pictures and run them out to the coaches.

I said, "Sure, that would be fine." On Saturday night, I hung out with the guys, and we had dinner at a great steak restaurant, Smith and Wollensky's. We had a good time. On Sunday morning, they woke us up and we went to Mass—I'm not even Catholic. Brett Favre comes in wearing shorts and a tee shirt for Mass at six o'clock in the morning at the Westin Hotel in Chicago.

We get to the game. Robert Brooks, Derrick Mayes and some of the players had been coming into my shoe store, so when I got down on the field, they said, "What are you doing down here?" The video director, Al Treml, pointed out the coaches on the field. I looked around, and it was just a mess out on the field with all those guys that are on the roster, and the coaches and the equipment guys and everybody. It seemed like there must have been 30 coaches—all dressed alike. They all had on green sweaters, all wore Packer caps, and there were about 10 blacks and about 20 white guys. I thought, "I'll never get them all figured out." I ended up figuring out who was who and just had a ball. After every offensive and defensive series, special teams—after kick-offs, punt-returns, whatever, I'd run the pictures out to the coaches who were standing out almost on the field. I just had a great time. That was a big deal for me.

——STEVE SCHMITT, owner, The Shoe Box, Black Earth, Wisconsin

I've been a Packer fan since the womb. Every Sunday, since we were four or five years old, we would sit with my dad, and he would teach us plays. He would tell us what was going on. Every Sunday, we watched Packer football—even when they weren't good—we still sat there and watched everything. My earliest memory is of how *bad* the Packers were. I remember, as a little girl, my dad throwing the foam Packer bricks constantly at the TV. My sister and I would have to go pick them up every quarter. My sister and I asked for tickets for our

Christmas present every year. We would always dress up. One year, we were bear hunters. We dressed up completely in green and gold camouflage. Another year, we were Santa Claus elves, all green and gold. One year my grandma made up these cow costumes at Halloween. She took all the black spots and painted them green and gold so we were Packer cows. It took her 55 hours to paint every spot. I dress up even if I'm watching the game at home. I'll paint my face, everything. I paint my face when I go to the bar to watch the game. My whole family does. I love the Packers. My bridesmaids' dresses are green and gold. My wedding band is actually going to be green and gold. I also have a Packer tattoo.

———TRISHA DENUCCI, Roberts, Wisconsin

I was in grade school, when the Packers played in the old City Stadium over by the school. We used to go in either through the fence, or over the fence, and sometimes you could walk in with an adult who had a ticket, and they would just push two through the turnstiles at once. Once you got in, naturally you didn't have a seat, so you either had to walk around the track, or lay in the end zone. I spent many games over there, as a kid.

One game, it had rained the day before, and the field was fairly soft. We were sitting in the back of the end zone. Leon Hart, a big tight end from Detroit, came tromping through and caught a pass. Naturally, we scattered. After he went through, we went back to where we had been, and there was a great big footprint right where I was sitting so I was glad I got out of the way. He was one of the real big players at that time.

———LLOYD STEINBRECHER, retired, Green Bay

The first memory of the Packers would be when I was five years old. I didn't live in Green Bay at that time but my grandparents did. When I was 14, we moved to Green Bay. When I was going to college, I worked for the Green Bay Board of Education maintenance department. One of the jobs we had each summer was to shore up the old City Stadium so it would pass the building inspection in the fall. I had the fun of hoisting 16-foot 6 x 6's into position to prop up the old wooden City Stadium. We used to say at that time, that Green Bay East High School had the largest high school stadium in the country…it held 33,000 people!

———DR. FRANK URBAN, Brookfield, Wisconsin

Chapter 3

Today We Ride

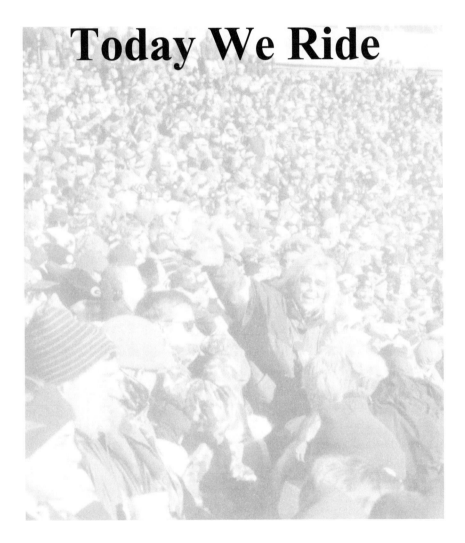

On the Road Again

A LOT OF OLD PEOPLE LIVE IN FLORIDA...WITH THEIR PARENTS

ROBERT GOODWYN

Bob Goodwyn lives in Beaver Dam, Wisconsin. He lived many years in Tampa Bay, where he was a founding member of the Tampa Bay Packer Backers.

October 10, 1937 is a day I'll always remember. My dad took me to a game at State Fair Park, in West Allis, which is part of Milwaukee. The Packers were playing the Chicago **Cardinals**, and the Packers won 34-13. You can't imagine how thrilled I was to see the Packers play, and to see them win. Marshall Goldberg was a rookie for the Cardinals that year, and he was really highly thought of, but the Packers really bottled him up good that day.

In the late 50s, I was able to invite a Packer player to come down and speak at a sports banquet that I happened to be the chairman of. I invited Tom Bettis, who was a linebacker with the Packers, a first-round draft choice out of Purdue. At the time, I was employed by a shoe manufacturing company here in Beaver Dam. For Tom's visit down here, he was paid with a new pair of shoes. I guess things have really changed, as today's players wouldn't walk across the room for a new pair of shoes.

Later, we needed another speaker, and we'd already had Tom Bettis and Willie Davis. We wanted to reach a little higher. We contacted the Packer office to see if we could get Coach Lombardi to come. His office said, "No, you can't get the coach to come to something like that. He doesn't make a lot of public appearances." But we weren't

> In the 1970s, a St. Louis football **Cardinals** fan bought an ad in the *St. Louis Post-Dispatch* offering to sell the "Official Cardinals' Playbook" with "all five plays illustrated, including the squib punt."

easily discouraged, and we thought if we could come up with an award for him, that he might come down to accept it. Then the question became, what do you give a guy like that who has already won everything? So we decided to name him, "Wisconsin's Outstanding Catholic Layman of the Year." The first annual award! And by gosh, if he didn't come down. He brought Tom Miller, the publicity director of the Packers, with him. I was the chief officer of that organization, which was a charity group, so I sat at the head table, and it was my job to introduce Mr. Lombardi.

I introduced him by reading the plaque we had made for him, and then said, "It's now my pleasure to introduce Coach Lombardi." I stepped back. The coach just sat there, looking down at his plate. I started worrying that he wasn't finished with his meal yet, but I wasn't exactly sure what was going on. I started getting kind of uneasy, shifting back and forth on my feet. I finally stepped back up to the podium and said something foolish like, "It sure was nice of the coach to be with us tonight." Finally, he got out of his chair and walked up to the front and shook my hand. He turned to the crowd and said, "I have received much recognition in my lifetime for my accomplishments in athletics, particularly football, but this is the first time anyone has recognized me for my dedication to my God and my religion. I am highly appreciative and am deeply moved by this award." I'm telling you that everyone in that room was on the edge of their seats for that whole talk. If he had told us to jump out the window I think we would have. Years later, I read that he said that in his life, his religion was first, his family was second, and the Packers were third.

I moved to **Florida** in 1972. I hung on to my tickets though, even though that was during the lean years. It was pretty hard selling your tickets when you're 1300 miles away, but I didn't want to give them up. I was delighted in 1976 when the NFL announced that Tampa Bay had been awarded a franchise and would be assigned to the "Black and Blue Division," meaning they would play the Packers

Gatorade is named after the mascot for the University of Florida. It was developed by a professor there under a grant from Stokely-Van Camp.

twice a year. What that meant for me was, that I'd finally be able to see the Packers on TV when the Bucs played in Green Bay, *and* I'd get to see the Packers live when they came to Tampa Bay.

It was at this point that I realized that there must be a lot of Wisconsin people in Florida who would enjoy getting together for a little social event when the Packers came to town. I talked to a few people I knew who were from Wisconsin. We decided we would form a group and we called it "The Tampa Bay Packer Backers." Our first event was a brunch that we held at the Admiral Hotel in Tampa. We promoted the event by word of mouth. We were pleasantly surprised to have nearly a hundred Packer Backers in attendance. One of the people who happened to be in the area was Ray Scott, who had been the voice of the Packers back in the Lombardi years. He retired from CBS after being the lead announcer on CBS's football broadcast. He'd been living in Phoenix, and was hired to do the radio broadcast for Tampa Bay that first season. He heard about our event and was happy to come and serve as our master of ceremonies. Another former player, Bob Long came. It was a great event and we had a good time, but there were some logistical problems. We had a really difficult time getting the fans from the hotel to the game on time, so we realized we didn't have the right format for what we wanted. The next year, we just decided to have a good old-fashioned Wisconsin tailgate party with beer and brats and the whole works. That year 346 people showed up! That's when we knew that we had something the fans wanted to be part of. We served all the brats they could eat, all the Miller beer they could drink, and even had souvenirs for them to take home. We brought a German polka band down from Madison and these guys were really good. They didn't even want any money; they just wanted four tickets for the game. Some of our guests that day were Bob Harlan, the president of the Packers; Tony Canadeo, who was on the executive committee. Also showing up were Ray Nitschke, Boyd Dowler, Hog Hanner, Mark Wagner the ticket director. The team photographer was even there taking pictures.

One year we got Frankie Yankovic to come. He was called "America's Polka King." At that time, he was getting kind of old, so he was more than happy to come. Something happened that was kind of funny with him. He was coming down to Tampa, and his wife was driving their fifth wheel truck, with Frankie asleep in the camper trailer being pulled behind. There was a fire back in the trailer and he had to get out. He had taken his false teeth out while he was asleep. When he rushed to get out of the trailer he had to leave his teeth behind. So, he went several days with no teeth!

Really at that time, Frank Yankovic wasn't 100 percent with it, but his name gave us some instant credibility. The band director playing with him knew what was going on, so when it came time to play, he gave Frank the songs, but never turned his microphone on. So for the whole show he was up there going through the motions, but no one ever actually heard him playing. It looked good!

Another funny story happened during the early years. We really weren't big enough to demand a lot of attention, since people thought we weren't for real. We had to get our beer through a local tavern, since we didn't have a beer license. We weren't selling the beer, but you did have to pay ten dollars to come to the party. This particular year, it was a really hot day. It was a one o'clock game so we opened our gates at ten o'clock. The guy who was supposed to be bringing the beer didn't show up. It got to be ten-thirty and he still wasn't there. These people wanted their beer! My gosh, it was hotter than hell down there in September. We got hold of this policeman who was there directing traffic, and he got on his radio and got the police department out looking for this guy. They finally found him and escorted him to the game. Everyone got their beer and everything was fine.

Speaking of the beer, we'd have six big beer trucks with two spigots on each side. People would line up and we'd have volunteers running the spigots. Once we turned those spigots on, we never shut them off. Somebody would have their cup under there and when it was full, someone else would be waiting to stick theirs under there. The beer would just continue to flow for the whole time the party was going on!

Everything we did was with Wisconsin products. The brats we served came from the Johnsonville Sausage Company in Johnsonville, Wisconsin; the beer was Miller Beer; and everyone that came got a souvenir towel that came from the McArthur Towel Company in Wisconsin. Other than Frank Yankovic, even the polka band came from Wisconsin.

We had police protection, not that we really needed it, but we had three officers there just mingling with the crowd. The last year I was there, we had 5,500 people. The police helped keep out gate-crashers and maintain a little bit of order.

We used over fifty kegs of beer and 2,400 pounds of brats! One year, the Johnsonville people brought down this special device for our party. It was called the "Big Taste Grill," and it was like one of those round milk trucks, or round gas trucks on a semi. They sliced off one quarter of this tank and built a grill into it. There were steps that led up to it, and we had seven guys up there grilling the brats. They had originally said they didn't take the trailer out of Wisconsin, but they did send it down to see us.

The night before the game, we knew there were a lot of people coming in from out of town. Something that helped us was that we could always get tickets. People could never get tickets to a Packers game in Green Bay, since they were always sold out. So, here these folks could come to Florida, go to a tailgate party, *and* get to see a Packers game. We'd purchase their tickets and they'd get to sit in a Packers section. One year I remember the total attendance at the game was 41,000, which is still only about half the capacity. And over half of the 41,000 were Packer fans! You'd look up at the crowd and there was more green and gold than Tampa colors. We also made a lot more noise!

From 1978 to 1996, when I moved back to Wisconsin—I was involved with the Tampa Bay Packer Backers. The group finally fell apart a few years later for a variety of reasons. After I got out of the organization, the whole thing finally fizzled out. One of the reasons was that the Tampa team started picking up, and they didn't want all those Packer fans there. They put a limit on the number of tickets the Packer Backer Club could get. Before I left, the Packers saw how many people we were getting to come to our tailgate party. They decided they wanted to put one on in Tampa also. They advertised it as "The Official Green Bay Packer Tailgate Party". OK, we weren't official! It didn't matter though, because people wanted to come to our party. They'd call and ask, "Is this the big one or the one that the team is putting on, because we want to go to the big one?" That made us feel good. We made people buy their tickets in advance, usually about a week in advance, so we'd know how much beer to buy, how many brats to buy, how many souvenirs to buy and so on. We actually made money on our party every year. Here the Packer tailgate party was charging three dollars for a beer, and we were giving them all they could drink and all the brats they could eat for ten dollars! People would come to our gate and say, "We thought we were buying tickets to your party and we found out we got them for 'America's Party' and we don't want to go there, we want to come to yours." Unfortunately, we couldn't take care of them because it was by advance tickets only.

We were the largest non-local fan club in the NFL. We also coined the phrase "The Battle of the Bays" when we were there. This past year the newspaper picked up that phrase and started using it, but actually we coined it fifteen years ago.

So many people came from out-of-state to watch the game and come to our party. They would come to Tampa and didn't know the city and didn't know what to do. So on Saturday night we held an event called "The Packer Polka Party." We'd hold it at a hotel where a lot of the people were staying, and we always got a big crowd for that. We also had a get-together at a bar in Tampa that was in a shopping center. Bart Starr was the coach then, and Bart Starr and his wife showed up and stayed for about twenty minutes.

If you try to find people who support the Packers, I'd have to fit into that category. When you look at what I was involved with in Tampa, you realize that we weren't doing it for the team—we were doing it for the fans.

In 1973, the Packers beat the Bears 21-0. The Bears were lucky to score 0.

VIKING FANS DON'T KNOW JACK.
MARY JO KNOWS JACK.

MARY JO LINK

Mary Jo Link lives in Minong, Wisconsin. She was born and raised in Shawano, Wisconsin, which is only 35 miles from Green Bay. She now lives 250 miles from Packerland, but after getting her parents season tickets, she rarely misses a game. Mary Jo is married to Jack Link, the owner of Jack Link and King B meat snacks.

My mom and dad went to all the games. They went with another couple so the other couple's daughter and I would spend Sundays together while our parents went to the games. About the age of 12, I really became interested in the Packers. My parents picked out their seats in the new stadium back before it was even finished. There used to be a lot of the original people in the north end zone where my parents had their tickets, but because of age, a lot of them have turned over to other people now.

Some days my dad would have to work on a Sunday, and I would end up getting to go since there wasn't anyone else they could get on a last minute's notice. I just remember how different the games were back then. My mom would dress in nylons, a fur coat and a dress. We would never dress like that today. We all wear jeans and end up getting beer spilled on us. But back then, it was an event to go to a game. You see pictures of the Ice Bowl with people wearing fur coats and dresses. The championship the year before was actually colder, because they didn't record wind chill back then. At that game, we had everything we could get on to stay warm. We had on long underwear, clothes on top of that, snowmobile suits on top of that. We stayed at a hotel across town, and tailgated at the Kmart parking lot near the stadium. We had to go to these port-a-potties, and they were so tiny that it was comical trying to use them with all those layers of clothes on. We brought Styrofoam to stand on, thinking that would be warmer than standing on the concrete. Once we got there it was amazing, because it wasn't even cold. It's always warmer in the stadium with all the people in there. It's a good thing too, because the Styrofoam broke apart the minute we stood on it. As the game wore on, and we knew we were going to the Super Bowl, it really got warm!

One other game I really remember was a rain game against the 49ers. It was a playoff game in January and it was so cold. It rained and rained and rained. We were just soaked. I remember walking into the stadium and having to wring out my mittens. We tried our best to avoid the puddles, but right before you got to the entrance, there was this giant puddle. You either had to walk through it or have someone carry you, so our feet were absolutely soaked by the time we even got inside. That same rainstorm in Green Bay dumped snow up in Minong, about fifteen inches. Driving home it was like a complete whiteout. It was really exciting.

The top dog of games for me was the Super Bowl in **New Orleans**. It was really special. Both of my sons went with me, since they weren't married at the time. We went through this company in Green Bay that put together the whole package. I managed to get our tickets upgraded, so we ended up in the end zone in the second and fourth rows. I let my sons have the second row seats. I don't know why, but we all ended up being on TV several times.

There weren't enough hotel rooms in New Orleans, so we ended up staying on a ship in the harbor. The only bad part of the trip was having to drive the 250 miles from Minong to Green Bay to meet the group that was going on the trip. Right before we left, a gas truck hit the plane we were supposed to fly on. We had to wait on them to bring another plane in for us, and they ended up not having anything stocked on the plane like beer or drinks or anything. Coming home we left at four in the morning on Monday. When we landed it was so cold…it was just terrible.

> **At halftime of a New Orleans Saints game in 1968, Charlton Heston drove a chariot and rode an ostrich while filming the movie *Number One*.**

We had to miss the parade when the players came back, because we had another commitment in Las Vegas. We were actually only home for one day before we left again. We were going to Las Vegas to a Safari Club International convention. I took my green and gold boa to wear with my black dress. Everyone just went nuts over that, because everyone loved the Packers. It was really fun, and it seemed like it never stopped.

We went the next year to San Diego, but it wasn't nearly as much fun, since we didn't win. In New Orleans, it was like we owned the city. We could do pretty much whatever we wanted. You could drink on the street, or whatever. At New Orleans, they made the whole event for the fans of the two teams. In San Diego, it was more like a big party for the people who lived there. They were nice to us, but it was just different. They had cages in front of buildings, where you couldn't walk outside if you had a beer. We went to one Super Bowl party with Brett Favre's family. I took pictures and ended up losing the roll of film. It was so funny out there, because they'd have a Super Bowl party and they'd run out of beer. Well, Packer fans drink a lot of beer, so they'd say "Somebody's coming with more beer." In a little while someone would show up with a beer cart and they'd have two cases on it. They didn't understand Packer fans.

I used to go to the Viking-Packer games, because we don't live that far from Minneapolis and we never had trouble getting tickets. I don't go anymore though, because they're just not that nice to us. I've been to Indianapolis; I got to go the inauguration at Soldier Field. The Bear fans were really nice, although I've talked to Packer fans in Milwaukee who say they can't stand the Bear fans. I'd heard all these bad things about Soldier Field, people said it was like a spaceship, but I really liked it. It's a city stadium, nothing we'd want in Green Bay, but I thought it was nice. We also went to the Packer-Bear game down in Champaign the year they were rebuilding Soldier Field. That was really neat. We had front row seats for that one. We have a friend, Jimmy John Liautaute, who owns Jimmy John's Sub Shops, who is from Champaign. The Bear fans just didn't want to travel to Champaign for these games, so there were always tons of tickets available. Jimmy John has a lot of business associates and friends, so he bought season tickets and brought in people who were interested in that particular game. He was so nice to us, and he gave us the front row seats. He really showed us a good time.

I have a whole room of Packers stuff. I have a life-size cutout of Brett Favre standing in the room. I have my tickets from the Super Bowls, I have beer from the Super Bowl, I have a beautiful picture of Mike Holmgren on his motorcycle. I have the bobble heads. I have some handmade items. I have this beautiful little outhouse that someone in our North Dakota plant made for me. It's painted green and gold, and it has a number four for the handle on the door. You can see the light through there, and it has two lights, a green one and a regular one. It has everything in there, and you can open the door and see all of it. My husband looked at it and said, "My god, who would ever spend that much time on something like that?" But I love it. My whole family room is decorated in Packer memorabilia. When we built the bathroom in this house, we put in off-white tiles with green and gold small tiles going around the edge of the room. The marble counter top has green and gold going all through it, and we have a forest green toilet. The first item I bought when I went to my first game after getting our season tickets was the picture of Bart Starr going across the goal line at the Ice Bowl. Everyone I know sends me Packer stuff, so I've got a ton of it now.

I'm on my third Packer-striped vehicle. My first one was an Expedition that I had "Go Pack Go" painted on the side in green and gold with a "G" flag on the back. Last year, I got a Lincoln Navigator. The guy who does my painting for me came up with a great idea. I wanted "Packer Fever-No Cure" on one side, and on the other side I wanted, "Leaving for Lambeau" with a Green Bay flag on the back. He came up with the idea to put the words on the back, with a squiggly green line that turns into a running football player on the door with a football in his hand and the number four on his jersey. People drive by us on the road and take pictures of the vehicle. We used to drive to games and park at the stadium. People would have their tables set up between their cars to party, and they'd see us and move their tables to get us to park next to them. I had pictures of my first vehicle on a Packers website called "The South End Zone." I got new plates on my vehicle, but I didn't want the Packer plates because they were yellow and I didn't want them against my green and gold car. So I got the traditional Wisconsin plate and had "MJ2GB" which excited me! Other things we tried to come up with just didn't seem right. With my name being Mary Jo, and my husband being Jack, it stands for "Mary Jo to Green Bay," or "Mary and Jack to Green Bay."

If my husband goes to the game with me, we have a big tailgate party. We're in the meat snack business, so we fly into Green Bay, and have one of the folks who sell for us bring in the Jack Links van. We stay at the Days Inn, which is right across from the stadium. It's a great place, because there are four bars. All the way around you, there are bands playing. We have beer and mixed drinks, and of course lots of Jack Link snacks to eat. The size of the tailgate party depends on who you're going with.

GREEN BAY PACKERS GREEN BAY PACKERS GREEN BAY GREEN BAY PACKERS GREEN BAY

Packers quarterbacks during a 1994 preseason game. (Left to right) Ty Detmer, Kurt Warner—yes, that Kurt Warner, Mark Brunell, and Brett Favre.

YOU CAN'T GET INTO HEAVEN UNLESS YOU'RE A PACKER FAN

JIM PILLEZZER

Jim Pillezzer, 44, is the pastor of the World Harvest Christian Center in Carmi, Illinois. He grew up in the Upper Peninsula of Michigan.

Growing up in the Upper Peninsula of Michigan, it was just natural to be a Packers fan, even though the Detroit Lions were the home state team. Where I grew up was only two and a half hours to Green Bay, and it was ten hours to Detroit. Of course, the Packers were the better team too, especially in the 60's.

I didn't get to go to my first game until December of 1977. Ironically, it was against the Lions. It was a cold winter day, and it was just wonderful! That was the Lynn Dickey era, and one of my favorite players was a defensive lineman named Dave Roller, I have an autographed picture of him. The Pack beat the Lions 10-9, so it was a perfect day. After the game, we ran down onto the field and it was just pure mud. It was the last game of the season, so they let us just run out there. It was quite an experience.

Even down here in Carmi, Illinois, which is in the deep southern end of the state, I run into Packer fans. At church, there are a few fans, and sometimes I wear a Packer tie with my suit when I preach. I have a tie with a G on it, and I tell them the G stands for God *and* the Green Bay Packers. I was over in Evansville, Indiana getting gas one day. I noticed the guy next to me paying with his Packer credit card. I struck a conversation with him, and he was a huge fan. Even here in Southern Illinois, where you would expect everyone to be either a Ram or a Bear fan, you constantly find Packer fans.

What's so neat about Green Bay is that you can drive through there and not see any skyscrapers. In fact, the tallest thing in the city is the lights at Lambeau Field. I was talking with a youth pastor that lives in

Rockford, Illinois the other day. He said he was just in Bismarck, North Dakota, and that all they bragged about was that Bismarck was the largest city in North Dakota. Then, you go to Green Bay and people brag about being the smallest city in the NFL.

I had two candy bars that they don't make any more, one was a Brett Favre and one was a Reggie White. One day my wife found the wrappers and figured out that our son had found them and eaten them. We were lucky though, and we found out that they still had some in the Hall of Fame and I was able to replace them.

My son is ten, and he's already a big Packer fan. Of course it's like it was when I was a kid, and you really didn't have a choice. We had a black and white TV, and when the game came on, you were told that you were going for the team in white, or if the Packers had on the dark jerseys you were told to cheer for the team in black. If you said, "No, I want to go for the team in white." You were told, "No, you're for the team in black." There was just no question.

I was so glad the Packers didn't tear down the old stadium. They did a great job of fixing it up and it's still Lambeau Field. The history is there, and it would never have been the same. You hear them talking about taking down Busch Stadium in St. Louis, and I know it will never be the same for **Cardinal** fans down here. They avoided that in Green Bay, and they've made it so much nicer now.

One year we were coming home from vacation, I told my wife I had to turn off and show them Green Bay. I said, "You have to see this, it's where the Packers play." I took them to the Hall of Fame and showed them the stadium. They're looking up at the stadium and they were going, "OK," but they didn't get the same feelings I did.

This coming week, a guy from church is going with me to Green Bay. We're going to take in the Hall of Fame, the stadium, and there's a McDonalds in town that's all decorated in green and gold with tons

> **Orlando Cepeda used more bats than any player in history. He felt that each bat had exactly one hit in it. When Cepeda got a hit, he would discard the bat. He got 2,364 hits in his career.**

of pictures on the walls. It's worth going to just to look at the pictures. The Packers are playing on Monday night. My brother is working on trying to get us tickets. If he can't, we'll have to just scalp some, because we really want to make it to a game. I can't wait to show him the sights. You're driving along and you see Lombardi Avenue, Holmgren Way, you see the houses painted green and gold, you pass cars painted in Packer colors—I mean it's the whole package.

Here I am 44 years old, and I'm planning this trip to Green Bay. I'm all excited, talking about getting there early and maybe getting some autographs, maybe getting some stuff. I am old enough to be most of the players' dad, and I'm still like that 17-year-old going to my first game.

To me, Green Bay is better than Disney World.

When Joe Paterno takes off his glasses, does his nose come off too?

THE PACKERS ARE AN ITCH THAT DOESN'T GO AWAY WITH ONE SCRATCH

CHARLES MUDGETT

Charles Mudgett lives in Waukesha, Wisconsin and is 71 years old. Formerly a sales manager, he has been retired for six years. He became a Milwaukee season-ticket holder in 1961.

A couple of years prior to the two leagues merging, the Packers played Cleveland in a championship game in Green Bay. I wrote for tickets to the game, and I got tickets. So a friend and I took a train from Milwaukee to Green Bay the day before the game. We stayed at the Northland Hotel. The next morning, we came down to the dining room for breakfast, and we sat at a table right next to Ray Scott and Tony Canadeo who were doing the Packer games at the time. We were impressed by that. I remember Ray Scott had a bowl of oatmeal for his breakfast. A big man, a famous broadcaster, and he was just eating oatmeal. We took a cab out to see the game, and then we caught the train back to Milwaukee that night after the game.

When the Packers played in the Super Bowl in New Orleans, I was drawn in the lottery of Packer ticket holders for Super Bowl tickets. My son, John, and I flew down to New Orleans for the game. We left on a Friday night charter flight and didn't get to New Orleans until two in the morning. We were to stay in Gulfport, Mississippi, which is a couple of hours away from New Orleans. By the time we got to the hotel, it was four in the morning. Then, the same morning, we got on a bus at eleven o'clock, and we were dropped off at the French Quarter in New Orleans. That's a place and a half! It was just loaded with Packer fans and New England fans. We stayed there until eight or nine that night and went back to our hotel.

The next day—game day—there was a big tailgate party in a little town called Bay St. Louis, the home of the famous author Stephen Ambrose, for the Packer fans. Then we went to the game and were taken back to our hotel. We were scheduled to come home Monday evening, so Monday morning, we got up and they offered to take us over to the casinos in Biloxi. Instead, John and I rented a car, and we drove thirty miles to Kiln Mississippi, Brett Favre's home town. There was a big statue of Brett Favre as you came into town. We went to the bar, The Broke Spoke, and that was a scene to behold. They had little bleachers set up in back and had a great big TV where people had watched the Super Bowl the day before. They had a big bin made out of wire, probably 8'x 8'x8', to throw their empty beer cans in. That thing was just about full of empty beer cans. I can imagine that was quite a Super Bowl party. We went into a restaurant for lunch and talked to people there. They told us where Brett Favre's dad lived, and we drove down a road trying to find it. But we must have done something wrong, because we didn't find his farm. That night, the plane bringing us home was late so we didn't get out of there on time, and we got into Milwaukee at five o'clock in the morning. Maurice, a guy from Fond du Lac, got on the plane wearing a tee shirt, pair of shorts and flip-flops. We got into Milwaukee, and there was a foot of snow and cold winds. It was funny watching Maurice try to get to his car.…

When we went to games in Milwaukee, we tailgated for every game. That last game in Milwaukee, the Packers played Atlanta. They didn't collect the tickets. They just marked the back of the tickets, and said, "You can have your ticket back." They ran out of programs at the game because people were buying them for other people who couldn't get tickets to the game. There were a lot of complaints from people who couldn't get a program. They republished the program and sent one or two to each Milwaukee ticket holder. I framed the two tickets and the program together. On one of the last plays of the game, Brett Favre dove into the end zone for a touchdown.…

There was The Vince Lombardi Charity Golf Tournament in Milwaukee every year. Back in the early days, after the games in Milwaukee, the players would come out to get on the bus, and they would sign autographs and talk to people. One time, I got to meet Ray Nitschke. We could go to practices, and I met some of the players there. They were much more open then than they are now. Some of them even drove their own cars when they came to play in Milwaukee. I remember Willie Wood and Bob Jeter coming out after the game and walking over to the parking lot and getting in their cars. Now, the players have their own parking lot in Green Bay, and you can't even see into that lot.

Comparing the Packer teams from both Super Bowl eras, if there was a way they could have played each other in their prime, I think the Brett Favre team would have won. Players are so much bigger and are faster now than they were in the old days. Lombardi's team had a lot of skill, but now the game gets faster, and the players get bigger. I don't think Lombardi ever had a player on his team that weighed 300 pounds. A 250-pound lineman was big then, and they weren't as fast as they are now. I think as far as quarterback skills, Brett Favre has much better quarterback skills than Bart Starr did—and he's a much better passer.

A lot of people were critical of the Packers when they quit playing in Milwaukee, but I think that's one of the best things they did. First of all, Milwaukee was a terrible place to watch a football game. It was a baseball stadium. Even though I had decent seats there, I thought it was entirely different the first time I went to Lambeau Field. It's such a fantastic place to watch a football game. The Packers treated the fans more than fair. They could have just said, "To heck with you Milwaukee fans," and could have given all the tickets to Green Bay fans. But they didn't, and I think it was a great way of doing it.

Randy Moss isn't smart enough to know he's dumb.

GASSIN' UP

Vince Lombardi is buried in a Catholic cemetery. It's 53 acres, so it is a large cemetery. He has a typical, gray, normal size monument, probably 3 feet wide by 3 feet high. It's inscribed Vincent Lombardi, date of birth and date of death. His wife is buried next to him.

A lot of people come, but probably not as many as in the past. People still come and bring stuff—footballs, helmets, some even put quarters on the grave, especially in the last ten years. The quarters are from the Jewish custom of putting stones on graves, so I find the pennies, nickels, quarters on top of the stones. I guess they do that to show they were there. There are flowers on the grave for some special days, like Fathers' Day, so I assume family members come, too. I get a lot of requests to take pictures of people while they stand by the gravesite.

One guy came and taped it, and then he went to the Super Bowl, then he came back and taped the stone again. Some people talk to him—"Vince, we won the Super Bowl," or tell him the time and day when they're there.

——JOE LUCIA, Superintendent, Mt. Olive Cemetery, Middletown, N.J., site of Vince Lombardi's gravesite.

Gilbert Brown came to Ladysmith with the Packer basketball team during the off-season to play in a benefit game. There he was, all three hundred-plus pounds of him, out there playing basketball. He'd be out there running down the court, and Gilbert would disappear into the stands. The ref would stop the game when they realized they were a player short, and there would be Gilbert up in the stands hiding behind a bunch of kids. I've never laughed so hard in all my life.

Even though we're over two hundred miles away, we still make it to games. I took my son to his first game when he was six. We were in Green Bay. There was a preseason game so I took him. He was so tiny he had to sit on my lap for the whole game. People around me asked if I had to pay for that seat even though he didn't use it. As he got older, I gave up my seat so he could go with his father. Now he's a cadet at West Point. Last year, he watched the first game of the season on a computer, because they don't have TV's at West Point.

He was watching on his computer with a fifteen-second delay, and the rest of the family was watching at home on TV. We were talking back and forth on the phone, and of course we knew what was happening fifteen seconds before him. He always tells me that it doesn't do any good for me to yell at the TV, since they can't hear me.

——**LEANNE BURCH**, Ladysmith, Wisconsin

Fuzzy's restaurant in Green Bay is one of our favorite places, and we have to make a trip there at least once a year. Fuzzy Thurston is the owner, and he's usually in there. As soon as you walk in, you have to endure one of his big bear hugs, he's really quite a guy. When the kids were little, we used to go up for autograph days. I can remember Donny Anderson, Eddie Lee Ivery, and some of those guys. Eddie Lee was always going around with his arm under his shirt saying, "My arm's broke, I can't sign today, my arm's broke!" My greatest memory of all is from when I was in the military in South Vietnam. I was fortunate to be in an infantry outfit that was pulling some guard duty around some artillery. We were behind the front, laid back around some sand bags. I got to listen to the Cleveland Browns-Green Bay championship game. I was lying there crying, because it was so neat. I always thought I was so lucky to be able to have listened to that game over Armed Forces Radio. Thirty-one years later I got to sit in the stands and watch the Pack win another championship game.

There's no doubt that the Packers are really "America's Team." The universal appeal of the Pack is that they're not some George Steinbrenner toy, they're our team. That's what appeals to everyone. They're owned by the city and the fans, and that's what makes them so special. I know I have my stock proudly displayed in my home. In fact, I threw somebody out of my house once because he objected to me calling them "our Packers."

——**RAY CATES**, 59, Senior Systems Analyst at Snap-on Tools, Kenosha

I went to law school in Minnesota, so when the Packers would play there, I would always go to the games...and be fearfully booed. That would have been in the mid-seventies, and the Vikings had Fran Tarkenton, but that's about all they had. They would typically have more Packer fans than Viking fans. That's even true up until the past two or three years when the Vikings stopped selling tickets to the Packer fans. They try to sell the tickets to Vikings fans first. Minnesota is one of the worst places to go for a game. It's a madhouse being in the Hubert Humphrey Dome for noise. I've even had situations where I've gone looking for a hot dog or a beer, and would be ignored by the serving person because I would be wearing Packer clothes. Some places, like Minnesota, Tampa Bay and Detroit, have begun to package the Packer ticket with another ticket so the Packer fans have to pay for two games if they want to go see the Packers play there. I travel, and as soon as you mention you're from Green Bay, most everybody loves you. We were in Atlanta this past summer, and when they found out we were from Green Bay, they couldn't have treated us better. We stayed at a hotel that had Atlanta Falcon cookies, and they brought us a dozen of those, but they put a big "G" on the box for Green Bay. When I travel, either on vacation or on business, I'll always put in a Packer T-shirt or a Packer shirt and wear it one day, usually the first day, to see what kind of results I get. They treat you extra special when they find out you're from Green Bay. More than a few of them ask if I can get them some tickets.

——JIM JOANNES, attorney, Green Bay

A couple of years ago I was walking down the street in this little town called Whitefish, Montana. I had on my Packer shirt, which is pretty usual for me, and this car came screeching to a stop next to me. The driver rolled down his window and yelled out, "There's a Packer bar two blocks down on the right, you've got to go in there and see all the stuff they've got."... My nephew and I went to the Super Bowl in New Orleans. We were walking down the streets of New Orleans with our cheeseheads on. This lady stopped us and told us that she was from Kiln, Mississippi, Brett Favre's home town, and that she really wanted to get a couple of those cheeseheads. We did *not* give up our cheeseheads, but we told her how she could get one.

——RANDY KUNSCH, 54, Phillips, Wisconsin

No matter where I lived, there were always Packer fans around. When I lived in Colorado Springs, there was a place called Wile E. Coyote's that was owned by a guy from Milwaukee. He had the whole bar decorated in Packer regalia. There was another bar called The Dublin House, and it was owned by a guy from Minnesota. His place was all done up in a Viking motif. Every year there was a big rivalry between the two bars when the Packers played the Vikings. Somebody would always end up stealing some memento off the wall and you'd see it at the other bar the next day. I remember the Dublin House had this life-sized poster of Tommy Kramer. One day it disappeared, and the next day it showed up at Wile E. Coyote's. When I lived in New Hampshire, there were a few fans, not as many as I would have thought, but a few. In Massena, New York there were quite a few. Living right next to the Mohawk Nation, there were a lot of Packer fans there.

I went to Tampa Bay for a game one year down at the old Sombrero. During the day it was about 80 degrees, and that night it dropped to about 38 or 39. Chris Jacke missed a field goal to cost the Packers the game. We had been all pumped up thinking we'd just go down there and kick their butts. The game was right before Christmas, late in December. The hotel we were staying in was hosting this big corporate Pepsi dinner, all black-tie-and-tux kind of party. All the Packer fans were staying in the same hotel. They saw this big party going on where no one was dancing or partying. Finally, the Packer fans started going out on the dance floor, and before you knew it there were fifty or so Packer fans out there all decked out in green and gold, and all the people in tuxedos sitting around watching. They let it go for about an hour or so, then finally they came on the microphone and said, "OK, Packer fans, it's time for you to go!" There were over 3,000 people at the tailgate party we went to before that game. It was so funny, at the game you'd look into the crowd and see more green and gold than Tampa colors.

——KEVIN MATZKE, 39, Green Bay

The only away game I ever went to was the monsoon back in '95 in Chicago. It was Halloween night. It was raining so hard you couldn't see across the field. The only people in the stands by halftime were Packer fans. One of the Bear fans said to me, "This is our kind of

weather." I started laughing and said, "Your kind?" He said, "Yeah, wet and cold." I said, "Green Bay is 200 miles north of here. We've really got cold weather there, let me tell you...." In the upper peninsula of Michigan, there are more Packer fans than Lion fans. Fifteen or twenty years ago, that part of Michigan tried to start their own state and call it the "State of Superior." I've been told by people who live there that, at times over the last several decades, they really, truly would prefer to have been associated with Wisconsin than with Michigan.

——**DAN DUNN**, 54, Hartford, Wisconsin

After the Packers won Super Bowl XXXI, Desmond Howard was at the Pro Football Hall of Fame to sign autographs. I grabbed one of my many *Sports Illustrated* magazines with Desmond on the cover and headed off to the Hall. As I was wandering around waiting for the session to start, I saw some folks with Packers stuff on so I went on over and started chatting with them. I asked them if they were there to get Howard's autograph. They said they were just returning to Upper Michigan from Florida and had never been to the Pro Hall of Fame. They didn't know Desmond was going to be there. I asked what they would have him sign? All they had was the ticket stub from there admission to the Hall. I told them that I lived just a few minutes away and that I would get them something for him to sign. I went home and brought them back a *Sports Illustrated*. They were really grateful. They said that they had gone through Kiln, Mississippi. They took my address and told me they would send some pictures from there. A few weeks later, I received the pictures along with a few extra copies to give to my buddies. That was so nice of them. About two months later, I received a big box in the mail from these same folks. It was loaded with stuff: a sheet of Vince Lombardi stamps, a Super Bowl XXXI mug, a stuffed monkey wearing a Packers uniform, lots of newspaper clippings from the Green Bay area with articles on the Super Bowl, a VHS tape full of the Super Bowl celebration party activities. I watched all six hours in one seating. There were Packers shoestrings, and even a Packer toothbrush. I thought that box would never be empty. There was a note enclosed, "Just wanted to thank you again for a lifetime memory."

——RICK NELSON, Canton, Ohio

I couldn't believe the way the Packer fans were treated in Minneapolis. One year, we went and they did so much slamming of the Packer fans. That was a year the Packers lost, so their fans were really mouthing off at us. I said, "That's okay. You guys still have to come to Lambeau in December." Then, when we were leaving the Cities, as we were driving under the overpasses, they had fans standing up above us on the overpasses holding signs down over the freeway saying, "Go Home Losers!" We couldn't believe it. Their fans are just very different from Packer fans.

——PAM KUNSCH, Phillips, Wisconsin, Teacher

My favorite team of all-time would have to be the one that won the 1997 Super Bowl in New Orleans. Not only from the standpoint of the team itself, but also because Brett Favre was from nearby Kiln, Mississippi. We stayed in Long Beach, which is adjacent to Biloxi, and of course we had to go over and check out where Brett Favre was from. There was this bar called the Broken Spoke, which was a biker bar, and it was doing land office business. Across the street from the bar was a pickup truck with a sign on it that said, "Stills Repaired" and a phone number. So, it was quite a culture change for us coming from the very staid Wisconsin. We drove into New Orleans for the game. Parking was $15 and another $5 for protection. It was about two hours before game time, and I realized I had lost my ticket. My wife had the foresight when we got out of the car to get her ticket from me, but I lost mine. Usually in a situation like this, I would issue a lot of expletives deleted, but this time it was such a terrible thing that I just broke out in a cold sweat. We were about two blocks away from the Superdome so we walked over there and saw a sign that said "Ticket Problems." We thought, "No problem." We'll just go over there and tell them what happened. They said, "No way," and were not the least bit helpful. We're walking back down the street, not sure what to do, when we ran into a New Orleans policeman, who turned out to be from Sheboygan, Wisconsin. We told him our story, and he told us to go back there and go to this one particular area and that they would take care of us. We followed his advice and went to the "will-call" office, but they weren't very helpful either. I said to my wife, "We've come this far; I'm not leaving." About that time, Ron Wolf, the general manager of the Packers came walking by. I walked up to him even though he didn't know me from a hole in the ground. I told him my story, and asked what could be done. He handed me off to one of his aides and we walked back to the will-call desk. After showing them my ID, they finally agreed to sell me a ticket at face value, which was $275 (At the time tickets, on the street were going for $2000.). Fortunately, I had the money in my pocket and was able to get in. No one ever did show up for the seat I'd lost the ticket to, so I guess it had just blown away when I'd gotten into my pocket.

———DR. FRANK URBAN, 74, retired state legislator

I'm very proud and honored to be associated with the Packers. They run such a clean operation. My wife and I have stock in the Packers. They are owned, not by a corporation, but by a whole group of people. I know that anywhere I go, not that I travel that much, but I spend quite a bit of time in Florida, and I have never, never heard any derogatory report about the Packers. In fact, I ran into an incident this last year when I was in a restaurant. A guy was waiting on me, and the food was delayed so we started talking. It came out that I was a Green Bay fan, and I showed him my card. First thing we knew, this veteran from the Iraq War is taking us to Disney World *because* we're Packer fans. He had worked for the Disney people so he could take guests, and he took us. This is the feeling they have. He told me that one of his friends in service named his son after Brett Favre. It's a nice feeling to know that people are that way.

———ED JABLONSKI, 79, Fans Hall of Fame member

One of the greatest memories I have was going to the Super Bowl in '96. We'd gone to a lot of games that year including Seattle. One of my best friends, Corey, and I have as one of our goals to see the Packers play in every stadium before we die. We've been to nine of them.

On our way down to New Orleans, we left on a Tuesday morning and were eating at a little restaurant in Mississippi with all our Packer stuff on. Some girls there said, "Are you guys from Wisconsin?" During the conversation, we learned one of the girls had graduated from high school with Brett Favre. They were a little leery but we convinced them we were just Packer fans who wanted to see where Brett Favre grew up. They showed us where to go and pointed down Irving Favre Road by a lumber company. There was this gate there, but it was open and there was a freshly paved, long driveway. Two of us wanted to drive down the driveway and two didn't think we should go. I said, "Hey, let's just go down there. If somebody tells us to get out, we'll just turn around and leave." It was probably a quarter-of-a-mile long, and we pulled in there. Here was an older mobile home and a black Humvee that looked brand new. There was also a house off to one side and an A-frame house off to the other side. We got out and this lady came out of the mobile home and says, "Can I help you guys?" I said, "Yeah, we're from Wisconsin. We heard this was Brett Favre's place." She said it was. We said, "Where is he?" She said, "I'm MeeMee Favre, his grandma." I said, "Is it okay to be here?" She said, "Sure, make yourselves at home." We talked to her for quite a bit. She said that was Brett's brand new Humvee he had won for being the MVP. She told us it had just come that day, and Brett hadn't even seen it yet. It was neat to see the A-frame. He's got his uniform from the Atlanta Falcons and a Packer uniform in there. He had a pool table, more of a party place with a swimming pool outside.

That night we went out on Bourbon Street and we were down at The NFL Experience. We got to meet a few old Packers. We got to see Brett Favre and Frank Winters as we were coming out of a restaurant. Being at the Super Bowl and in New Orleans and having tickets and then the Packers winning—it may sound crazy but I'd say the birth of my children, my wedding day and, then, that Super Bowl are the greatest four days of my life.

——MIKE ZURFLUH, "Mr. Packer" in Wisconsin Rapids

It was only after Brett became famous that the bar became a "Packer" bar. We have all kinds of pictures of Brett Favre on our walls, and Brett's dad, Big Irv. Now, we get plenty of Packer fans who come here to our bar room to watch the games. At the last game, we probably had 35—40 from Wisconsin here to Mississippi to see the game in Brett Favre's hometown. Every Packer game, we get a lot of people from Wisconsin and plenty of home-town people. They buy tee shirts, caps, shot glasses that say "The Broke Spoke," cigarette lighters and stuff like that. During all the Packer games, we serve free food. Last game I cooked a big pot of spaghetti and cole slaw and garlic bread. And for all Monday Night Football games, I cook up a big pot of red beans and rice. These fans are wild whether the Packers are winning or losing. The last game, the Packers lost, and we still had a good time. They pull loudly for the Packers and cuss them a little bit when they're losing.

When Green Bay played in the Super Bowl in New Orleans, the Friday night before that Super Bowl, they estimated there were 5,000 people here—4,000 of them were probably from Wisconsin. Our bar will only hold about 50 people, so we set up a bar outside for that crowd. They closed down the street out front so traffic wouldn't go by because there were so many people. Kiln is a town of about 1,800 people. We don't have a big town, just a couple of stores and restaurants. We're pretty close to downtown. When all these people came here to town, they were scattered all over the place. Some of them even stayed right here at the bar because we stayed open 24 hours for nine days in a row. We never closed the doors. The Monday after the Super Bowl, we probably had 200 people come through here heading back home to Wisconsin. They were celebrating. A couple of months after the Super Bowl, we were averaging 75—100 Wisconsin people every day. Even now, in the wintertime, we probably get 20-30 Wisconsin people a day, and we get eight to ten tour buses from Wisconsin come through here. The only food we serve here is heat-'em-up pizza.

——STEVE HAAS, owner, The Broke Spoke bar in Kiln, Mississippi

In 1996, we went to the Super Bowl in New Orleans. While we were there, we decided to take a drive over to Kiln, Mississippi to see where Brett Favre had grown up. We drove over there and found his house. After we got out of the car, my husband started saying that we shouldn't go up to the house. I said I'd come all this way and I wasn't going to stop now. We went up and knocked on the door and Brett's father came out. We told him who we were and where we were from. He was so nice to us. I took a picture of him with my husband, then he said, "Don't you want a picture too?" So, my husband took one of the two of us. I asked him what it was like being the father of a superstar. He said it was nice but there was some sadness, too. I didn't really ask him what he had meant by that. He wasn't in any hurry for us to leave. He told us about the restaurant in town that his family owned. It was closed at the time, but we went back a few days later and met more of his family. We had quite a talk with one of his daughter-in-laws. Brett's dad said that if we ever came back to Kiln we could probably always catch him at that restaurant.

——MARY DUROCHER, former Packer employee

During the 1997 Super Bowl, we were on about the 20-yard line. There was an area for the auxiliary press next to us. We saw various people from the media. One guy kept looking over at us. We were all in good spirits before the game and cheering and having a good time. I looked around, and it seemed to me that it was well over half Packer fans. They had their yellow towels and were waving them. They had their cheeseheads on and several people creatively had blinking Christmas lights built into the cheesehead. One guy in our section stood up, looked around, and said, "Okay, let's hear it. This is the last *home game* of the year." Before the Packers were popular, a lot of people would wear their orange deer-hunting coats to stay warm. That was a little bit of a tradition. This guy, as kind of a throw-back thing, wore his blaze orange deer-hunting outfit inside the Superdome, which was about seventy degrees. We saw every kind of outfit there. This guy from the press who had been looking at us said, "You guys are scary." I said, "Why?" He said, "I've covered several Super Bowls. I've never seen anybody cheer and be that enthusiastic about every little thing." They had been putting up on the scoreboards quotes and pictures of different Packer people, from Bob Harlan to Ron Wolf. Whenever anything would come up on the screen, we would all cheer and go nuts. On Monday morning, we were able to rent a car and go over to Kiln, Mississippi and see some sights in Brett Favre's home town. At the Broke Spoke, the owner was out there in his khaki pants, with a rake in his hand, raking up beer cans and bottles. I asked him, "When did the party start?" He said, "I think about Tuesday of last week when the press started to come in." This was about eleven on

Monday morning, and I asked, "When did the party end?" He looked at his watch, "About two hours ago."

——JOHN MUDGETT, 44, Waukesha

 In 2000, we decided to go to Lambeau to watch the Christmas Eve game against Tampa Bay. The original plan was for my husband, my dad and me to go to the game. My sister, who is not much into football, planned to stay home with my Mom who was very sick with breast cancer. We ordered our tickets through www.packerfantours.com and got three pretty good seats. We were really looking forward to going to the game; however, my mom took a major turn for the worse and passed away just before Thanksgiving.

My whole world crashed down around me. We decided that since Christmas wouldn't be the same for us that year, we would still go to the game. Now we had another problem…we were in need of one more ticket because we didn't want to have someone sit alone. I called the people at Packer Fan Tours and explained my situation, hoping they could at least get us one ticket very near our other three seats. They did even better. That wonderful staff sent me four new tickets—without shipping charges. They billed my credit card for the extra ticket *and* sent me a shipping label so I could return the original three tickets. I fully expected to see charges on my credit card for a total of seven tickets, thinking I would get a credit once I returned the three tickets. However, all I was billed was the original charge for three tickets, plus the one new one! Thanks to Packer Fan Tours, we were all given the chance to spend a day together without any stress and were able to put aside our sad feelings for four quarters! Also, the atmosphere at Lambeau was unbelievable. The temp was -15, but we were still very warm. I have never been to a stadium or a town where the people were so friendly and welcoming. Our family tradition is to go to at least one Packer game a year. We started that five years ago now, and we are doing good so far.

——TRISH KEARSCHNER, Indianapolis

It has amazed me that no matter where I go, I run into Packer fans. I've started traveling now that I've retired, and I am constantly meeting fans. I was at the ruins in Mexico and saw a little boy wearing a

Packer shirt. I was in Martha's Vineyard and there was a Packer fan. I've gone on two Packers fan cruises. Ahman Green has been on both of the cruises; LeRoy Butler and Donald Driver were on the last one. They have an autograph session, and then they have a question–and–answer session, followed by a cocktail party. After that, you leave them alone, but it's still really something being on there with them. That's going to be an annual event for me.

I've been to Kiln, Mississippi and had my picture taken in front of Favre's hometown plaque. It probably sounds silly for a woman my age, but I'd really like to meet Brett Favre…I guess me and about fifty million other people. I asked if he might ever be on one of the cruises, but they say he's not into that kind of thing. Because of the security concerns, it would probably never happen. My impression of Brett is that despite all of his fame and success, it has never gone to his head. We have a man in town named Bill Quimby who was an NFL official and had worked with the Packers over the years. He says that Brett is just a fine young man, and that he was always impressed with his attitude and how well he could get the team going. He just confirmed what I already thought about him. I don't know what I'll do when he retires—I know someone else will come along, but there will never be another Brett Favre.

——BETTY DeBROWER, Cedar Rapids, Iowa

Difference between government bonds and Viking wide receivers??... Government bonds mature.

Chapter 4

It's Good To Be An NFL Owner

Let's Hear From Our Employees

DEVINE INTERVENTION

BOB HARLAN

Bob Harlan is the President and Chief Executive Officer of the Green Bay Packers. He has been with the Packers for thirty-four years, sixteen of those years as the President. He started with the organization on June 1st, 1971 as assistant general manager. Prior to joining the Packers, Mr. Harlan worked in public relations with the baseball Cardinals in St. Louis, and as the sports information director for his alma mater, Marquette University in Milwaukee.

I grew up in Iowa listening to **Harry Caray** doing Cardinal games on KMOX. I started working for the Redbirds late in the 60s. They moved into the new stadium in 1966 and won the World Series in 1967. I was at spring training for the Cardinals in 1971 when Dan Devine was named the coach and general manager of the Packers. Dan was a good friend of Bing Devine, my boss with the Cardinals (no relation). Dan called Bing and said he was looking for someone to come in and help him since he was doing both jobs. He wanted someone to be able to handle the contracts and the paperwork so he wouldn't have to deal with it. Bing knew that I had gone to school at Marquette and was a big Packer fan. Bing told me it would be a big jump in salary and a jump up in jobs, so if I wanted him to, he would throw my name in. I told him I wasn't looking to leave the Cardinals, but that I'd be interested in talking to them. Dan Devine flew down to St. Petersburg and interviewed me, then brought my wife and me to Green Bay a few days later and offered me the job. It hap-

Page Two. In 1941, the news director at a small radio station in Kalamazoo, Michigan hired Harry Caray away from a station in Joliet, Illinois. The news director's name was Paul Harvey. Yes, that Paul Harvey! "And now, you have the rest of the story......

pened very quickly. Bing is now in his mid-80s, and I still see him from time to time. Whenever he sees me, he always says, "Don't forget, I'm the guy who got you that job."

A lot of the problems in major league baseball and professional football are very similar. Of course, the jobs I had were very different. With the Cardinals I was in public relations, which meant I was basically a friend to the players. Here in Green Bay I'm the guy who negotiates contracts and such, so it's a different kind of relationship. As far as dealing with player problems, stadium problems, financial problems and the like, it's very similar. I've said one of the huge advantages of the NFL is that it only plays sixteen games a year. Playing **one game a week** means that every game has playoff implications. It's tough to say that about other sports where they're playing 82 or 162 games a year.

The other thing is that the longer I've been here, the more I appreciate the system that the NFL has. That's what saved Green Bay. The fact that Pete Rozelle convinced the other owners in the early sixties to share revenue is enormous. If we didn't have television revenue, we wouldn't have been in business this long. Secondly, when the most recent collective bargaining contract was signed in the early 90's, it included a salary cap. We knew that free agency was coming and we thought that if we had total free agency with no cap we would be in trouble. We did get a cap and the system is working extremely well. The stands are full, the league is very competitive, the advertisers love us, and we're in very good shape. Our biggest concern now is that the system remains in place, meaning we always have the revenue sharing and we maintain the salary cap. We can exist and compete as long as that system is in place. Other sports are not as fortunate as we are. Bud Selig is a good friend of mine, and he's always saying that he'd give anything to have the system the National Football League has. It's just been a huge boost for a city of 110,000 people. If we didn't have the system in place that we have today, we wouldn't be here.

The difference between a .250 and a .300 batting average is one hit per week.

The competitive balance in the NFL is wonderful. Everyone goes to training camp in July thinking that they have a chance. Look at Carolina making the 2004 Super Bowl.

We had a huge battle in Green Bay around our new stadium. We unveiled our plans in January of 2000 and the vote was taken in September of 2000. For those eight months, we had a battle both in Madison, where the state capitol is, and also with the Brown County board here in Green Bay. During that time frame, we made fifteen trips to Madison to deal with the legislature, then in spring we had to deal with the county and with the City of Green Bay. I guess what I learned, being new to politics, was that the word "tax" really bothers people. It was going to be a half-cent sales tax in Brown County. The state fiscal bureau did a report and showed that it would cost the average citizen thirteen cents a day or forty-six dollars a year! You would have thought we were asking for ten-thousand dollars a year. The battle was just enormous. The final vote was fifty-three percent to forty-seven percent, so we just barely got it through. All along, the opposition kept saying, "Just vote no, because they have a back-up plan." By the time we'd dealt with the legislature, the county board and the city, we were already at our Plan B. What now gives me the most pleasure is that, four years after that vote, the stadium is doing exactly what we said it would be doing. It's elevated the team in revenue; we've jumped from twentieth last year to tenth this year in revenue. It's going to keep the franchise viable in the NFL for the next generation. It's bringing visitors literally from around the world to Green Bay to see the stadium.

We actually did look into the possibility of moving the stadium. We never got to the point of looking at land, but the first thing we did was look at the bowl to see if it was even in good enough shape to keep playing here. With the weather conditions and the age, we were very concerned if it could last another thirty or thirty-five years. As soon as we got the clearance on that, we never even considered going anywhere else. This is where the tradition is. This is where the Lombardi teams practiced and played, this is where the Holmgren teams practiced and played, and that was important to us. We could have gotten some farm ground and built a new modern stadium, we could have even called it Lambeau Field, but it would never have been the same. I heard from so many fans that said, "Please don't leave that stadium." I mean it showed that the fans love the stadium as much as they love the team.

With the new stadium, we increased our seating capacity from 62,000 to about 72,500. We've been sold out for every game since 1960. We had two people come off the waiting list for tickets last year who had been on the list for 34 years. We have people who come in with their newborn children and put them on the waiting list, hoping that when that child is in his mid-thirties he might be in line for tickets! It's just a tremendous fan base that is very loyal and very patient. I'm not sure if they'd be as patient now if we started to decline, because we've had some great years. We've raised the bar, and they expect bigger things from us. We had some lean years in the 70's and 80's, but once we took off in the 90's, that bar was raised quite a bit. A lot of people had the feeling that when the Lombardi era came to an end, that we would never get back to those glory years. Then, when free agency came into being a lot of people said that the first team that would suffer would be the Packers. The thinking was that not many players would want to come to Green Bay to play, but once Reggie White came here, it made a lot of other players take notice. It's a great place to play football—you're adored by the fans, you play on grass, it's a great stadium, and the facilities are top-notch. We've had twelve straight years of .500 or above football, and the last time the Packers had a winning streak like this was 1934 to 1947, so the fans are a little spoiled now. That's OK, they deserve to be.

Late in the '91 season, when Ron Wolf came in, the Packers really began the build-up to the Super Bowl and the years we've had recently. We had struggled through the 70's and 80's and just couldn't find a consistent way to win. We needed to find a good solid football man who could come in and take charge of the situation. I had known Ron for some time…not as good friends, but I knew that he had worked for Al Davis and the Raiders for twenty-five years. I knew that anyone who could do that had to know a lot about football and has to be a very dedicated worker. I offered Ron the job late in the '91 season and he accepted. He had been offered the job as general manager in 1987 and had backed out right away. I thought I knew why he did, because I felt like he didn't know what kind of control he'd have with a 45-person board of directors. I hope I gave him the information he needed in '91, because he accepted. We brought him in during the middle of the season because I wanted him to live with the team and the coach, attend practices, see what was going on with the team, instead of having to spend an off-season trying to figure the team out from watching tapes. Fortunately, he was scouting with the **Jets** then, and they gave me permission to talk to him. I interviewed him, offered him the job, and he accepted. He came in here and right away he fired the head coach, Lindy Infante, with two years left on his contract, brought in Mike Holmgren, made the trade that brought Brett Favre here, got Reggie White as a free agent, and we went to the playoffs for six straight years and won the Super Bowl. So he just turned it around dramatically—it all started with Ron Wolf.

Brett Favre came to us in a trade from Atlanta, where we traded the Falcons our number-one pick for Brett. I heard from a lot of fans that wanted to shoot Wolf for giving up a number-one pick for a quarterback they'd never heard of. Of course, it sure worked out for the best. We've made some pretty good trades over the years. Just recently, we were able to get Ahman Green from Seattle, and he's been a tremendous running back for us.

Even in the lean years, we had some great players. Lynn Dickey was a great quarterback for us. James Lofton, who went into the Hall of Fame last year, was a superb receiver. Paul Coffman was a great tight end, and Larry McCarren was a great center. We had the stars but we just couldn't put it all together to win. When I was down the hall working for the gentleman who preceded me as president, I used to hear two things all the time. The first thing was that we didn't care if the Packers were 2-12 or 12-2, since we were sold out for every game no matter what. The other question that came up all the time was, "Who is making the decisions there?" We had a huge board, and people didn't think there was anyone in charge. Once Ron came on

> **During Super Bowl III, the Jets' amazing upset of the Baltimore Colts, Joe Namath did not attempt a pass in the fourth quarter.**

board, all those questions went away. The first thing Ron did was fire Lindy Infante. We were basically paying two head coaches for two years, and that ended the speculation that we didn't care if we won or not. It also showed that Ron Wolf was running the show, or he wouldn't have had the authority to do that. That's really where it all turned around. For the last ten years, we've had the best record in the NFL. It's showed that the little city can compete with the big guys.

I will always have a warm spot for Brett Favre. He's just such a competitor! Before I came here I always said the most competitive guy I'd ever known was Bob Gibson. I mean you just didn't want to get around him on a day he was pitching because he was so focused. He was just ready to go and get anybody. He was just a super athlete, people forget that not only was he a twenty-game winner, but he was also a consistent Gold Glove winner. But it's tough now to beat Brett. There are weeks now when he's walking around the locker room on crutches, and by gosh, he's running out on the field on Sunday and he's ready to go. In 2003, he played with a broken thumb on his throwing hand for most of the season, and still threw a league-best 32 touchdown passes. He's just a gutsy, competitive kid who has never let his notoriety go to his head. He's still the down-to-earth guy he was when he first came here and nobody knew who he was. I've always respected him for that.

What also makes the Packers so special is the fact that we have 110,000 shareholders! We've had four stock sales in our history, the most recent in 1997. At that point, people paid $200 for a share of stock. We added twenty-four million dollars and 106,000 new shareholders. Those people don't get dividends, interest, tickets, nothing for that stock. They get to come to a shareholders meeting once a year, they get to vote on new directors, and that's it. It's small town America…it's blue-collar America…and the team is owned by those fans. There's no owner who can take the team and move it. The source of the team's appeal is that it's a wonderful story that just happens to be true. It's warm and fuzzy as no fiction can get. It's the most wonderful story in all of sports.

We had our shareholders meeting recently at a building right across the street from the stadium. We had about 2,300 people there. They had asked me if there was any way the shareholders could see the new stadium. I made plans that we would bring them up here and let them walk through the players' tunnel out onto the field. You would have thought I had a bunch of kids who were six years old! I walked them up the street, which was about two blocks from the stadium. There were only 2,300 people at the meeting, but I think I had about 10,000 people by the time we got to the stadium. People on the street saw us and figured they'd tag along to see what was going on. I had this one lady tell me, "I've been a season ticket holder since 1958 and I just got down and kissed the grass!" It's just a love affair and it's a lot more like fiction than reality, but it's all true. I compare it a lot to the Notre Dame Subway Alumni. That's a group of people who never went to Notre Dame, but love the school anyway. That's the kind of fans we have. They're fascinated with this little town, and how it can keep surviving and thriving. We're also very popular with the league office. Every time we're on television, the ratings go right through the roof. The league recognizes that and talks about it.

I've told people that I've worked for the two greatest traditions in all of sports, the baseball Cardinals and the Green Bay Packers. When you look at those two franchises, it's pretty hard to beat.

The margin of error in Dennis Green's play-calling is plus or minus 100%

A WOLF IN PACKER CLOTHING

RON WOLF

Ron Wolf spent nine and a half years as general manager of the Green Bay Packers, from the 1992 season through the year 2000. Prior to that, Wolf spent 25 years with the Raiders as Director of Player Personnel, (both in Oakland and in LA), and three years, (two football seasons), in Tampa Bay in 1976 and 1977. He is now retired from football and living in Annapolis, Maryland.

I came to the Packers at Thanksgiving of 1991. To me, Green Bay is as unique a place as there is, in any form or fashion in the sport of football, be it college or professional. The people in Wisconsin are unique football fans. The people that support the Packers are the finest fan base anybody would want. The thing that surprised me, and that I always took note of, was when we went away, the number of fans who came to see us play and root for us even though we were not very good and hadn't been very good for 24 years. Before I got there, the Packers had four winning seasons in 24 years. After I got there, the Packers never had a losing season. That'll be on my epitaph. You can see right there the uniqueness of that franchise, which was stumbling. It personified losing. They had forgotten what it was like to be associated with or affiliated with winning football. We were able to bring that back. To me, the uniqueness is how the people supported the team, even when they were bad.

When I got there, the waiting list for season tickets was under a thousand. I think it's back up now to 60,000 waiting for tickets. When we got there, you could always get tickets for games.

I was there through all the planning and the renovations. I left after it passed. I felt all along, because of the marvelous support of the people there, that it would pass. One of the great selling points in Green Bay, Wisconsin, when we took it over, was people wanted what Green Bay had to offer. I'm talking about the fan base, the accessibility. A traffic jam in Green Bay is five people at a stop sign. You're 15 minutes from work no matter where you are in the area. It's easy to get to work. The schools are magnificent. The living is tremendous for your family. It's an ideal place for a family man. If a player comes there, his kids are going to go to a great school. They're going to be treated like royalty. All we ask them to do is conduct themselves accordingly, like they are professional athletes. By and large, most of them did.

The city gives you an opportunity to be yourself. There can't be a better working relationship between community and team than there is in Green Bay. Bob Harlan gave me the opportunity to run the football operations. We did that, and, I think, did a pretty good job of it. We brought respectability back to Green Bay. Many people said that if we had free agency, it would destroy places like Green Bay. Green Bay has the best won-loss record, as of now, in the free-agency period.

Brett Favre is exactly what you see on Sunday. He's a dominating football player. When he's on your side of the field, the field tilts in your favor. I thought it was a must that we get a quarterback of that caliber. That was a heck of a trade for the Green Bay Packers. It was a heck of a trade for me, personally, but more so for the Packers. He's given stability to that operation, and he's just a great football player. He may be one of the greatest ever to wear the Green and Gold.

Favre was a second-round draft choice, and nobody had ever heard of him. He threw six passes his rookie year, none of them were complete. In spite of all that, he was the one guy I knew we had to have if we were going to be successful. We were able to work out the deal and get him. We did it by giving up a first-round draft pick. We traded that pick to Dallas. They got a "one" and a "four." The guy that was picked by Dallas was a defensive back from Texas A&M. He was a good player, but he was no Brett Favre. Brett Favre is the only three-time Most Valuable Player in the history of the National Football League. To get a player like that for what we gave up is unique, plus what he's meant to the foundation. Another big trade I made was for Ahman Green. He is now the single-season leading rusher. He may be the all-time leading rusher now with the Green Bay Packers. I was able to get him from Seattle for a guy named Fred Vincent, an absolute steal.

Reggie White was signed by the Packers as a free agent. That was a great recruiting job done by Ray Rhodes. People looked at that Reggie White deal and said, "Hey, with a player of that caliber going to Green Bay, then Green Bay must be a heck of a place." That opened the eyes of a lot of people. You can't underestimate the power of that player network. We appeal to a certain group of player, a player who has a family, who wants to just go play football. Those are the kinds of people who came to Green Bay.

Mike Holmgren left before I left, and I replaced him with Ray Rhodes, and after a year, replaced him with Mike Sherman. Mike Holmgren is a brilliant man and a great football coach. I'm sure he saw a lot of his peers having the opportunity to run their own deal and felt that, as smart and as capable as he was, that he would be able to do it. Unfortunately, it didn't work out for him in **Seattle** quite that way. Now that he's back just being a coach, people are picking him and the Seahawks to win it all this year. He's a tremendous football coach.

When I came to Green Bay, I tried to make that as unique a place as there is to play. The approach Mike and I used was that everybody looked at the schedule, noted when they would be playing Green Bay, so they just marked a "W" next to it. We said, "What we have to do is we have to eliminate this to make this a terrible place to come and play." We were able to do that. At one point, we had 25 or 26 consecutive wins in that place. We did a heck of a job. It got to where teams

> **Mike Holmgren was an eighth-round pick by the St. Louis football Cardinals in 1970. He was a back-up quarterback at USC.**

> **During the Seattle Mariners first year in 1977, they measured their distance to the fences in fathoms. A fathom is six feet. For instance, where a park may have a sign that denotes 360 feet, the Kingdome would have the number 60.**

didn't want to come there to play against us. We started something that is still going on there. When I was there, we played the Chicago Bears, as bitter a rivalry as there is in American football anywhere. The Packers had beaten the Bears in Chicago ten straight years. That's unbelievable. No one ever did that. Lambeau didn't do it. Lombardi didn't do it. Halas didn't do it. Ditka didn't do it. Think of all those great coaches. All the time, Holmgren and Rhodes and now Sherman—they've done it. That's an incredible record.

GREEN BAY PACKERS GREEN BAY PACKERS GREEN BAY GREEN BAY PACKERS GREEN BAY

* Mike Ditka

WORKING WITH THE PACKERS IS LIKE PLAYING HOOKY FROM LIFE

LEE REMMEL

In the gloried history of the Packers, perhaps no person has seen more nor done more than Lee Remmel. He has been a Jack of All Trades and master of several: team historian, executive director of public relations (1974-2000), a writer and columnist for the Green Bay Press-Gazette *for almost 30 years. He is a member of the Packer Hall of Fame and the press box at Lambeau Field was named for him in 2003.*

My father was a huge Packer fan. We lived in Shawano, 35 miles northwest of Green Bay. My dad, my older brother and I listened to Packers games on the radio—there was no television then. That's when I cemented my relationship with and my allegiance to the Packers. I went to my first Packers game in 1944 at City Stadium, against the Chicago Bears, and I learned that all I'd heard about the Packers-Bears rivalry was true. The Packers jumped out to a 28-0 lead. The Bears stormed back and tied it 28-28. The Packers pulled it out with two fourth-quarter touchdowns.

In 1946 through 1956, the last year City Stadium was used by the Packers, I worked on the sidelines. I interviewed the head coaches and their respective teams after the games and then wrote "Sidelights." That was my first 11 years of covering the Packers. In 1959, I was still doing that at the new stadium, when Lombardi came here about mid-season, and he stumbled over me at the sidelines, and said, "What the hell are you doing here?" That was the end of that. I've been in the press box ever since. Lombardi was difficult with the press. I wouldn't say he had a split personality, but during the regular season, he'd give you a lot of monosyllabic "yep" and "nope" answers because he didn't want to give any comfort to the enemy. He didn't want his remarks ending up on somebody else's bulletin board.

During the off-season, he was a great interview. I was usually asked by the editor and publisher of the Packer Yearbook to do some kind of overview of the team looking to the next season. I did that with Lombardi all the years he was here. I had to make an appointment and have my questions prepared, and he would give me full and comprehensive and eloquent answers to every question. It was great stuff…could have been etched in stone.

The coach before Lombardi was Ray "Scooter" McLean, who was head coach for only one year, the most disastrous year in Packer history. His record was 1-10-1. Following that season, Red Smith wrote that "The Packers had overwhelmed one opponent, underwhelmed ten, and whelmed one in 1958."

In 1974, when I joined the Packers, Dan Devine was in the fourth and most tenuous year of his time at Green Bay. The man who had been director of public relations, Chuck Lane, resigned to join Bart Starr in Bart Starr Distributors, dealing in NFL merchandise—wrist watches, pennants, clothing.

I called Dan Devine in **Miami** where he was attending the National College Coaches Convention to get confirmation of the fact that Lane had resigned and to ask what he wanted to do about naming a successor. He asked me if I would be interested in the job. I said, "Under the right parameters." He figured I was suggesting his (Devine's) position was highly tenuous, which it was. He said we'd talk when he got back to Green Bay. We talked and he suggested I talk with the president, Dominic Olejniczak. That's what I would have insisted on anyway because I knew Devine's position was pretty shaky. We talked and finally arrived at a salary that was acceptable. That wasn't a long process, but he was notorious for being frugal. I asked about a contract, and he said, "We don't give contracts to front office personnel. I can't imagine why you would ever have to leave the Green Bay Packers organization." I took the job and was called Director of Public Relations.

> **Do you confuse Miami (Ohio) with Miami (Florida)?**
> **Miami of Ohio was a school before Florida was a state…**
> **When Don Shula retired, he had more victories than over**
> **half the NFL teams.**

At the same time this was going on, there was considerable promotion for Bart Starr to succeed Devine as head coach and general manager. The team was floundering during that season. Signs began appearing in the stands, "Fresh Start with Bart." By the time the season ended, there had become a great groundswell. I don't think the executive committee of the Packers had any choice but to name Bart Starr as head coach and general manager to succeed Devine. Devine resigned on Monday morning following the final game of the '74 season. At that time, Bart Starr seemed like a great choice. Unfortunately for him and for the Packers, his nine-year term didn't work out.

Chuck Lane returned and Bart worked out a shared arrangement where I was a director of publicity and handled all the releases and press conferences, did the writing and editing of the game programs and that kind of thing. Chuck came back in as director of public relations and advancing games....

When Lombardi came in 1959, he turned it around right away, and the Packers went 7-5. The second year, he had them in the NFL championship game against Philadelphia, which the Packers lost. In an eight-year span, the Packers were in the NFL championship game six times, which is a feat that no other team has ever performed in the history of professional football. The Packers are the only team to have won three consecutive championships—one under the standings method in 1929-30-31...then in 1965-66-67. The Packer players finally realized they had the wherewithal to do it...and did it.

In 2000, the vote was taken to do a renovation of the stadium. I did a couple of speaking appearances, mostly on behalf of Tony Canadeo, one of our great players. Because of his health, he was not able to go out publicly. I wrote some releases in support of the referendum. There was considerable, well-organized opposition to the referendum so I was concerned that it might not pass. The vote was 53 to 47 percent, which is hardly a mandate. If it hadn't been for Bob Harlan putting his personal integrity on the line, I really don't think it would have passed. He was a huge factor—his integrity and his honesty. Throughout that period, he would be out at five in the morning welcoming workers coming off their night shifts. That same night, he would be back out at some high-school football game doing the same thing—shaking hands with fans when they came into their stadiums.

I have no clear picture in my mind of what might have happened had the referendum been turned down. It would have been very difficult if that had not passed. I don't know where the organization would have been able to set up the kind of financing needed to do the substantial renovations. The Packers had already committed to more than half of the $295 million needed to complete the job.

In talks I've given lately, I made note of the fact that everything Bob Harlan predicted the renovation would do for the Packers and the city of Green Bay has happened and is happening. That's remarkable. Even above and beyond what he predicted has happened.

In the sixties, I once interviewed the team founder, **Curly Lambeau**, after he had been elected to the Pro Football Hall of Fame. I said, "Curly, did you, when you founded this team in 1919, at the age of 21, ever have any thought that it would reach the level of interest it has evoked around the country at this point in time?" He said, "Heck no. I just wanted to have a football team and play football." In other words, he sort of flew by the seat of his pants. But, he became an innovator. He has been credited with being the first head coach to have daily practice in the NFL, the first head coach to film daily practice, the first coach to film games, and certainly the first coach to fly his team to road games. In 1938, he started flying the team to road games in two DC-3s. He wouldn't allow them to fly in one airplane, fearing an **air disaster** that could wipe out the franchise.

> The Oakland A's colors are green and gold because their late owner, Charles O. Finley, grew up in La Porte, Indiana and loved Notre Dame...when he bought the Kansas City A's, he changed their uniforms to the Notre Dame colors. The Green Bay Packers also adopted Notre Dame colors because Curly Lambeau played at Notre Dame.

> When Knute Rockne and seven others were killed in a 1931 plane crash, it was the largest disaster in U.S. aviation history up until that time.

Curly Lambeau was 21 years old, he'd had one semester at Notre Dame playing fullback alongside the immortal George Gipp, when he launched the Green Bay Packers. Curly had some help from George Whitney Calhoun, the sports editor of the *Press-Gazette*. He publicized the organization and the start of the team. Curly was the key element in the overall process. In 1922, when they temporarily lost their franchise for using an ineligible player, Curly put in a few bucks of his own money and persuaded a friend of his, Don Murphy, to mortgage his Marmon Roadster for two hundred bucks so they could go back to Canton, **Ohio** and buy back the franchise for $250. At the time he was launching the team, Curly was working for the Indian Packing Company. If you check the old newspaper issues of the *Green Bay Press-Gazette*, you will find that the Packers were referred to as the "Indians" because of the Indian Packing Company sponsorship.

Curly and Calhoun decided to call a meeting and see what would happen as far as organizing a team was concerned. At that time Curly decided to put together a team, so he went to the general manager of the Indian Packing Company and got him to put up $500 for jerseys for the team. Oddly enough, the Indian Packing Company went out of business, quite possibly before that season was over. Another meat packing company, the Acme Packing Company succeeded them as sponsors. That's how the Packers nickname came about. Calhoun started calling them the Packers probably in the third or fourth week of that first season in 1919…and it's been the Packers ever since.

In the early twenties, the team had been having financial problems. A man named Andrew B. Turnbull, a publisher with the *Green Bay Press-Gazette*, got a number of the local civic leaders together and launched what became the Green Bay Football Corporation, the first official corporation. That put the team on a businesslike basis for the first time. They sold a share of treasury stock for five dollars. It's always been non-profit and non-dividend stock. For a long time, The American Legion was listed as the beneficiary if the organization

> **NFL footballs are made in Ada, Ohio. Each team uses one thousand per year.**

were to be dissolved. About ten years ago, it was suggested that changing the beneficiary might be a prudent thing to do. Within a year or two, a decision was made to change the beneficiary to the Green Bay Packers Foundation, a foundation that distributes cash grants to various organizations and charities. That is now the beneficiary if there were a dissolution of the franchise. It has a 45-active-member board. There are a number of meritorious members who are non-voters.

Last year a sportswriter from Switzerland came to talk about the Packers. His key question was, "Why do you think the Packers have been able to survive in Green Bay when many other cities of similar size, which were in the NFL earlier, have fallen by the wayside?" I said, "This may sound like oversimplification, but I suggest that a can-do spirit that is here absolutely has refused to let this franchise leave Green Bay. They've always found a solution to whatever problems may have arisen."

Refrigerator Perry suffered from Anorexia Ponderosa

WHY DID LARRIVEE ONCE ANNOUNCE BEAR GAMES? HE WAS REPAYING A DEBT TO SATAN.

WAYNE LARRIVEE

Wayne Larrivee was the radio voice of the Chicago Bears for 14 seasons before he joined his life-long favorite team, the Packers in 1999. Larrivee broadcast Kansas City Chiefs games for seven years, as well as the Iowa Hawkeyes, Quad Cities Angels baseball, the Chicago Bulls and Chicago Cubs. Larrivee, 49, is a native of Western Massachusetts and a graduate of Emerson College in Boston.

I grew up in Massachusetts and was a Packers fan back in the sixties. Who wasn't? I'm one of these people who follow the same team all my life, and I've taught my kids that, too. You pick out a team, as a kid, for whatever reason. I thought the "G" and the colors on the Packers uniform and on the helmet were really neat, so that's why I became a Packers fan. And they just happened to start winning championships.

I loved the New York Yankees because I thought the "NY" and the **pinstripes** stood out. As a kid, I thought that was a neat insignia, and that's how I became a Yankee fan. Then, they just happened to be winning at that time, as well. In my broadcasting career, I've always said, "If I ever get a chance to do the Yankees or the Packers, I'll have to do that." No regrets, but Green Bay is the only job I would have left the Bears for...and that's what happened.

You can work in Atlanta and make a nice living, but who cares? Nobody even goes to the games. You can work in New Orleans or Houston or any of those other towns, but it's not the same. When you're covering a team where the fans are really passionate, it makes

> **Yankees owner Colonel Jacob Ruppert added pinstripes to their uniforms to make Babe Ruth look skinnier.**

all the difference in the world. That's a big deal. That's a lot of fun as a broadcaster. That makes every game more important. Green Bay football on Sunday is as religious as anybody could ever be.

During the Ice Bowl game, I was at a ski area with my father, who was a ski patrolman. He had insisted that we go skiing every weekend. I was sitting in his old Mercury with the radio on in sub-zero weather at this area in Pittsfield, Massachusetts listening to every play of the game. I felt I was out there with the fans but not quite as cold as those people at Lambeau Field.

As far as favorites, of course, Bart Starr, and Jim Taylor are certainly among them. In fourth grade, I used to carry a lunch, and I had an NFL lunch box, one of the first marketing things the NFL did, which had all these team insignias on it. I would carry that. It had Jim Taylor on the front of it with #31 in the green and gold uniform. I loved Carroll Dale, wide receiver. On defense, Dave Robinson, the linebacker, was one of my favorites along with Herb Adderley and Bob Jeter. I thought they were one of the best cornerback combinations ever to play the game, in any era.

Every time I go to Lambeau, even for practice in the middle of the week, it's special. There's no doubt about that. This is my sixth year there, and that hasn't worn off at all. On game day, in the morning, I go down and walk on the field, walk over to the south end zone, or the one-yard line and remember what happened in the "Ice Bowl" and other things. To me, it's still a thrill to go there.

In Chicago, we looked forward to the Packer game in Green Bay because a lot of us on the crew are big football fans. A game in Green Bay is special. If you're going to do NFL radio sixteen weeks out of the year, what better place to do it than in Lambeau Field on a Sunday afternoon? It's just one of those special places.

The first game I ever broadcast in the NFL was a pre-season game in 1978. The Chiefs played the Packers in Lambeau Field. Back then, Lambeau Field looked a lot more like it did in the sixties—before sky boxes and everything else. I was with Walter White, a tight end on the Chiefs, and we were walking on the field before the game. He asked, "Where did Bart Starr go over for that touchdown?" I thought,

"That's amazing that one of these current players has an understanding of history and would want to know where this historic touchdown took place." I told him where I thought it was, but we walked over and asked one of the Packers people, who happened to be Bob Harlan. I didn't know him at the time. He took us over to the yard line and showed us a spot on the one-yard line near the south end zone.

Bob Harlan is a special person. There are three key people in Packers history. The first, of course, is Curly Lambeau, who started the whole thing. Then, there's Vince Lombardi, who personified the entire Packers myth. Then, there's Bob Harlan, who restored the franchise. What's amazing is that his son, Kevin, was working with me in Kansas City when Bob was named to the job. I remember Kevin saying to me, "They had darn well better promote my father to that job. He's ready for it. He's the guy it should be. If he doesn't get that job, he's going to leave there." I said, "Well, I hope he gets that job." He did, and it wasn't too long before they turned that franchise around. He did it with great common sense. He's a "people person." He personified the whole organization.

That's the way they should be because they're community owned. It's a community team. If you pick up the phone and dial the Packers and ask for Bob Harlan, he'll pick up the phone. It's a little more corporate today, and it has to be, but for a long time, you could just walk into Lambeau Field offices and walk right up to Bob's office and pull up a chair and talk to him. There was that kind of an openness about it that was really special. He restored the Packers. Without Bob Harlan, they wouldn't have hired Ron Wolf. That was Bob's choice. He'd known Ron Wolf for a number of years based on a previous hiring that didn't go so well, and that was Tom Braatz. Bob made the choice for Ron Wolf. Ron Wolf made the choice to hire Mike Holmgren. Together, they settled on Brett Favre to be their quarterback. In free agency, they made the pitch and got Reggie White to come over to the Packers. Ron was telling me one day, "Reggie was getting wined and dined in all these big-time restaurants in San Francisco. We had him down here at the Red Lobster. That's where we closed the deal." None of that happens without Bob Harlan moving into the position he's in.

Furthermore, if you need further amplification of Bob's contribution, it's the stadium. They don't get the stadium passed without Bob Harlan going door-to-door to all of his neighbors all over the town in Green Bay and Brown County and knocking on their doors and saying, "We need this. This is crucial. The future of the Packers is at stake here." Any number of us could have done that. Any number of people in the organization from head coach to general manager, and the people wouldn't have bought it. But, they bought it from Bob Harlan because of his incredible integrity. He's the reason that stadium is what it is today and why the Packers have a future in the NFL.

Trust me. The Holy Trinity in the Packers is Lambeau—Lombardi—Harlan.

I know Kansas City fans are passionate, but they're nothing like these fans—not even close. I wouldn't want to be anywhere else. I hope I'm here for a while. I realize that if you're anywhere long enough, you're going to see the good and the bad of it, that's for sure, in my business. But I just hope it lasts forever.

When watching the Dallas Cowboys, do you root for the defense...or the prosecution?

IS THIS HEAVEN?
NO, IT'S A PACKER HOUSEHOLD
IN IOWA

BETTY DEBROWER

Betty Debrower is a retired operating room super-visor in Cedar Rapids, Iowa. She retired from the medical center in Cedar Rapids two years ago. She has four children.

I'm not sure why my husband became such a big Packer fan. He was born and raised in Iowa.—just like Bob Harlan. He always had a lot of Packer memorabilia. He had the bumper sticker that said, "The Pack is Devine" when Dan Devine was the coach, and "The Pack is Back". I can't count how many times I've seen that bumper sticker over the years, even when they didn't come "back."

My most memorable Packer moments are of going to the shareholders meetings. It's so neat to rub shoulders with these people, and you can do that there. I love those meetings. They're real meetings too—a lot of people picture it as a big party—but they really do work at it. They pick members of the board of directors, they give a report of the previous year, Bob Harlan does a presentation, and then they talk about the upcoming year. It's really well done. Then, in addition to all the reports, they have a question and answer session. The first year I went, they had the meeting at Lambeau Field. A lot of people showed up just to finally get to see Lambeau, since you could never get tickets. At the shareholders meetings, Bob Harlan took the time to answer questions for about a half an hour. He used to go around the field, but when they moved inside the meeting room they had micro-phones in strategic places. This year I didn't like the format as well, because I liked hearing the other people's questions, too. There is just such a special feeling being there. It's just like I said before, it's like going to Mecca.

I just got information that it might get easier to get tickets this year. They're starting a program where people that have tickets and can't go to the game can put their tickets up for sale at face value plus twenty-five percent. The extra goes to the Boys and Girls Clubs of Green Bay. That's just one reason why I'm so impressed with this organization. They take care of their fans.

What possessed me to buy that share of stock was that I did it as a Christmas present to myself in 1997 in memory of my husband. I saw an article in the *Cedar Rapids Gazette*. It didn't say how to go about getting the stock. I was at a party with a friend of mine who was more computer-savvy than I, and he went online and found out how to go about buying the share. It was a great Christmas present, and I've had more fun with it that just about any other present I've ever gotten.

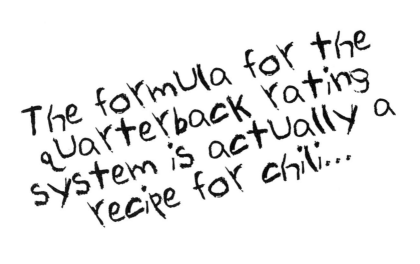

The formula for the quarterback rating system is actually a recipe for chili...

QUICK HITS AND INTERESTING BITS

My dad would take us to games periodically. Up until 1971, you could still get in for free at halftime, so I went to a lot of games to see the second half. Whenever we could scrounge up tickets we'd go, too. The second game we went to was Dan Devine's first game as head coach. One of our guys intercepted a pass and ran down the sideline and got pushed out of bounds right into Dan Devine. Devine ended up breaking his leg on the play, and I can still vividly remember that whole play....About twelve years ago, my uncle knew this guy who wanted to get rid of two tickets. This was before they passed the rule that you could only pass tickets down to your immediate family. So I went over and met this guy and he sold me his season tickets for face value. He said he'd call the ticket office to make it official, and sure enough at the end of the season the tickets were put into my name. Ironically, the tickets I got from this guy are in the same section my uncle and I sat in during the Ice Bowl. So now I have two season tickets to Lambeau Field. One of the owners here at Horseshoe Bay is on the board of directors and we have access to tickets. We never miss a game, unless it's pre-season, then we let someone else have the tickets.

——RICK HEARDEN, Egg Harbor, Wisconsin

I haven't gotten to take my son to a game yet, but we're hopeful. With the skyrocketing price of tickets, you realize you can get a lot better seats in front of your TV. I'm sure it will happen some day. My wife wasn't a real fan, but having lived with me all these years, and having had to put up with me watching the games every Sunday, I think she's become a fan. The breaking point for her was when we were watching a game one day and I had to take the dog out. When I came back in, I asked her what had happened. She said, "Oh, they're in the Red Zone now." I just looked at her and said, "What?" She explained that it meant they were inside the twenty-yard line. She just laughed, because they had just explained it. Today, she actually arranges her schedule so she can watch the games with me. As a mom, she can't always just flop down on the couch like I do, but she enjoys watching the game.

What makes the Packers so special with fans everywhere is the fact that they're in a small town. The big towns have their fans of course, but more of the country is made up of small towns, and fans can identify more closely with Green Bay. You look at some of these other towns and there are all these quiche eaters, and in Green Bay you've got the brat-eaters with a hunk of cheese. The Packers are running a commercial right now where a guy is holding on the phone with the ticket office and a voice comes on and says "You're number 62,000." And that's literally correct. It's just a strong community feel with the team that even people who don't want to be part of it become wrapped up in it.

A few years ago there was a commercial where a family was saying a tearful goodbye to someone leaving the area. As soon as the family was out of sight, everyone hopped in their cars and bikes and scooters and rushed to the ticket office to see if they could get the family's tickets.

———REX BECKER, 49, Janesville

When I was 23 years old, I bought a bar and restaurant and became friends with a lot of people pretty quickly. One was an assistant manager at the paper mill. He had pretty good access to tickets so we'd go to quite a few games. At the end of the year, he'd always get a lot of free tickets from vendors, so we'd get a bus load and go down. It was probably around '94 that I'd average going to at least half the home games. Now, I'm in real estate, and my wife is a nurse. She decided to get her real estate license so that if I'm not around, she could answer a real estate question without violating any laws. When she went to Green Bay to take her tests, I went to Lambeau Field. I signed up for season tickets and asked, "How do you do the Milwaukee tickets?" They gave me an address, and I sent the form in requesting those tickets. Then, four or five months later, I get this letter. I thought it was a joke. Now, this was the year they had quit the Milwaukee games. There were enough people that didn't take their tickets so my name came up, and I've been on the Milwaukee package, two regular season games and one pre-season game, ever since it first came to Lambeau Field.

———MIKE ZURFLUH, 43, Wisconsin Rapids

In 1973, I had put my name on a season-ticket waiting list for Packer games. In 2001, I finally got a call that my name had come up for tickets. I had waited 28 years for season tickets. Finally Packer tickets in my name—a pretty proud moment. I'd been able to scrounge tickets and get tickets through other people all through the years, and we had always been able to go to every game, but to get them in *my* name was special. Actually, these seats are probably the worst ones I've ever sat in. They're corner end zone about fifty rows up.

In 1983, the highest-scoring Monday Night Football game was the Redskins and the Packers. We had some friends coming from central Wisconsin and I tried all week to get tickets and couldn't. I decided to just go down to the game and park in the parking lot to see if I could pick up tickets there. I put a sign around my neck that said "I need 2 tickets." We couldn't have been there 15 minutes when this guy came up and said, "Hey, Bud, you need a couple of tickets? I've got two of them for sale." I said, "How much do you want for them?" I'm figuring the guy's going to scalp them on me, since it was the Monday Night Football game, and the Redskins were the World Champs! He said, "Just give me face value—thirteen bucks." I said, "Thirteen bucks apiece. Great. Where are they?" He said, "Forty-yard line sitting right next to Bart Starr's secretary." I said, "You're kidding me." Sure as heck, we got there, and the seats were just awesome and it really was Bart Starr's secretary. The Packers end up winning the game 48-47—another one of those nights when we were out really late. We had a blast. My buddies from out of town already had their tickets, and here I came down with no tickets, and I ended up sitting on the forty-yard line next to Bart Starr's secretary. A great night.

———**LARRY PRIMEAU**, Neenah, Wisconsin

Years ago, I was a waitress, and one of the guys at the restaurant had three sets of tickets. Everyone else always took his Bears tickets, because it wasn't very good years for the Packers at that time. But I said I'd take them for the whole year. The next year he said if I wanted them for the whole year he'd sell them to me, because he'd seen me at the games and said anyone that loved the Packers as much as I did deserved the tickets. I tended to get a little bit involved in the games, so he knew I was a real fan. He continued selling me his Packer tickets for years. I never knew when he was going to show up, he'd just pull up in my driveway and toot his horn, and I was expected to run out to his car. He'd tell me how much they were that year and I'd pay him. Sometimes we'd just be coming home from camping and he'd pull up…it didn't matter, I always got my tickets. Then, one year he had a stroke and I didn't hear from him, so I called his house and his brother answered. He told me his brother had had a stroke, but that he had said if I called to make sure I got my tickets. That was the last year though, because he died later that year and his tickets went back to the team.

After that, I was only able to go to games when I could get tickets. Anybody that had tickets for sale knew how crazy I was about the Packers. They would sell me tickets. If they had it on the radio that there were tickets available because it was too cold and a lot of people weren't going to go, I'd make sure I got them. A few years ago I had the chance to go on December 24. I told my kids and grandkids not to expect any baking that year, because I was going to the game! The first game I ever went to was in the 50s. That was back in the days when women wore high heels and fur coats and corsages to the games. It was nothing like it is today with people wearing snowmobile suits and blue jeans. Back then it was really an event to go to a game.

——PAT EISCH, 68, Packer fan for over 50 years

I've been a Packer fan ever since I came home from overseas in 1955. In 1960, I was working for a CPA firm in Green Bay on an audit. The girls in the office came back from lunch and said the team was taking applications for season tickets. I went down there on my lunch hour, filled out the application and turned it in. Then they asked me how many tickets I wanted. I was living in Sheboygan at the time, so I thought if I was going to drive all that way I might as well bring a carload. I said I wanted six tickets. A week later, I got a letter from them saying that I had six tickets in my name.

It sure is a lot different today. About three years ago, there were some new people in front of us at a game. I asked them how long ago they had put their names in, and they said they'd been on the waiting list for 32 years. I'm in section 129, seats 1 through 6. I've had the same seats all along. I paid the $8,400 licensing fee a few years ago to keep the seats. I originally paid $4.50 per seat for them. I'm in row 52, and there are 60 rows in the general admission sections.

——KEN RAMMER, 73, Appleton

I started having my tickets in 1957 when they built on to Lambeau Field, and I've been there ever since. I got my tickets because I was a Packer fan who grew up with the team. My parents bought me a single ticket in 1957 when the stadium expansion happened. For a few years I had a seat in the kids' section, down in the end zone. The following year I had the chance to move up to where I am now: section 122, row 55. My seats are on the home side of the field where the old press box used to be. If I was down about twelve seats I could use the press box as a backdrop. From my seats you can see the whole play forming—it's a great seat. It's like a family reunion in that section because I've had the same seats since I was a kid. The difference now is, that in the beginning years, I was the kid and there were grandparents sitting around me. Now, I'm the grandparent and those people's kids and grandkids are sitting all around me. I've probably only missed eight or nine games in the forty-seven years that I've had my ticket. I go to every game, no matter what the weather, no matter how much snow, or how cold it is. If it's freezing like the Ice Bowl, I still go, but now I have the clothes for it and I'm not going to stay away. I keep going even if they're having a bad year too. I know that someone has to win and someone has to lose, so I don't get upset if we lose. I do get upset if I don't think they've tried their hardest though.

——**WENDY SMETANA**, Green Bay city bus driver

The way we got our Packer tickets was kind of unusual. Nowadays, they have a waiting list of 60,000 or 70,000 people to get season tickets, but back then they didn't have anything like that. In 1957, I was in a hardware store and they had a display with applications to buy Packer tickets. I looked at them, and wanted to share the tickets with my best friends, Chuck and Pat Heeter. I picked out four tickets on the thirty-five yard line about half-way up on the east side, facing the press box. I called up Chuck at his office, and told him I was at the hardware store, and that they had Packer tickets available. I asked him if he'd like to go in on these tickets, and he said, "I don't know." Can you imagine that today, someone saying they didn't know if they wanted Packer tickets? Anyway, we bought the tickets, and we've had them ever since. I don't go to games any more, but I gave the tickets to my son. Chuck Heeter has since died of prostate cancer, and when he died, since the tickets were actually in my name, I had to pass them to his son. So now our two sons go to the games in the seats of the original owners. That's the way tickets are passed down in Green Bay. Tickets are handed down generation to generation and any extra tickets are snapped up right away. Originally, if you were a season ticket holder you couldn't pass your tickets down, you had to turn them back into the club. Then they finally saw the light, and said you could pass the tickets down to someone in your family with the same last name. Of course that opened it up to generation after generation having the same tickets. To thank me for passing the tickets to Chuck's son, their family bought me a brick from the old stadium. They etched on it, "For Dr. Harold Gross and his thoughtfulness." That brick is now on display at the stadium.

——DR. HAROLD GROSS, 90, retired physician

My husband didn't really want me to go to work in the first place, but when he found out it was for the Packers he was really excited. One of the things that he was so happy about was that since I worked there, we got tickets to all the games. We sat with the players' wives and the coaches' wives on the forty-five yard line. When I left the job, Coach Lombardi called me into the office and asked if I wanted tickets. I just said, "You know it!" He laughed and told me the only problem was that the only tickets they had available were in the end zone, but if I'd stop in periodically, they'd try to upgrade them. We gladly took them, and even when we had a chance to upgrade, we didn't. We love those seats, because they're up high enough to see the whole play. After we moved into the end zone, my husband said, "This is where we belong." While we sat with the players' wives, we were hooting and hollering and drinking a few beers, and the players' wives were so poised and reserved. It was really strange. It was almost like they weren't at a football game. We got used to it, but we liked the end zone a lot better. We still have the tickets, but we don't go that often. Two of our sons use them now. I ask myself all the time why I didn't ask for four tickets. We had two children at the time and could have used the extra seats. But at least someone in the family is getting to go to the games.

——MARY DUROCHER, retired, former Packer employee

Chapter 5

Tailgreat

Beer: More Than
A Breakfast Drink

RAY NITSCHKE WAS JUST A REGULAR GUY WHO SOMETIMES WORE A CAPE

KAREN ELLIS

Karen Ellis, 58, is a fanatical Packer fan in the heart of Chicago Bear territory. Her home in Bristol, Wisconsin is just three miles from the Illinois border. She recently retired after 40 years with the same company.

I became a fan watching the "Ice Bowl." We've been fans ever since, and Ray Nitschke and I have become very close. Back when Kohler built their new plant out in Pleasant Prairie, they had a promotion there to open the plant, and Ray Nitschke came out. My boss had taken him on a plant tour. I told my boss, "If you ever do anything for me, let me meet Ray Nitschke in person because he is my idol." So, my boss was down in the pump factory with Ray and called me and said, "Huggie Bear, come on down here. I have something for you." I went down there. He introduced me to Ray, and I was speechless.

So Ray Nitschke called me one year at Christmastime. I had just finished supper. I'd had a real rough day at work. I had a migraine headache so I told my husband, "If anybody calls, take their number, and I'll call them back." I took some medication for my headache and lay down. I wasn't down five minutes when the phone rang. My husband said to the caller, "Well, she's not feeling good. Who is this?" He said, "It's Ray Nitschke." My husband said, "Karen, you're not going to believe it, but Ray Nitschke is on the phone." I said, "Yeah, and I'm President of the United States." I took the phone and said, "Okay, if this is Ray Nitschke, tell me something to make me believe that you're Ray." So over the phone, Ray said, "You came down to the shop to meet me, and I had a red blazer, a white turtle-neck and my chrome dome showed so pretty, but you couldn't even talk, Blondie." I forgot that I had a migraine.

Ray Nitschke started me on my collecting. He gave me an 8x10 black and white photo of him holding a football and signed it, "To Karen Ellis, a beauty. Good health and happiness always. Love you. Be good, Blondie. Ray Nitschke." Then he put all his stats underneath his name. That was my first picture. I now have 150 autographed pictures on my family room wall and three-quarters of the way across the ceiling. I've also got helmets. I've got all sorts of collectibles. And all of them, except for one, are strictly Packers. Another favorite of mine is Terry Bradshaw, and I had him autograph a picture. I put that up on the wall, too, and my husband keeps telling me I have to take it down.

I have a helmet telephone. I had gone up to Racine to pick up a rookie card on Don Beebe for my nephew for Christmas. When I got there, the door was locked. I knocked on the window, and the lady came to the door. She says, "We have somebody in here, and that's why it's locked." I thought maybe someone had tried to rob the place. This was the year Reggie White had that pneumonia problem right before Christmas and didn't get to play a lot. When I went in, Reggie was in there setting up an appointment for an autograph session. When he walked out of the back room, I was so shocked. I never expected to get to see him in person. He walked out with me. At that time, my green truck was a '95 Chevy pickup, which I had done in green and gold. I had a little black football player, with #92, painted on the side of the truck toward the back by the tailgate area. We had John Jurkovic painted on the other. I told him, "Jurko was my husband's buddy. When we would go to Green Bay, he would meet us at Prime Quarters for supper sometimes." But Reggie was my driving force. I'd heard him preach three sermons. I had always said, "If you weren't a believer before you went, you would be when Reggie got done with you."

Reggie White looked at my truck and said, "Oh, I love your truck, sister." He got a kick out of that little black football player on our truck. I told him, "When my mother passed away, you were her favorite football player." She had never gotten into football until after my dad died. Then, she was around us all the time so, of course, she had no choice but to like football. She always liked Reggie. I told him that the guys I worked with, when my mother died, took up a collection and gave me the money and told me to buy something of the Packers to remember my mother by. So I did. I bought the helmet telephone. I told him, "I want nobody to autograph it but you. But, I can't afford this $200 autograph session." He said, "Well, you come next week and be in the parking lot before I go inside the building. If I go inside, my agent will be there, and you'll have to pay for the autograph. Meet me in the parking lot. Make sure the helmet is warm, and I will autograph it for you." He did. He autographed it, "Reggie White, #92, I Corinthians 13"

I have a white autographed football I paid $49.95 for at the Pro Shop in Green Bay the year the Packers won the Super Bowl. That summer, my husband and I spent two weeks in Green Bay. We chased all the players and the coaches. I was able to get 77 autographs while we were there…every player, even the ones that didn't make the team, and all the coaches, the year of the Super Bowl. That is under glass.

Bart Starr autographed a football for me. That's under glass too. All my pictures are autographed. Now, I've had a mural painted on the back of my new pickup, which I bought when I retired. On one side of the tailgate, it's got the Ice Bowl, with Ray Nitschke, real large and in full color, and shows all his facial features…crooked nose and all. On the other side of the tailgate, I've got the Super Bowl and Brett Favre in full color. Behind him is the first play of the Super Bowl, and the picture I have is of him running off the field with his helmet in the air. On Ray Nitschke's side, I have the winning touchdown that Bart Starr did. On the bottom, I have "Winning isn't everything. It's the only thing." So in the upper part of the tailgate, on the left-hand side, I've got Vince Lombardi—gotta have the trench coat in there—talking to Bart Starr. Then in the background of that, I've got a defensive play with Ray Nitschke bent over because Ray was my favorite. It took Jay Wright, the artist, 45 hours to do it. I gave him 15 pictures, and we sat down and laid it out and he airbrushed it.

Brunswick made a Super Bowl bowling ball that year. They cut 250, of which the first 100 went to the Green Bay Packer Association. It didn't even have Brunswick written on the ball. It's just got the two teams, the Super Bowl number, and the score of the game. My brother drills balls in Kenosha at Sheridan Lanes. When they came in, my brother was able to get 50 of the balls for resale. He took one and held it aside. The lower the number of a collectible, the more it is worth—my ball is #104. He held it aside until the following year for Christmas, and he gave it to me. I treasure that. My husband keeps saying, "You've got to get that thing drilled." I said, "No, I don't."

Frank Emmit, the cheesehead pilot, was up there for a promotion for the Packers on September 1st in 1997. He had a cheese wedge on a Ritz cracker, called "Cheese on a Ritz." He autographed the hat and a Frisbee and gave it to me. His plane crashed, and when he was going down, he had one of those foam cheesehead hats in his hands, and he said he put it between him and the dash of his plane, and they claimed that was what saved his life.

I won't buy autographs. I chase people for all of mine. I'll even chase them in the heat. When I got that football autographed by all the players, the two that gave me the hardest time were LeRoy Butler and Edgar Bennett. Every day, they'd tell me, "Catch you after practice." My husband and his buddy, Randy, were there. Randy says, "Karen, you're not going to succeed this time." I said, "Oh yes, I am." On the last day we were up there, I told the players, "I'm leaving tomorrow morning. I need the autographs." They said to me, "Well, we'll catch you after practice, Blondie." I said, "I know which truck is yours so I will be waiting for you this time." I sat on the fender of their truck, and when they came out of the locker room, they both started laughing. I said, "I'm not leaving." Bennett goes, "Blondie, you've worked hard enough for this. I'll give you your autograph." Edgar took the ball, and he autographed it, then LeRoy ran across the parking lot, and Edgar threw the ball to him. I said, "If you drop that ball, or he drops that ball, you're going to get me a new one and get it re-signed with all those signatures." He just laughed. They both autographed it. I grabbed the ball and ran back to my husband and his buddy yelling, "I got it." When the players were leaving, they stopped the truck, got out of it and came over and gave me a hug. They said, "You worked hard for this one, Blondie."

We have to get a release from the PR man at Green Bay for our tailgate. Jerry Kramer took a picture of it when we were tailgating two years ago and said he might use it for some of his campaign ads. Bob Harlan called me at home one morning and said, "Karen Ellis?' I said, "Yes." He said, "This is Bob Harlan, president of the Green Bay Packers." I said, "What?" He said, "When are you going to be in Green Bay again?" I told him we would be coming up the next week for the game. He said, "I'm looking at a picture of a pickup truck, and I would love to see this truck in person." We went up there, and he met me in the parking lot. He had his picture taken by himself. Then, he had one taken of him and me standing by the truck. Jethro Franklin got out of a car and was going toward the locker room, and he stopped and said, "Boy, is that thing beautiful? Can I have a picture with it?" I took a picture of him standing by the truck and blew them all up and sent them up to Green Bay. They autographed them all and sent them back to me. Bob Harlan hung one in the locker room. He said that Brett Favre had fun with saying, "Look who's in full color. The rest of you guys are shaded down to black and white." I thought Fuzzy Thurston was going to hug that truck. I took it over by his place to show him and he said, "I love this truck." I said, "No, Fuzzy, it's not for sale." Bob Harlan said it would be nice to put the tailgate, if we ever decided to get rid of it, in the Packer Fan Hall of Fame. But I've told my husband he had to bury me in that truck. It's my pride and joy."

I sent a lot of stuff to Ray Nitschke in Green Bay wanting him to autograph for Christmas presents. He never went to the bottom of the box. He called me and said, "What do I do with this stuff? Where do I send it?" I said, "Ray, if you went all the way to the bottom of the box, you would find an envelope, with money to mail it back, and an address." He went to the bottom of the box. He didn't use the money. He used his own money to mail it back to me. I never paid him for anything, but he did numerous helmets and footballs for the kids, hats and all kinds of things. He took a tee shirt that had Ray Nitschke on it and he autographed it "To Art." I told him "I owe you one for that." He autographed it to my husband instead of to me.

When we would go to Green Bay, we would meet him at Skip's Place. There's the Hutson Center, the practice field, and then there's the Ray

Nitschke practice field, and then down from there on the corner at the backside of the practice field, just off Lombardi, there's this little hole-in-the-wall restaurant that makes the best doggone breakfast you'd ever want. Ray came in there for breakfast all the time. Around the corner at the bar where the stools are, he sat on one stool all the time. If somebody was sitting in that stool, they had to move when Ray came in. When Ray died, they had that stool embroidered, "Ray Nitschke, #66, we'll miss you, and we love you." Then they covered it with plastic. Most people, when they come in, have enough respect that they don't even bother to sit on that stool. Some people just ignore it and sit on it, but I don't know how they can.

I want Brett Favre to see the tailgate. I need a written release from him because Jay Wright and I want to do a painting of that tailgate. He's the artist, and he asked my permission because it was my idea, and he's done an oil canvas. According to that PR guy from Green Bay, we need releases from Brett Favre, from Ray Nitschke's daughter, Amy, and from the Packer organization, and one from Dallas and one from **New England** because they're the opposing teams. Even though you can't see facial, you have to get a release before you can make a print. We want to make 1500 prints. Then we want to take 100 of them and have Bart Starr and Brett Favre autograph their respective sides. Then we want to sell them, and all the money would go to the Vince Lombardi Cancer Foundation because I'm a cancer survivor, to the Bart Starr Boys Ranch, and to Make-A-Wish Foundation because they sent my best girlfriend's family to Disney World for a week for their daughter, Jennifer. Every year I support the Make-A-Wish Foundation. They call me and ask if I want to buy something they have that's Green Bay Packer that year. Most of them are pictures, but I always support them because they've been so good with Jennifer. Other than printing costs, all the money would go to those charities.

The New England Patriots once played a regular-season home game in Birmingham, Alabama, in September 1968.

I've written to **Dallas** and New England but haven't received any response at all. That's my biggest thing to cross first because I don't think I'll have any trouble with the rest of them. Bob Harlan doesn't think I'll have any trouble getting the Green Bay side done.

Before they had the gated area for the players to park in, the players parked on the side of the stadium and went in from there. Bart Starr would drive down in the stadium and would park inside at the old atrium so he wouldn't get bombarded by the kids. One day, he parked outside, and when he came out of the locker room after practice, the kids didn't realize he was there, and I followed him to his truck and asked if I could have his autograph on a football. He told me, "If I autograph your football, I'm going to have to autograph for every one of these kids, and I am running late. If you want your football autographed, go behind the stadium, sit in the middle of the parking lot, and I will stop and autograph it for you." He and his trainer came across the parking lot. He actually stopped his truck, got out and autographed my football. I thanked him, and he said he had respect for older women. I said, "It pays to be a senior citizen."

Mike Holmgren always signs right across the leather stitch, the criss-cross ones on the footballs. I got to Chmura before I got to Mike, and Chmura signed it right where Mike always signs. Mike said, "He'll pay for that in practice." Chmura said, "I beat him. I'm taking those lines."

I had Gilbert Brown autograph a shovel for me. It says, "Grave Digger" on it. He and I were standing in the parking lot talking when my girlfriend's daughter, Clarissa, saw us. She was about five years old at the time and had a little Packer cheerleading dress on. As soon as she walked up to me, she said, "Grandma Karen." Gilbert was a softie for little kids, especially little girls, and he looked down at her and picked her up and put her on his shoulder and walked her all the

Coach Jimmy Johnson and Janis Joplin were high school classmates at Thomas Jefferson High School in Port Arthur, Texas. Jimmy Johnson didn't know she sang. They hated each other. She called him "Scarhead" and he called her "Beat Weeds."

way back to the locker room. I got a picture of the two of them together. I made him autograph that picture, and I put it up on my ceiling. Then the day we did the baseball game, after about the third inning, all the players were letting some of the kids run for them when they would hit. They were pulling little boys out of the stands all the time so I said to Bernardo Harris, "Do you mind if my girlfriend's little girl comes out to run." She ran and got a home run for him.

I've got many pictures of myself with different football players. My favorites are the ones with Ray Nitschke. He was so loveable. He was at Carthage College in Kenosha once when we were there. I stood next to him, and he put his arm around me, and my husband, Art, took our pictures. He cuddled me real tight, and he said, "Oh, that feels so good." I went to walk away, and he said, "Wait a minute, Blondie, come here." He asked Art if he had more film in the camera, "Get on this side. We'll check this side out, too." So he had to have a picture of me with him on both sides. He said, "Do you know what current football players like Favre would get to sign something for these kids? Back when I signed things, I'm lucky if I got fifty cents." He was an awesome man.

I live for football. I love it. I just love football.

PACKER TAILGATING:
A LITTLE LIQUID FORTIFICATION
AGAINST THE UNKNOWN

JEFF MEINHARDT

Jeff Meinhardt is 42 years old. He remembers sitting on the floor with his grandfather and father watching Packer games. They would get up at halftime and go outside and play football, during the Forest Gregg years. Meinhardt runs a successful bar and restaurant business.

I remember the feeling of walking into Lambeau the first time. Just the walk through that thing, it isn't enclosed, but open-air—to see the Ring of Fame and the Bart Starrs and the Ray Nitschkes. I don't exactly remember when it was because we do a *good* job tailgating before we get in. Once we get in, we don't drink any more because we've got to get home in a couple of hours. You don't want to miss any of the game while you're relieving your social pressures.

There's an ice company here called Home Town Ice. They have these Home Town ice chests where they load up about forty bags of ice. This freezer had been just recently emptied so it was still somewhat chilled. I don't know how this woman, who was very drunk, found out about it, but she said, "Come here. Look what I've found." Next thing you know, I'm crawling in this Home Town chest. It was a pre-season game so it was very warm at Lambeau that day. All of a sudden, here I am in this darkened ice pit with this woman. Needless to say, football took a backseat that day. It was unbelievably fun.

A frustrated hippie, I grew up in the seventies and eighties, there's nothing different between a **Grateful Dead** show and a Packer game—except the extra-curricular goings on out in the parking lot is

> **Do you know what Jerry Garcia said to Elvis when he first saw him in heaven?**
> **"Hey King! Guess who your daughter married."**

a little bit different. The camaraderie is the same—if a guy needs a beer, here it is. We may be drinking beer and eating brats and not the black bean burrito and the imports, but it's the same feeling at a "Dead" show as at a Packer game. To me, that was the biggest irony. That and, when they play YMCA, all these red-neck conservatives get up there and dance to that song. The irony of that is just unbeliev-able. If they knew what the YMCA was all about. Here are 60,000 people, basically conservative and middle-class, all dancing like it's the gospel truth....

When the Kansas City Chiefs came up in 2003, the Packers were ahead the whole game until the fourth quarter, and then the Chiefs pulled ahead and won. The Chiefs have good fans. You know what it is? It's the teams that have been around long enough that are educated. Kansas City Chiefs have educated fans. Packer fans are educated. This is no kidding. You go to the shopping malls in Green Bay. Down the middle of the malls, they'll have banners explaining the different ref-eree signals—what off-sides means, what illegal procedure means. It's an educated town. Here, there's nothing else to do but watch football.

When I first started dating my wife, the first time I brought her home, there was a pennant on my front door, and she's wondering what the hell kind of guy she'd gotten involved with—he's 37 years old, and he's got sports pennants on his front door. I'm not going to say we went as far as having a test before the wedding, but remember the movie "Diner" and the Baltimore Colts—not too far off. If you're going to spend your life with somebody.... Let me put it this way, I just recently got her to accept the green and gold color combination. She thinks it's a terrible color combination, but she can tolerate it now....

Nitschke would be one of my all-time favorite players—just because of his heart. Beyond anything, I'm a huge Brett Favre fan. There are two people in this world I'd love to meet—Giuliani, the ex-mayor of New York, is one; Brett Favre would be the other. I've told my wife, "Once Brett retires, we'll give him a couple of years, but we are going to be taking a trip down to **Mississippi** to find him." He's been

> The speed limit on the University of Mississippi campus is 18 MPH in honor of Archie Manning's uniform number.

through so much professionally. The guy's got the record for most starts—the guy has done things I've never seen anyone else do before. To have him on our team, every year he's here, you can almost count on going to the Super Bowl—or, at least have a good chance—because we've got Brett Favre.

We're holding our collective Packers' breaths right now just wondering when he's going to announce his retirement. I think we've still got another year or two left after this one, barring major injuries or anything like that, God forbid. Other players may leave and go to other teams, but Brett Favre's loyal. I just can't see him, the way he talks, leaving for contract problems to go to any other team unless it may be the Saints. He would be forgiven for that because it's closer to home. I could see him leaving Green Bay for—maybe—a shot at home. He's so close to retiring now, though, that I think he'll stay here.

You know why the grass in Wisconsin grows to the south? Because Chicago sucks! There's nothing better than beating Chicago. They're so damn arrogant down there. They just think they walk on water, and they just suck.

I seat about 110 here in my bar, and we have tons of Packer fans in here to watch the games. We have beer specials—free beer until the first one pees. I tell you it gets real interesting for a while. It brings them in. We've got a green and gold toilet seat that person has to wear for the rest of the half.

The Bears think it's like golf...low score wins.

BITS AND BITES, BEGGED, BORROWED AND STOLEN

I don't like the Falcons' new stadium. I just don't like the Georgia Dome. There's an old story about Green Bay. If you fly over the city on a Sunday you can see stadium but you can't see the parking lot—it's all smoke. The city fathers in Atlanta built this new covered stadium and wanted everybody to take public transportation to the game. That's fine, but you can't have a tailgate party in a subway station! I heard rumors that the new owner went up to Green Bay to ask how the Packers keep their fans so happy. Now he's bought up parking spaces around the stadium and I think that will help. At least we can have a decent tailgate party.

No matter where you go in the world you can meet Packer fans. There are a lot of them in England, as I'd be walking down the street with my Packer shirt on and someone would eventually yell, "Hey Packers!" There are a lot of fans in Italy too. I never realized the Italians were such big football fans. They all love the Packers, and when you tell them you're a stockholder they get all excited. It really makes you feel proud knowing you're part of something that big.

——HERB BARNES, retired, Atlanta

My wife has been ill for the last seven years, and has periods of feeling good and bad. At the time of Super Bowl XXXI, she was not feeling well so we decided not to go to it. We had a huge party here and just had a blast. It was a winter day with snow. We fixed tenderloin and lobster and lots of stuff and had tons of friends over. After the game was over, we decided to take a run down to the stadium. Everybody piled into our Packer van, and we got down there, parked the van, opened it up and started playing Packer tunes. Horns were honking everywhere. Everybody was just ecstatic and electrified. It had been thirty years since the Packers won a Super Bowl. I never truly thought I'd ever get to see them win a Super Bowl. I had been with them through the seventies and the eighties and the nineties before Brett got here. There were so many not-so-good seasons then. To have the Packers win a Super Bowl is unbelievable, and to actually be alive when they won it and to be a part of it was absolutely incredible. The Lambeau parking lot was packed—like a tailgate party—huge snowflakes were coming down—an absolutely perfect night. We rolled in back home about three o'clock in the morning.

The next day, there was a big welcome-back celebration so about four hours later, we packed the van back up again with what we could and took off back to Lambeau. We set up and did more tailgating until the team arrived. There was zero to minus-ten wind chill that day. They had the players on buses bringing them slowly through town. The players rolled down the windows and were greeting the fans. They got to Lambeau about seven that night. We were all freezing. It was a long two days, and we were all exhausted when it was over. We had gotten so stressed out over the whole thing—wanting them to win the Super Bowl so badly and the anxiety of the game and then the celebration of the victory and the homecoming. It was great.

——**LARRY PRIMEAU**, engineer, Kimberly-Clark

I still make it back to Green Bay for three or four games each year. The one thing all my friends look forward to is the tailgate parties. They're not fancy, with pretty much a set menu of hamburgers and snacks and peanuts and Bloody Marys and beer in good weather. In bad weather, dad will boil hot dogs and put them in a thermos. Then, we'll just have hotdogs there. My friends look forward to being there at the tailgate parties and talking to my dad. They have specific rules for these parties: 1) the youngest person empties out the coals from the grill—that means my dad knows he'll never have to do it! 2) No vegetables. One time, somebody brought spinach dip, and my dad asked, "What's that green stuff in there?" They said, "It's spinach." He said, "Well, that's a vegetable." They said, "We thought it would be okay because it's surrounded by fat." He said, "Nope, that doesn't count." With that, he put them on probation.

——**MARK RAMMER**, Austin, Texas

One year I won a bowling tournament and won three hundred bucks. I told my wife that the Browns were coming to town and I was going. This game was right after the incident when the Brown fans were throwing beer bottles on the field—in fact, it was the next week. So I called my brother-in-law up in the Dells and told him I had this money and that we were going. It was on December 23rd, and everyone was dressed in Santa outfits and green and gold. The funny thing was that this was the period when they were renovating the stadium. The whole thing was ripped apart, there was no bathroom available, and it was probably the worst it's ever been. They had no parking, and they had like three hundred porta-potties outside—it was a disaster. In our infinite wisdom, we decided to get there early. In the meantime, the NFL decided to kick the game back from a noon start to a three o'clock start. They knew how much everybody loves the Packers, and they knew what it did for their ratings. There were these rows of houses near Lambeau Field the owners rented out their yards to fans. They were even opening up their houses for people to use the bathrooms. We got to our tailgate spot and put out our stuff and ran up our flag. There were people on both sides of us partying and we absolutely had a gas. The superintendent was driving around and no one was feeling threatened or worried, and this was right after 9/11. I mean everyone was just having a good time. There were these two girls who came walking by. They were just rushing by us right at noon. I could tell by the way they were walking that they were thinking they were late. They were all decked out in green and gold and had their faces painted and everything. We yelled at them and said, "Hey ladies, the game's been kicked back for three hours, it's not starting at noon." And their jaws just dropped. They had driven six hours from the Quad Cities in Iowa to come to this game. So naturally, the only thing to do was to invite them to our tailgate party. We were cooking brats, drinking beer, throwing the football around—we just had a blast. The game is only about half the fun at Green Bay.

——BOB BACON,

The Packers, coming out of the sixties, coming out of winning, established new territory—maybe things they'd been recognized for that other people hadn't been recognized for. The biggest thing for the Packer fans is their tailgating frenzy. A lot of different teams take pride in their fans and their tailgating. The Pittsburgh fans are kind of the same way in their elaborate tailgates. I think the Packer fans put first dibs on that. They have recognition for their bratwursts and their cookouts and being at Lambeau Field at a time when it may not have been happening at other venues. So, to me, playing for the Packers or the Steelers was fabulous—we're two sister teams, from the mentality of the people, and the pride of the people in their teams, blue-collar kind of guys. When you think about Wisconsin, you think about the mills. When you think about Pittsburgh, you think about the mills. Paper mills and steel mills. It's a shot and a beer kind of a place. Not fancy, not city, but more country. Pittsburgh has its own ethnic. The Fox Valley has its own ethnic. Pittsburgh is dotted with their ethnic cultures. You had Green Bay. You had De Pere. You had Kaukauna. You had Appleton. You had Neenah and Menasha. You had Little Chute. Who's in Little Chute? The Dutch. The Irish were over in Menasha. The Hunkies were in the South Side. There were all those things that people identified with. Getting back to the Packers and the fans was not only about winning, but it took on its own identity as far as fan support and they took great pride in their tailgating. It wasn't just with one region, but it was with an entire state. It wasn't as if the Steelers were just out of Pittsburgh, but out of Pennsylvania. That was the identity that Packer fans were all over.

——ROCKY BLEIER, Appleton native

Some would say that Randy Moss is the backbone of the Vikings...others wouldn't go quite that high.

Chapter 6

Put Me In, Coach

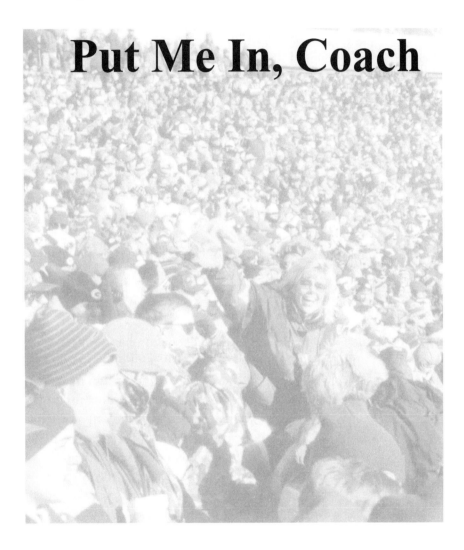

It Was A Ball

FUZZY WENT OUT FOR BASKETBALL BUT THEY DIDN'T NEED ONE

Fuzzy Thurston with Sue and Larry Primeau (Packalopes)

FUZZY THURSTON

*Wisconsin native and Green Bay restaurateur, **Fuzzy** Thurston, is one of the fans' all-time favorites. He played for the Pack from 1959-1967.*

I was a Packer fan from Day One. I'm also a Wisconsin Badger fan and love both of them. I never thought I'd ever get a chance to even see them play, much less play for them. That was kind of nice.

My first year with the Packers was Coach Lombardi's first year, 1959. I was with the Baltimore Colts when Weeb Ewbank was their coach, and we had just won the '58 World Championship in sudden death in New York. At the end of the season, Vince Lombardi traded for me. In 1968, I retired from Green Bay. I was the only Wisconsin-born-and-raised guy on the team for most of those years. I was born in Altoona, Wisconsin. I went to a small high school, and then I went to Valparaiso on a basketball scholarship. I played two years of basketball, and the coach told me I'd probably better quit basketball so I went out for spring football for the first time my sophomore year and was starting my junior year.

When I first heard that I'd been traded from the Colts to the Packers, I was a little upset because the Colts had a World Championship team. The year before, the Packers had won one game and lost ten. But I

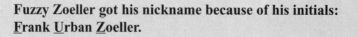

Fuzzy Zoeller got his nickname because of his initials: Frank Urban Zoeller.

was happy, too, about going back home. That made me feel good. I didn't know anything about **Vince Lombardi** when I was first traded. He didn't have much of a name at that time because he'd just been an assistant coach, he'd never been a head coach. There wasn't too much said about him. He'd been with the Giants. In '68 when I retired, I would never even have thought of playing for anybody else. After that great success, with those great teams, and the great coach, when I heard Coach Lombardi was going to retire, I thought I might as well, too. We both retired that same year, but Lombardi stayed around as a GM and then he went to Washington. Every year in September, as many as 25 guys from those teams come back, and we have a great time. I see Jerry Kramer three or four times a year. Actually, Jerry Kramer didn't write his book—I wrote it for him! No, he did a great job with his book.

The Green Bay team is so different from everybody else. We were able to become friends with a lot of the fans. A lot of the people who go to the games, you also see around town and get to know them. If you play in Chicago or play in New York, you don't get to know the fans. Being such a small city and a small state, you'll likely meet a Packer player wherever you go. It's a great relationship. There's no question in my mind that the Packers have got more fans in the world than anybody else. When you go to games some other places, their fans are terrible.

The first Super Bowl you win is always special. The first championship in '61 was just as great. Just because they put a name on it, Super Bowl, it doesn't mean that it's any better than it was when we were World Champions in '61, and '62, and '65. Sometimes, they forget those players in those games. I think all those championships should be regarded as the same.

In '61, the Packers won the championship by beating the Giants 37-0. That was Y. A. Tittle's year. Y. A. Tittle came to the 'Title

> **"Winning isn't everything, it's the only thing." That line was first said by John Wayne in the 1953 movie, "Trouble Along the Way."**

Town,' and we sent him back without a title. We almost sent the Giants back without a Tittle.

Green Bay fans are great, and thank God they love the team as much as they do. We appreciated them very much when we played. No matter what we did, no matter if we did lose, they were all just great people all the time. I don't think there are any fans in the world like the Packer fans. It's been a great life for me to be able to play in front of all of them. I still have so many friends in Green Bay.

Thank you for interviewing me.

GREEN BAY PACKERS GREEN BAY PACKERS GREEN BAY GREEN BAY PACKERS GREEN BAY

HERE'S SOMETHING THAT'S HARD TO BELIEVE: RAY NITSCHKE WAS AN UGLY BABY.

BILL ANDERS

Bill Anders is Director of Operations for a college book company in Atlanta. He was raised in Green Bay and went to his first Packer game when he was seven years old. He has gained considerable fame as a Ray Nitschke look-alike.

This is our fourth year to live in Georgia, but I've lived in ten different states. Whenever I would move to a new state, I would get newspapers or get online and find where the closest Packer bar is located. But with NFL Ticket and all this other stuff on TV and having so many more football games being shown, I can keep up. I lived in Texas for five years, and I think I got a total of two Packer games in the whole five years down there—and one just happened to be when the Packers played the Oilers so I got to go to that game. You just find a Packer bar—and when you get there—there'd be all kinds of people in there, and somebody would have some kind of feed or you'd just sit around and watch for scores to come through. So every Sunday, I was always amongst Packer fans and friends.

I remember one time in Houston, all my friends there knew I was a Packer fan. I brought everybody that worked for me and everybody that I knew over because the Packers and Chiefs were being televised. I got ready, sat down for the game, and the announcement came on…it was almost like "Heidi"…that this game will be interrupted for Disney's "Cat From Outer Space." I damn near threw the TV out the window. The party was a short one.

I've been to the Silverdome and Hubert H. Humphrey, and I go once a year to Soldier Field for the Packer-Bear game with my father-in-law, but I used to go with my brother when he lived there. I've been to a game in Houston too. I saw them in Denver when I went to school in Colorado. I've been a lot of places to see them. Last year we went to the preseason Atlanta-Green Bay game. Outside of Green Bay, I've never been anywhere where I've gone in and said, "Wow, this is a great atmosphere." It's terrible down here. The Georgia Dome is more of a DJ party than it is a football game. I had season tickets for the **Houston Astros** one year. I enjoyed it, but being in the **Astrodome** just didn't do it for me.

I was at a Monday night Packer-Bear game at Soldier Field in '94. My brother Rick is a Packer fan, but not like I am when I jump around and go goofy. He follows them, and he loves the games, but he's just not that rah-rah about it. He called me one day and said, "I've got Monday night football tickets. Can you make it?" I lived in Bloomington, Illinois at the time. I wasn't that far away, and I said, "Sure." He said, "Look, I know how you are. You've not really been around Soldier Field a lot, and I live in this town, so *do not wear anything Packer!"* I said, "There's no way. I'm not coming." He said, "No, you can do it. Just don't wear anything Packer." So I said, "Okay."

I didn't wear a stitch that was Packer clothing, which probably made us stick out more because we didn't have Bear stuff on. We went to the game and we sat in the end zone about half-way up. We were just kind of clapping—we're jumping around—'cause my brother had read me the riot act about getting goofy. He said the fans were a little rougher on out-of-state people, especially Packer fans. "Don't do it." Favre threw the 99-yard touchdown pass to Robert Brooks, and it came out of our end of the field...right where we were sitting. We just went nuts.

> **The public address announcer for the Astros (Colt '45s) in 1962 was Dan Rather.**

> **In 1976, the Pittsburgh Pirates were "rained in" at the Astrodome after a ten-inch torrent flooded the area. The teams made it to the Astrodome, but the umpires and fans did not.**

Those Bear games back then, and still to this day, have a big portion of Packer fans in there. In the section we were in, there were very few. When the play had ended, there was just my brother and me—standing up and jumping and high-fiving each other. We heard all these people yelling, "Sit down. Sit down." Then we turned and some guy yells, "Hey, Nitschke, sit down." We sat down, and my brother looked at me and said, "You know. I never thought of it, but you look like Nitschke."

Rich Heard and I are best friends. We played football with Ray Nitschke's adopted son who was a year behind us. We got some exposure to Ray, and he was just a teddy bear and a gentleman away from the limelight. When he got that gravelly voice and got going, everybody thought he was this fearsome guy…but he really wasn't.

That year the Packers made the playoffs when nobody expected us to go anywhere. We had Atlanta at Lambeau Field. I got some dorky glasses and I put some tape in the middle, and wore a Nitschke jersey. Rick and I and a bunch of friends were at a tailgate party, and NFL Films happened to come by. They backed away and said, "Ray, say something into the camera." I just did the gravelly voice of Ray Nitschke and said, "The glory days are back, baby. We're gonna do it again." That became the opener for the Brett Favre Show for two years. It's in the "75-Year History of the Green Bay Packers" video. It's just everywhere. Every time it was shown, people would call my mother in Green Bay and say, "Was that Billy on TV?" The next year we made the NFC championship game and played in Dallas. There was a possibility we could get by Dallas, and it was going to be a good game.

So Rick and I and his father and brother and uncle jumped in a van and drove down to Dallas. I got some shoulder pads and some eye black, and I went a little bit more "Ray." I shaved the middle of my head, which was just very sparsely covered with hair anyway. I looked even more like Ray. Everybody got a really good laugh out of it.

We had to park about a mile away from Texas Stadium in a terrible gravel parking lot where most of the Packer fans were sent. People were tailgating there, and they kept coming over and saying, "Hi." We had this Packer love-thing going on. It got to be time for us to go in for the game. We were walking along, cracking jokes, goofing around. People were coming up and throwing me footballs and playing around. Before we knew it, there were 300-400 people behind us. It looked like this Pied-Piper thing. I was marching into Texas Stadium with everybody behind me. The Dallas fans were throwing stuff. They recognized me right off. They were yelling, "Nitschke, go home! Nitschke, you're retired."

It turned out that Ray Nitschke was the Honorary Captain that day so he was down on the field, and I was up in the stands in my 'Ray' outfit, so we had a pretty good laugh about it. A bunch of the Dallas fans in our section were saying things like, "Wait a minute. He's down there? There are two of them. No wonder he was so good."

Then, one year, Rick got me a real pair of the authentic Packer pants, and we got some pads, got some old black cleats, and I started blacking out my two front teeth. I got the arm pads just like he had. Everything was so true to what Ray used to wear except that he used to wear a helmet. I got one, but I quit wearing it because I got the snot knocked out of me every time I had it on. The Packer fans got so excited and they would start banging my head so I stopped wearing the helmet. I've been told by many people that you can actually take a picture of me and then compare it with a Ray Nitschke picture and go, "Wow."

My wife Karen, from central Illinois, is a Bears fan. When we were dating, when the Bears scored, she started jumping around. I almost left her apartment because I couldn't stand that. Then, we had to come to an agreement where, "Okay, you can be a Bears fan, but don't cheer during the game." Then it became, "Okay, if we go to a game, you can't wear Bears stuff." Before long, she was totally converted and she is now a Packers fan. Now, even her father is, too.

But Karen never got the "Ray" thing. When we'd be planning to go to a game, she got to where she'd say, "I'll stay in Green Bay with your mother. You go to the game." She'd always give me this look like, "I'm married to a dork!" every time I'd go out the door wearing all my stuff. One day, she finally decided to go with Rick and me. I was in the full "Ray" outfit. We were walking in, and everybody stopped me for pictures, "Ray, how you doing?" They kept high-fiving and yelling. My wife and Rick's wife, Andrea, were behind us. I turn around and look at Karen, and her eyes were just sticking out. Andrea looked at her and said, "See. Now, do you get it?" She finally got it.

When I go to a tailgate party, it is so much fun. I can't eat or drink anything because people are coming up for pictures the whole time. One time I was standing there at our tailgate, and I got a tap on the shoulder. As I'm turning, a voice is saying, "Ray, come to our tailgate. I've got some people I want you to meet." I looked and I didn't even realize who it was right off the bat. One of my buddies was standing next to me, and he said, "Billy, go. That's Tommy Thompson," who was our governor. I went over to his tailgate where there were a bunch of legislators and other people. Every one of them had pictures taken with me. We had a lot of fun with it.

You constantly hear, from the younger kids, somebody saying to somebody else, "Who is that?" An older person will always answer, "You don't know Ray Nitschke?" Then, they'll start to tell them the story. My brother and I joke about it. He said, "Bill, you really need to work this thing because in about ten or fifteen years, nobody's going to know Ray, and you're out of a job."

If it's a really cold game, I will get out of the 'Ray' outfit to go into the game because it's not that warm. But other times, I'll just stay in it the whole time. The joke that Rich always uses is "I look more like Ray Nitschke than Ray Nitschke did." One time, Matt Millen had the camera put on me during his broadcast and said, "Geez, that guy looked more like Ray Nitschke than Ray Nitschke did." One time my wife and I were at a game, and I got out of the 'Ray' outfit. As we were coming back down through the tunnel, there was Ray Nitschke. I really wished I had stayed in it because I wanted a picture with him, and would have loved to mess around with him a little bit. I do goofy stuff there. I go over by the players' entrance and act like I'm walking in. I think I've stunned the security guys a little bit, because a couple of them have let me in. I'll get just so far in, and then they'll stop me. I'll go, "Oh, I just thought I was playing today, fellas."

WHEN JON GRUDEN WAS A PACKER COACH, VANDALS DID $400 DAMAGE TO HIS CAR. THEY STOLE IT.

BOB MCGINN

Bob McGinn, 51, is the Green Bay Packers beat writer for the Milwaukee Journal-Sentinel. *He lives in Green Bay. Here he remembers when Jon Gruden was on the Packer coaching staff.*

When I see Gruden competing on TV, or holding the Super Bowl trophy, I think about how he started out…one of his jobs was as the driver for Mike Holmgren. The Green Bay practice field is more than a quarter mile from Lambeau Field. The team doesn't go anywhere during training camp. They stay in the dorms at St. Norbert College, about six miles away, but all the practices are right at the Packer facility. The coaches would be maybe half a mile away in a headquarters area right smack on Lambeau Field. They would have to drive down or walk the half mile to this practice field. In his first year, Gruden's job was to ferry Mike Holmgren back and forth.

I would be talking to Holmgren after practice and there would be Gruden with the car warmed up in colder weather. They would be practicing outside in October. Just outside the gate, Gruden would be out there waiting—and that was his job! He would drive the guy back and forth.

Gruden was always talking to me about the Arena Football League. His brother Jay plays in the Arena League for the Orlando Predators, and Jon was always talking about that and about how he was scouting the league on his own, coming in early in the mornings and watching film. He knew everything about the Arena League. I assume he was probably scouting the CFL and every other damn league at this time too. He was just so into it.

This was a young coach who was originally in quality control. I didn't really know that much about how hard he was working on his craft to know the system, how much he was bugging Lewis and Holmgren to teach him things. A real good friend of mine was Bobb McKittrick from San Francisco. I knew him really well for a lot of years. We always talked about Holmgren and Sherman Lewis and Dennis Green and different people like that, but I know Gruden has said he has learned so much from McKittrick.

The first year, Holmgren had Sherman Lewis coach wide receivers, in addition to his job as offensive coordinator. Then, the second year, he promoted Gruden from quality control to wide receivers coach. In 1992, Gruden was offensive assistant quality control. Green Bay was in the throes of a twenty-five year downturn, and it was just horrendous. People thought they could never win here again. That's what Frank Deford basically wrote in *Sports Illustrated*. From that staff, who went on to became head coaches? Okay, we've got Ray Rhodes, Jon Gruden, Dick Jauron, Steve Mariucci, and Andy Reid—five head coaches out of that staff. Sherman Lewis moved on as offensive coordinator with Minnesota and Detroit. Greg Blache became a defensive coordinator with the Chicago Bears. Gil Haskell became an offensive coordinator in Carolina and Seattle. Three guys became coordinators. That was quite a staff.

In 1993, Gruden was promoted to wide receivers coach by Mike Holmgren in the off-season. Then he coached wide receivers for the next two years. Immediately, the question was: could this twenty-nine year-old guy handle Sterling Sharpe? Sterling Sharpe was brutal. He was really tough on coaches, writers, and teammates. He was kind of an overwhelming personality. Coaches would say if he didn't want to practice, the team wouldn't even practice. If his mood was down and if he was screwing around at practice some days, they just couldn't turn the thing around. This was probably Gruden's first major test in coaching. That was when Sharpe was not talking to me or almost anybody else in the Wisconsin media. I remember talking to Gruden and to other players about that. All indications were that

Sharpe respected Gruden almost immediately and I didn't see any problems they had at all. I thought that probably kept him in good stead when he had to deal with Ricky Watters in Philly.

They were a crazy bunch—Ty Detmer's crazy sense of humor, Favre would have been in that, Gruden, Mariucci. They had a good time. In 1994, the Packer quarterbacks in camp were Kurt Warner, Mark Brunell, Ty Detmer, and Brett Favre.

Jon was with some really veteran coaches, guys who had a million Super Bowl rings in San Francisco and Green Bay. Jon was just so young. I do remember that he would ride his bicycle through the snow at Green Bay. That would be down that half mile slope from the locker room area down to the practice field.

After games, it always helps to have a position coach explain good plays and bad plays in the locker room. After Gruden became wide receivers coach, he was always willing to do that. He was a young coach, in his late twenties, and he did not shy away from that. I relied on both him and Mariucci. I tried to get one or both after games. Jon was more than willing to explain good and bad, to stand there after defeats, just the two of us. One day, I said, "You know, this is probably going to help you when you become an offensive coordinator. That may not be too far from now." I never realized he was going to be a head coach sooner than later, either.

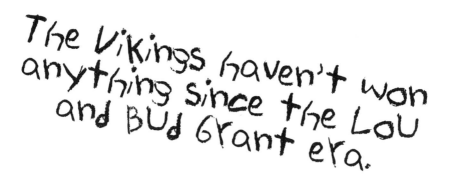

The Vikings haven't won anything since the Lou and Bud Grant era.

YO, VIKINGS. OUR FOURTH-TEAM QB IS A MVP—TWICE

STEVE MARIUCCI

Steve Mariucci is the head football coach for the Detroit Lions. From 1992-1995, Mariucci was quarterbacks coach for the Green Bay Packers. In 1994, he had the unenviable task of releasing Kurt Warner because the other three quarterbacks in camp were Brett Favre, Heisman Trophy winner Ty Detmer, and Mark Brunell.

In 1993, we signed Kenny O'Brien from the Jets 'cause he had 12 years in the league. We had Brett who had one year, and Ty Detmer who had one year. We drafted Mark Brunell in the fifth round and we had Kenny O'Brien. We thought we might keep four. Well, you don't keep four. Somebody had to go. We felt the best guys were the young guys and we said, "Gee, do we want to do this? It's gonna be the youngest group of quarterbacks ever assembled in the league, with nobody with more than a year experience." We ended up doing it.

When Kurt came the next year, we still had a young bunch. Yet, luckily, Brett played every game; he didn't get hurt. Not that Ty or Mark couldn't have done it, it's just that when you're training young guys and they don't get all the practice work—Good Luck! It doesn't happen like it's supposed to when they're not getting all of the work. We had to alternate Brunell and Ty Detmer active and inactive every other week, just to keep them happy. I don't know if that was the best thing or the worst thing to do. If they're all good enough to play, you simply can't hang on to them all. They're gonna go elsewhere because they all want to start. They all deserve to start so you can't hold them back.

Kurt Warner at the Packers proves timing is everything. You have four quarterbacks on your team: Brett Favre, Ty Detmer, Mark Brunell, and Kurt Warner. It was not Kurt Warner's time. He was a youngster who didn't get a lot of reps at all because the others were very young and deserving to show us what they could do. They were all second-year players or so. Kurt was there as a youngster, just getting his feet wet, just learning what pro football entails. You'd love to be able to keep all those guys and know the future and be able to predict. Needless to say, the Packers have only one of them remaining and it's Brett Favre, and he hasn't missed a game. The others moved on and do their thing elsewhere. Ty has done it, so has Mark, and so has Kurt. It's a matter of being patient and waiting for the right time and the right place, and being opportunistic when you get that chance. Whether it's because you've been traded to the right team, or there's an injury or two in front of you, or whatever the reason might be when you get your chance. All four of those people have done well when given their shot. It took Kurt just a little bit longer to show what he's got.

We were handed him. He was signed by Ron Wolf, the Packers general manager. Back then, Kurt was not ready yet. He was just beginning, in the infant stages of learning what pro football was all about. We were in a situation where we didn't have the time to train him and evaluate him like you would hope to because of the other guys being so young and already on your depth chart and already having proven that they deserved to be there. They're getting all the reps. Kurt was simply a young guy who'd sit and learn in meetings. I know he enjoyed being there, because Brett, Ty, and Mark gave him a lot of grief and had a blast with him. Favre called him Chachi. He may have had a lot of nicknames. They were a fun group of guys. He did fit in, he really did.

I don't know who told Kurt he was being cut. Typically, there is somebody from the front office who would do that as a general rule. After a guy is cut, you wouldn't know that you would ever see him again. I would be lying to you if I said, "This guy I knew had potential. This guy is going to be an MVP some day. This guy is gonna do great things." You'd sound like some sort of genius who could foresee this and see the potential in the young man. But I'd be lying to you if I said that.

GREEN BAY PACKERS GREEN BAY PACKERS GREEN BAY GREEN BAY PACKERS GREEN BAY

> **On January 4, 2000, Kurt Warner was on the *Late Show With David Letterman*. Letterman asked Warner what it felt like to be cut by Green Bay. Warner said, "Well, I was a little disappointed." Letterman responded, "It made you feel cheap! It made you feel cheap and dirty and like a loser, didn't it?" Both Warner and the audience roared.**

PLAYIN' FAVORITES

My favorite players are Brett and Bart, naturally. That's easy to pick. I was in a restaurant once, and there was a picture of Brett and Bart standing with their arms around each other. I told my daughter that if I had a purse big enough, I'd take that picture home with me. Lo and behold, that Christmas she got me that picture. It's my favorite present of all time. I've got a Packer jacket with autographs all over it. I only get the ones that mean something to me. I don't bother with the ones who haven't shown me anything. I've got a spot saved for Brett Favre's autograph, but I don't think I'll ever get it. Darren Sharper is very good when you go to get his autograph. He's so friendly. I really liked getting his, because sometimes you get a guy who is very blah about giving them, but sometimes you find the really nice guy. I go to the Brett Favre softball game every year too, and you see the players being more like themselves at that.

What makes the Packers so special to fans everywhere is that we don't have a lot of arrogant players like you see on a lot of teams... not mentioning Minnesota or anything. I don't think we've had a lot of those over the years. The coaches do a good job of keeping the players down to earth.

——PAT EISCH, 68, Packer fan for over 50 years

Sterling Sharpe was my favorite player, and then, of course, Favre. My sister's favorite player is Reggie White. About six years ago, my dad sent Sterling Sharpe and Reggie White group pictures we had taken at a ball game and asked them to sign them. Sterling never sent back the picture or signed anything. This was during the time when he had been hurt so maybe he was just too busy. Reggie White sent back the picture, signed, with an extra note, saying, "I hope you have a Christ-filled Christmas. Reggie White."

——TRISHA DENUCCI, Roberts, Wisconsin

I also loved Jan Stenerud. When I used to live in Green Bay, I'd drive by the practice field and Jan would be the only guy out there kicking. I also loved him because he was an old guy. My mom is a good friend of Fuzzy Thurston. He's a super guy and I don't think there's anyone who appreciates Green Bay people as much as he does.

I even planned my own wedding around the Packers. My husband is a big fan and his father was a huge fan. My husband's retirement dream is to go to every Packer game in a season. He wants to go to all the away games and every home game. We'd love to see all the other stadiums, but we already know that there are no fans like the ones in Green Bay.

——**LEANNE BURCH**, Ladysmith, Wisconsin

I'm a Packers fan, but my biggest thrill was meeting Johnny Unitas. I love Bart Starr, but that was really a thrill. I mean two minutes after you meet him he's treating you like an old long-lost friend. I'll tell you someone else who's like that, Fuzzy Thurston. He makes you feel like you've known him for years. I also met Jerry Kramer out in Denver on a sports show and he's a great guy. I met Max McGee once and he seemed like he was a super nice guy. Once, when I was stationed in Fort Knox, we went out to dinner one night and we ran across the "Golden Boy," old Number 5. We hollered at him and he came over and thanked us for our service and talked to us. He was just a super nice guy.

Back in 1996, the Packers lost all the receivers to injuries. We picked up Andre Rison from the Falcons and he did a great job. After a game, this reporter asked him how he could play for the Packers, since the town was so small. Everyone knew everyone else's business. Andre said, "You don't have to worry about it if you keep your nose clean." The reporter said, "Coming from you?" I mean this was the guy whose girlfriend burned his house down while he was in Atlanta. But I saw the interview, and he said he wished that every player in the league could play one year in Green Bay. He said, "I've been out to dinner by myself and when I get ready to pay my bill, and the waiter says that it's already been taken care of. I don't even know who did it. I go out to get gas, and when I go to pay the guy, he gives me a free car wash." I think the best story I've heard is about the away games. The airport is only five miles from downtown Green Bay, and the players all drive out to the airport and leave their cars. The guys leave their keys at the airport, and fans come out and start their cars for them when they are due to get back!

There's something about the Packers that's almost like family. I've talked to people who have been to the new stadium and they tell me it's really something. They say there are people to greet you, you can meet the players if they're around, and it's open every day except Christmas and Easter. There are great restaurants there and you can hold meetings there, weddings there…it's just a great place.

———HERBERT BARNES, 83, retired Lt. Colonel, Atlanta

Bart Starr was, and still is, my favorite and idol to this day. The thing that impresses me most with him and what I always loved about him was that even after he left the area—he lives in Alabama now and owns car dealerships—he still does charity work in this area. He still has a home for orphans, the Rawhide Ranch. As a true gentleman, he's just my favorite.

———BILL ANDERS, Lawrenceville, Ga.

It would be tough to say my favorite player, but I guess it would have to be Willie Wood. He was with the Packers in the glory years, a free agent who was not even drafted out of USC. He not only made the team and became a starter, but eventually worked his way to the Hall of Fame. There's also always been a place in my heart for number 66, Ray Nitschke. When he retired my uncle and aunt sent me a pin that said "I love Ray," and I wore it proudly as a high school student in northern Wisconsin. I admired not only his aggressive style of play, but also the fact that he had tremendous pride in being a Packer. In more recent times, I'd say Gilbert Brown is my favorite. This is a young man who couldn't make the Vikings, then came to the Packers and dedicated himself to the team. At one point he had a chance to leave the Packers to make more money and he turned it down to stay in Green Bay, even though it was for less money. To me, those three players exemplify what it means to be a Packer.

———RANDY KUNSCH, 54, Phillips, Wisconsin

 I became a Packer fan when I was three years old, and I actually thought the game of football was called "Packers".… I've seen Sherman Lewis in a bar a few times. He's a great guy as long as you don't talk football. I was sitting next to him one night in 1996 when he was the offensive coordinator. He'd sit there and buy me beers all night as long as I didn't talk football. He said

he had to do that all day and he didn't want to at night.... I met Ray Nitschke once. I was walking out of the supermarket and he was walking in. I said, "Hey, you're getting a little bald there, Ray." He stuck his fist up in my face and said, "These are getting bald too, you want to mess with them?" I said, "No, I don't want mess with them," and walked away.

On draft day in 1998, my friend Dave and I were watching the draft on TV. Randy Moss was available in the draft, and I felt he was the best player in the whole draft. I kept watching, and Randy Moss kept dropping and dropping. I knew that if the Packers didn't take him, the Vikings would. I told my friend, "Get on the phone and call the Packers and tell them to draft Randy Moss. Tell them that if they don't, the Vikings will, and we'll end up facing that guy at least twice a year and he's gonna be great." So my friend got on the phone, called the team, and said, "Let me talk to Ron Wolf." Just like that, they patch him right through to Ron Wolf. My friend told him that they need to draft Randy Moss, but Ron told him they've already made their pick. The Packers picked Vonnie Holiday, the Vikings got Randy Moss. The next year the Packers home winning streak came to an end against the Vikings and Randy Moss. I'd worn a jacket to every home game for 29 straight games, and I'd never worn that jacket to a losing game. After that. it was all over. I couldn't believe my friend got right through to the president of the team like that, but I guess they thought he was from some other team or something. I just wish they would've listened to him. I still have dreams of Brett Favre and Randy Moss on the same team.

People like the Packers because they're the underdogs. They really are America's underdog, coming from the small city. They're not the Dallas Cowboy Crack Heads or the Minnesota Viking Chokers. If there's one team I hate it's the Vikings…and the Bears and the Lions.

——BRETT VAN DRISSE, 38, Green Bay

Last year I went to the Legends breakfast and was talking with a gentleman and his son who had flown in from New York that morning. As we were talking, I told him the story about the ceremony. When we got done talking he reached into his bag and pulled out a shirt. He said, "I brought some of these to give to local firemen, but I think you'd appreciate one." He handed me this shirt and I opened it up and it said, "Steven Siller" on the front. He was a fireman in New York that was off duty on 9/11. When he heard the towers had been hit, he hurried back to the station, got his truck and equipment and rushed to the tower. That was the last anyone saw of him. It's just amazing to me to have this shirt. It has his name on the front and the words, "Ground Zero-Hero" with a cloverleaf. One side of the cloverleaf says, "NYPD" the other side says "9/11/04" On the back, it has a U.S. flag with the words, "God Bless America."

My all-time favorite player is Willie Wood. When he comes here for the Legends events in Green Bay, I've seen him a couple of times in the supermarket parking lot. I feel so sorry for him, because these guys today are making such big money, and back then they just didn't. Here he was walking with two canes, and could hardly walk. I went over and started talking to him and he gave me his autograph, but he could hardly stand.

——WENDY SMETANA, Green Bay

In 1959 at Christmas, I received some football gear, shoulder pads, hip pads and a helmet, as a gift. The helmet was a Packer helmet, but it was blue, and it was signed by Tobin Rote, who was the Packers quarterback at the time. I was nine, and I asked my dad, "How come, since it's a Green Bay helmet, it's blue?" He just explained to me that was the colors they used then. At that time, their colors still had the blue, and they hadn't turned over to the green and gold.... I remember thinking, "Who is he?" when I heard they had traded away the number-one draft choice for Brett Favre. I had never heard of him. But that's why Ron Wolf is in the position he is, and why I do what I do what I do for a living! That's the bottom line. At the time, Packer fans were still rallying around Don Majkowski. He never got them over the hump and into the playoffs, but he still had the potential until he got injured. I do remember thinking we could have used that number-one draft choice to draft a really good "known" player, and, "Who is this Brett Favre kid?" Well, nobody has to ask that question anymore. I think that reaction was the consensus of all Packer fans.

——DAN DUNN, electrical specialist

From my standpoint, there's a big different between the players of today and the ones from the great Packer teams of the past. The early players stayed around longer, and I got to know them personally very well. Nowadays, I call it the 'revolving door.' It's a matter of free agency, and they're off again. They keep going in circles. They're not a team like it used to be. One time I went out to Ray Nitschke's house and took pictures of his kids in their back yard and in a tree house there. Also, my son, Jim, and I took Brett Favre's wedding pictures here in Green Bay. Their small daughter walked down the aisle in front of them dropping rose petals. There were 18 people at the wedding…we had to keep it quiet. Nobody knew about it. He didn't want it to be published. The Public Relations staff called me and said Brett had asked if I would take the pictures of the wedding for him. They asked me to keep it quiet. He got married in Green Bay at St. Agnes Catholic Church. After the wedding, we were invited over to his house, which they had just bought, but it wasn't yet furnished. Then we went over to his friend's house. That same year, I took pictures of Brett, his wife and his daughter for his Christmas card.

———**VERNON BIEVER**, Packer photographer since 1941

At work, we deal with Warner Electric quite a bit. One of the owners called and asked me if I'd be interested in going to the Lombardi Legends weekend thing in Green Bay. I told them I'd love to go, so they told me to show up at the stadium and some people from Warner Electric will meet me and show me up to the box. We got there, and I brought my helmet and a football. They met us and took us up to the box. We began to take pictures and look out over the room. Pretty soon I see all these old Packer players walk out on the field. I believe this was every living Packer player! We were talking and commented, "Look at all those old Packer players walking out there." A lady comes over and says, "Well, are you guys ready to go?" I said, "Where are we going?" She said, "You guys are going out on the field, too." I said, "You're kidding me." I walked out there and didn't know where to go—there were so many players—Hornung, Starr. You could meet them, shake their hand, talk with them. If I had died that day, it wouldn't have mattered. That day and the whole weekend were just awesome. We got to meet these players and we got stuff signed. They took a big group photo in the stands. We were able to go up and have our picture taken with all of them together. That was a great time getting to meet all these players and getting their autographs.

———**LARRY PRIMEAU**, Neenah, Wisconsin engineer

My folks were Packer fans when I was a tot. We would vacation in northern Wisconsin, and we got to go see the Packers practice. We'd stand in line to get autographs, and my parents took a picture of me getting Bart Starr's autograph just before he was getting on the bus. It was a hot day and he was just the most patient guy. They had been working out, but he stayed there for everybody to get an autograph or a picture. That really impressed us. A lot of athletes today are good about signing, but some really aren't. He was just a class act, a tremendous individual.

————JOHN MUDGETT, 44, Waukesha

Don Hutson was one of the legends we of a certain era grew up with. Greatet team: Chicago Bears. Greatest runner: Bronko Nagurski. Greatest receiver: Don Hutson. You didn't question it; it was simply accepted.

I just missed seeing Hutson play, but I heard the stories about him. Used to swing around the goalpost with one hand and catch a touchdown pass with the other. Once caught a pass in full stride, one-handed, with his palm facing downward. All the stories.

Ten years ago I met him at an old-timers' reunion and asked him about those tales. "Well, the goalposts were on the end line in those days," he said, "so I kind of used the post as a pick. Swung around it? Well, yeah, I used to do that. As for catching a ball from on top…if I did that I was just showing off."

The 6'1", 180-pound Hutson came into the NFL as a two-time All-American at Alabama, where he was known as the Alabama Antelope. Pro football wasn't ready for him. Back then defense ruled the league. The year before Hutson showed up, the average team completed just four passes per game. Within five years he owned all the receiving records: 11 stood for at least 50 years. In 1942 he caught 74 passes, more than four of the league's ten teams. Short and long posts, square-outs, down-and-ins, hooks, stop-and-go routes, deep flies, he had them all. Hutson also played safety and kicked for the Packers. In '45 he scored 29 points in one quarter against the Detroit Lions by catching four touchdown passes and converting five extra points.

In 1989, I flew to Green Bay and spent an afternoon in the Packers' film room watching footage of Hutson. I wanted to see the legend come to life. What I saw was a Ray Berry on the possession routes, blessed with the grace of a Lynn Swann, plus a great hunger for the ball at the point of the catch, like a Jerry Rice. For 11 years—99 touchdowns, three championships, a pair of MVP awards—he was the best.

I ran one catch back frame by frame, an impossible reception on a sideline route. His momentum was pulling him out of bounds, but he somehow corkscrewed his body back in and kept extending his arms—they seemed five feet long—and the ball stuck to his finger-tips. I've seen only one other like it, Swann's against the Dallas Cowboys in the 1976 Super Bowl.

He was an unexplained force in the NFL, a meteor that lit up the sky. An original. A legend.

——PAUL ZIMMERMAN, writer, New York City

In 1998, Robert Brooks missed practice one Friday. Nobody knew what was going on with him. It was a big mystery, "Where's Robert Brooks? Is he going to retire? Is he not going to retire?" Then, all of a sudden, on Saturday, he walks into my store, The Shoe Box. I said, "Robert, what are you doing? Everybody in the Midwest is looking for you, wondering what you're doing." He said, "Well, I just had a lot of thinking to do. I just thought I'd get in my car and drive and think things through. Before I knew it, I wound up at your place here at The Shoe Box." He was a buddy of mine. That's the weekend he decided to retire—to get out of football. With his wife, Diane, and his two children, in San Diego on vacation, and his soon-to-be-former teammates getting ready for practice, Brooks found himself sitting in the parking lot alone, not sure what to do. He said, "Then, I just went and drove. I just got in the car." By the time the emotion-filled drive was over, he found himself at, of all places, buying shoes at The Shoe Box." By then he had found peace with his decision.

——STEVE SCHMITT, Black Earth, Wisconsin

Warren Sapp can't be on the $25,000 Pyramid 'cause he doesn't have a clue.

Chapter 7

Throw Another Log On the Fire

The Ice Bowl

THE ICE BOWL WEATHER WOULD HAVE BROUGHT A TEAR TO A GLASS EYE

RICK HEARDEN

Rick Hearden is 42 years old and lives in Green Bay, Wisconsin. He is President, operator and part-owner of the Horseshoe Bay Golf Club in Egg Harbor, Wisconsin.

When I was five years old, my family moved from Kaukauna, Wisconsin to Green Bay. We moved into a small house on Ridge Road, two blocks from Lambeau Field. We actually moved there on December 12, 1967. The famous Ice Bowl was played on December 31, 1967. Back in those days you could go to the Packer games and get in for free at halftime. So at halftime of the Ice Bowl, my mother bundled up myself and my uncle, who was thirteen years old at the time, and drove the two blocks to Lambeau Field and dropped us off. My uncle and I walked in at halftime for free, and that was my first Packer game.

I remember three things from the game. First, I remember walking into the stadium and sitting down in one of the stairways between the bleachers. I remember this "older" gentleman, but of course when you're five you think everyone is older. But anyway, this older gentleman motioned for us to come over to him, and he said there were two empty seats next to him if we wanted them. Probably about five minutes later, my 13-year-old uncle was nudging me on the shoulder, and was pointing to this guy sitting to my right. This guy had been sitting there for the entire game and his nose was running. This formed an icicle on the end of his nose. My uncle was whispering in my ear trying to get me to tweak the icicle off this guy's nose, but I didn't ever get up the nerve to do it. As a five-year-old boy, that was my biggest memory of the Ice Bowl. The last thing I remember was that we were in the south end zone, which was where Bart Starr made his famous sneak across the goal line. I can still vividly remember that when the gun sounded to end the game almost the entire crowd swarmed onto the field. It was one of the most incredible sights to this day that I have ever witnessed. You hear stories today of people having pieces of the goal posts, and I believe them, because people carried off both of the goal posts after the game. My uncle was apparently smart enough to keep us from being swept onto the field, because we probably would have been crushed. We stayed up in the stands and eventually got out alive.

The joke is that Lambeau Field seated about 50,000 people at the time of the Ice Bowl, but there were about 200,000 people who claim they were there. Well, I believe there were more than 50,000 people there, because I was there and I didn't even have a ticket! The only way we got to sit down was because people either never showed up, or left early because of the cold....

Every Packer fan felt like 1996 was going to be our year. One of the things few people remember about that season was our defense. The Packers actually set the NFL record that year for fewest touchdowns allowed. People always talk about the Bears and the Ravens and how great their defenses were, but the Packers had an outstanding defensive unit and you still never really hear about it.

As you can tell, I'm a Packer fanatic. I was born into the Packer family. My grandfather, Lester Hearden, played for the Green Bay Packers in 1924. My grandfather's brother, Tom Hearden, played for the Packers in 1926 and 1927. So that's pretty cool, having two relatives who played for the Packers. But the really interesting part of the story is that in 1920, the starting backfield at Green Bay East High School was: my grandfather, my grandfather's brother, and a guy named Jim Crowley. Jim Crowley was one of the Four Horsemen of Notre Dame. My grandfather went to college for two years, and won the 100-yard dash at the Penn Relays, which was the biggest track event of the era. He was just a speed merchant. My uncle Tom also went to Notre Dame where Jim Crowley played, although my uncle was there the year after the Four Horsemen. He was actually the captain of the team in 1925. The interesting thing about those three guys being in the backfield, besides the fact that they all went on to have great football careers, was that the head coach of Green Bay East

High School that year was a guy named…Curly Lambeau! He was the head coach of the Green Bay Packers *and* the Green Bay East High School team at the **same time**. Obviously, two of his high school players came back to play for him as professionals, and Jim Crowley went on to glory as well. The other link here is that Jim Crowley went on to become head coach at **Fordham University**, where one of his players was…Vince Lombardi, one of the Seven Blocks of Granite. It's amazing how this little small town developed these great athletes and then created these ties all around the country. It was almost foreshadowing that Crowley coached Lombardi, and one of Lombardi's best friends was Red Smith. Red Smith, a Notre Dame graduate, was a big sports reporter in New York, and he was from Appleton, Wisconsin. Red Smith was Vince Lombardi's biggest supporter when it came to getting Lombardi to Green Bay. Vince Lombardi had all these ties to Wisconsin and didn't even know it till he got here.

Curly Lambeau wanted to carry on the Notre Dame colors at Green Bay. Originally the Packers colors were blue and gold, not green and gold. If you watch when the Packers wear the throwback uniforms, they're blue and gold. Back then, the Packers colors were either blue and gold or green and gold, depending on who the coach was at the time. Notre Dame wears both blue and gold and, occasionally, for big games, green and gold

In 1969, the fiftieth anniversary of the Packers, my grandfather went to the alumni banquet. All the players there got a Green Bay Packer helmet lamp. It was an actual helmet that had been turned into a lamp, and when he passed away I inherited it. He played one year with the Packers, and he played the same position as Curly Lambeau, so he didn't get much playing time. He did score a touchdown that season so he's in the record books. At the end of that season, he went

> **In 1941, Buff Donelli was the head football coach for the Pittsburgh Steelers and Duquesne University.**

> **The Rams, who began as the Cleveland Rams, were named for the Fordham University team.**

up to some town in northern **Michigan** that had a team. That team came down to play the Packers in a game and just got demolished. After that he decided pro football wasn't going to pay the bills and left the game. He retired as an engineer. He was only in professional football for three or four years....

That leads to another story that I just learned about ten years ago. I was at a Monday Morning Quarterback club meeting, and I was actually the host this day. It was a group that met on Mondays to discuss the game from the day before, and we always brought in a player to talk about it. I was the host and was sitting at the head table with Frank Winters and Lee Remmel, the long time PR guy for the Packers. Anything you want to know about the Packers, Lee Remmel can tell you. He has a memory like you wouldn't believe. I introduced myself to Lee Remmel and sat down. He said, "Hearden, are you related to Tom Hearden?" I told him it was my great uncle and he said, "Let me tell you a story about Tom Hearden." So he starts telling this story about my great-uncle. He said, "Tom Hearden was one of the finest football coaches ever, not just in the history of the Packers, but in all of football. In 1946, his St. Norbert's football team was undefeated and ranked 19th in the country, and that included all schools in the country. Notre Dame, Michigan, etc. were all in the same ranking as little-bitty St. Norbert, which had a student population of about 1600. In 1958, unfortunately, Tom Hearden had a stroke. At the end of the '58 season everyone knew we needed a new football coach. If Tom Hearden hadn't had the debilitating stroke, no one in Green Bay would have ever heard of Vince Lombardi, because Tom Hearden would have gotten the job!" I'd heard stories of what a good coach he was, but hearing it from Lee Remmel really brought it home. On one hand, you wonder if they would have had the success they had if Lombardi hadn't been there, on the other hand, the Super Bowl trophy today might be called the "Hearden Trophy!"

The state of Michigan has more golf courses than any other state in the Union.

ICE BOWLS, SNOW BOWLS, AND SUPER BOWLS

My oldest son and I attended the Ice Bowl game…we really did! You talk to a lot of people now who say they were there, and they really weren't, but we were. We got up that morning in Milwaukee and it was about 14 below zero and a bright, sunny day. We debated whether we would go or not, but we finally decided we would.

When we got there we saw about 48,000 other nuts, so we didn't feel so bad. It was interesting to see the Packers in their heavy clothing, and then to see the Cowboys in their light clothes, trying to adjust to the weather. Of course, they never did. It was so cold that day that when you took your thermos and poured it in your cup, if some of the coffee dribbled down the side, it would freeze before it dripped off! We were actually sitting on the 20-yard line on the west side of the stadium, right near where Bart Starr made his famous sneak. Right before it happened, I told my son, "Jimmy, I don't think they're going to pull this out." This woman sitting next to me started giving me holy hell because I could even think that the Packers could lose. When he made his famous sneak, she started yelling, "See, see!" and shook her finger at me. People were dressed in snowmobile suits, and other people had paper bags wrapped around their feet, anything to stay warm. Out of that game grew the famous "frozen tundra story" that Green Bay is known for.

——**DR. FRANK URBAN**, Brookfield, Wisconsin

During that "Ice Bowl" game, I was up in the press box. It was bitter cold—to this day, they say it's the coldest air-temperature game played in the history of professional football. There has been one game with a lower wind chill, and that was the Charger-Bengal game in 1981—which had a wind chill of 59 below. Our wind chill was 46 below, but the air temperature at kickoff was 13-below zero. It was nine-below at Cincinnati for their 1981 game.

——**LEE REMMEL**, writer, at that time, for the *Green Bay Press-Gazette*

We went to the Ice Bowl—that was exciting. We stayed for the whole thing too. It was so cold, and in those days people used to be able to bring thermos bottles. We brought a thermos of "Old Fashioneds" and we stayed warm drinking those. We were so proud of ourselves for staying the whole game, but when we got to our car, our transmission had frozen up, so we had to call a taxi to get home. It was a fantastic game though.

——MARY DUROCHER, Green Bay

I first became aware of the Packers in the late 60's, after they had their great run with Vince Lombardi. I did attend the world famous Ice Bowl, at the age of nine. I really didn't realize the implications of what was going on. I grew up less than a half a mile north of Lambeau Field, so as a little boy I'd always run up to the games with my friends and try to rush the gate, or sneak in somehow. Before the Ice Bowl, there had been a significant amount of snowfall, and they had piled up the snow from the parking lot. There was a large amount of snow pushed up against the fence, and at that time the fence was only about eight feet high with a little barbwire on top. To us, with the snow, it was just like a ramp up one side and down the other. We just waited until the officer watching a particular area walked away and we scaled the fence and were inside. To be honest, I don't remember anything about the game at all. I remember being shooed out of a lot of areas. We'd just keep moving around until an usher made us move. I do recall being at the south end zone right on the goal line at the beginning of the fourth quarter. I was in the perfect spot for what was about to happen. Unfortunately, the weather got to the nine-year old, and when Bart Starr made his famous sneak I was already at home soaking in a tub of hot water. So my main memories of the Ice Bowl are of sneaking in and being shooed out of various areas by the ushers.

——PAUL MAZZOLENI, 45, Arlington Heights, Illinois

I've seen some exciting games. Everyone remembers the Ice Bowl on December 31, 1967 when the Green Bay Packers were playing the Dallas Cowboys for the National Football League championship in Green Bay. The winner would get to go on to the Super Bowl. Back then, we always stopped at the airport for lunch on our way to Lambeau Field. The plane carrying the Dallas fans had just landed when we got there. The women were in high heels, fur coats, leather

Ellen Dahl

gloves, and nothing on their heads. If they weren't lucky enough to have seats in the enclosed boxes, I'm sure they didn't even see one quarter of the game. I was dressed in so many layers that walking up all those steps to our seats was a chore. We had scarves around our head and neck, caps, earmuffs, and liquid fuel hand warmers inside double woolen mittens. Then, we even sat in sleeping bags. The weatherman said it was thirty-five below zero wind chill. I wasn't exactly warm but I wasn't freezing either. At the end of the fourth quarter, we were on our feet hoping and praying for a miracle because the Packers were behind 17-14. Conservative Vince Lombardi called for a quarterback sneak. Bart Starr made his famous sneak, and the Packers won to go on to their second Super Bowl victory.

You rarely hear of the "Snow Bowl," but it was memorable to me. It had been snowing since mid-morning on Saturday. On Sunday morning, both the radio and the TV were advising all motorists to stay off the roads unless it was absolutely necessary. We knew they couldn't have been talking to us! There was a Packer game in Green Bay and we were going. We loaded our car with usual gear, adding extra blankets and four shovels. We stopped in Stevens Point to pick up a friend. The plows had been out since early morning but heavy snow had wiped out all evidence of it. We traveled Highway 54 at a very careful speed. Traffic was almost nonexistent—some people had listened. About four miles from the Waupaca County line, we became stuck in the middle of the highway. Out we got, retrieving our shovels and shoveling the snow from the road so we could go on. Turning back was *not* an option. A four-wheel-drive Jeep passed us, and we jumped in our car so we could follow in their wheel marks before they were filled with blowing snow.

We made it. Lambeau Field had a seating capacity of about 60,000. That day there were 2,500 devoted fans there. All of them true-blue…maybe not on the outside, but on the inside. We were dressed warm enough, but our binoculars were of no use at all because the snow completely wiped out our view. It was snowing so hard, the only way to see was to hold your hands on each side of your face to make a tunnel to look through. We never made it to our seats.

We just pushed the snow aside and sat down. Not surprisingly, the Packers won the game....

I bought shares of Packer stock for myself and all my grandsons who were interested. When that sale was not adequate to fund the upgrades at Lambeau Field, I willingly paid the $1,400 licensing fee for each of my seats. I invite fans who aren't as fortunate as me to come to games with me. I also get a lot of brownie points with my sons and grandsons. Of course, the grandchildren get the really cold games while I watch on TV. Age does have its privilege!

———ELLEN DAHL, 81, Wisconsin Rapids

My brother, Bob, and I went to the Ice Bowl game. I just got to go because no one else wanted to go because it was so cold. I was pretty young, probably about 20, but we did stay for the whole game. We took our sleeping bags—and they were really good ones. We sat down and zipped those sleeping bags all the way up to our neck. We stayed pretty warm that way. This lady in front of us sat there in a dress and a fur coat and nothing on her ears. She wasn't dressed for a game in Green Bay, and I don't think she made it past the first quarter. During the game, we noticed that Bob Hayes, the Cowboys speedster, wouldn't leave the line of scrimmage if it wasn't going to be a pass play. I'm sure if we noticed it, the Packers did too. It was just so cold he didn't bother running if it wasn't a pass. I remember being there and seeing all the things you see on TV now, but at the time we didn't think of it as being all that significant. My brother still has the tickets so we can prove we were really there.

———DAN WELLENS, 59, Green Bay

I went to the "Ice Bowl" game. At the time, I worked for a company in Waukesha. The owner of the company was a big Packer fan and he invited some customers to go to the game. On the Friday before the game, there were still a few seats left on the bus so I called the Packer ticket office at Milwaukee County Stadium and asked if they had any tickets left for the game. They said, "Yeah, we've got three left." I told them to save them for me, and I'd be down to get them. I drove from Waukesha to County Stadium, 20 miles away, picked up the three tickets, came back, and was able to ride the bus to the game.

In those days, the people could run out onto the field after the games. The last play, they threw a pass and the ball sailed out of bounds. We were sitting a couple of rows up on the east side of the stands on about the 30-yard line, and I came close to getting that ball. That was on New Year's Eve day. When our bus arrived back in town, several people, who had left their cars parked outside, could not get them started because it was so cold.

——CHARLES MUDGETT, 71, Waukesha

 I became a Packers fan in 1930 when I went to my first game back in that same year. I don't remember much about that game—it's been too long ago. But I do remember going to the Ice Bowl game. We sat there with big sheets of plastic covering us. I stayed warm, but the guy that went with me left before the game was over. When I saw him the next day, I told him he missed the best part of the game. He said he hadn't missed it, because when he got down to the entrance he heard it on the loud speaker. Back then there wasn't any giant screen to see it, so all he got to do was hear it—but I got to see it. I was getting a little shaky about our chances that day, but the way they took the ball down the field on that final drive, I knew we were going to win.

Another game I remember was so cold that I thought we were all going to freeze. In the parking lot that day this guy had a jug he was carrying in, and he bumped that jug up against a car's bumper and it went "ding" and that jug just shattered. That's how cold it was.

——ARNOLD DOEPKE, 92, Rothschild, Wisconsin

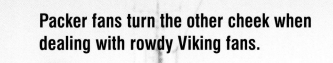

Packer fans turn the other cheek when dealing with rowdy Viking fans.

Jon Gruden—Green Bay Packers, 1992

"Ray Nitschke" and St. Vincent.
"Nitschke" is Packer Fan Bill Anders.

Green Bay Packers Coaching Staff, 1992

Front row, left to right: Greg Blanche, Nolan Cromwell,
Jim Lind, Dick Jauron
Second row: Bob Valesente, Sherman Lewis, Mike Holmgren,
Ray Rhodes, Kent Johnson
Stairs: Jon Gruden, Gil Haskell, Steve Mariucci, Tom LoVat, Andy Reid

Karen Ellis Knows How to "Tailgate"

The woods are full
of long hitters...
like Brett Favre

Celebrating the first public viewing
of the new Lambeau—2003

Credit: Jim Biever

Brett Favre was riding high in 1993.

Brett Favre prior to 1993
L.A. Rams game.

Credit: Tom Lynn

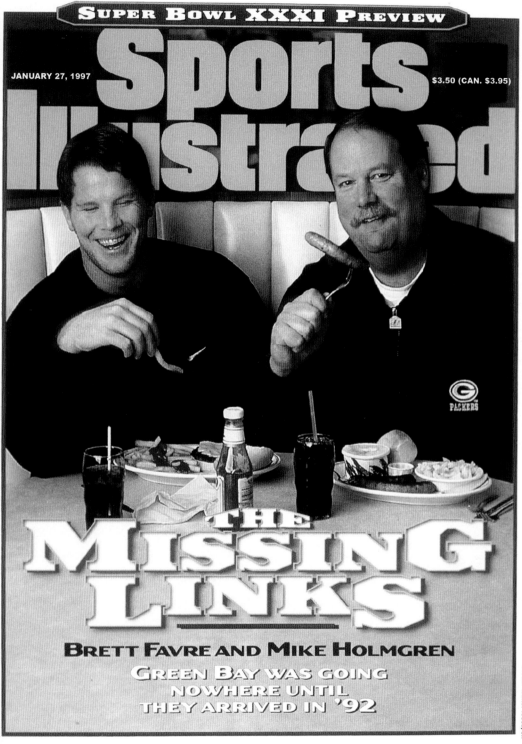

Sports Illustrated

JANUARY 27, 1997

$3.50 (CAN. $3.95)

THE MISSING LINKS

BRETT FAVRE AND MIKE HOLMGREN

GREEN BAY WAS GOING NOWHERE UNTIL THEY ARRIVED IN '92

Chapter 8

PackerPalooza

IF YOU RUN NFL FILMS BACKWARDS, IT LOOKS LIKE THE PLAYERS ARE HELPING EACH OTHER UP AND SHOWING THEM ON THEIR WAY

STEVE BOETTCHER

Steve Boettcher of Milwaukee is a documentary filmmaker. His The Legends of Lambeau Field *opened to rave reviews in 2003. Boettcher was raised in a die-hard Packer household in Appleton. You can check out his film at www.legendsoflambeaufield.com*

T*he Legend of Lambeau Field* is a documentary that took us two-and-a-half years on the project. It was commissioned by the Packers as a commemorative film on the re-opening of the stadium after the new construction. We went back and interviewed forty current players, former players and Hall-of-Famers and coaches from all the eras of the team. I talked to guys who were play-ing with the teams in the very early years to the guys who are playing today. In a sense, I collected all the history and all the great moments that happened at Lambeau Field.

As a filmmaker, you look for those hidden gems. One thing we found of real interest was—a fan that had brought his motion-picture camera into games. He shot the "Ice Bowl" from his seat with his camera. He would sit there with freezing hands and wind up his little camera. He even snuck in the day before the "Ice Bowl" and filmed both teams working out and stood right next to Vince Lombardi and filmed him working out his team on that Saturday when the weather was nice. He got Dallas getting off the bus—it's rare footage that had never been seen before. The Dallas players were getting off their bus, kind of cocky, just walking through their plays pretty confidently. They didn't know, that within a few hours from the shooting of that film, the world was going to change for them dramatically—weather-wise and the outcome of the game! Some great little nuggets were found producing this film. It's like seeing the game from a different perspective, literally shot in the stands right down with the goal-line sneak of Bart Starr to win the game. You just see the breaths of everyone. It's like an eerie, ominous feeling of everybody exhaling together and everybody breathing in together. All this steam was kind of shrouding around this winning touchdown. It's euphoria in the stands after that. It's a really neat perspective to watch this classic moment.

The film was silent, of course, so it was amazing to just see the power of the image…just to watch this rare inspirational tribute to this moment in history. It was very exciting to see.

We interviewed Ron Kramer and some real old-time guys like Tony Canadeo. It was great to get their views on what this team and what this franchise has meant to the small town of Green Bay, Wisconsin—kind of "The David and Goliath" of professional sports.

Here was this storied stadium in this small, hard-working, middle-class town of Green Bay and how it became such a legendary landmark. Early in the film, we interviewed the **Monday Night Football** guys. John Madden said, "When you think of hallowed grounds in football, the first one that comes to mind should be Lambeau Field." That's where we began the film—talking about the hallowed grounds of Lambeau Field. It was a great opportunity for us to interview fans who have done strange things—like maybe marrying someone in Green Bay because they had really good season tickets, just knowing that "if I marry this individual, I'll get one of these two tickets, and it's worth getting married to this person because they have great seats." People who have spent every one of their fall Sundays, when there's a home game, sitting in that parking lot tailgating at 7:00 a.m. in the morning. And, they're there when that sun goes down, still tailgating and reminiscing about the game. The whole state of Wisconsin really rallies on a Sunday when there's a Packer game.

> **John Lennon's death was first reported to the nation by Howard Cosell on Monday Night Football.…In 1999, Monday Night Football became the longest-running prime-time entertainment series ever, breaking a tie with Walt Disney at 29 years.**

We shot tons of the footage at tailgate parties and got all the extreme tailgating that goes on. There's a fine art and a craft to tailgating. The fans in Green Bay have really defined what tailgating is. I'd like to believe that they are some of the first ones who have really done tail-gating right to the point of fine linen tablecloths and grilling the finest foods—really making it an event—not just simply hamburgers on a grill. It's become much, much more than that.

It's weird in a way, but a good weird, I guess. It's very unusual. It's something you have to see sometime. It's like a shrine you have to visit in your lifetime. One of the "Seven Wonders of the World" is going to Lambeau Field and watching a game there and seeing all that goes on.

A great moment there is a Bears game. It's just two Midwest teams that have always gone head-to-head for years and years and years. The proximity of the two cities, where many fans drive up from Chicago just makes such a great rivalry. I mean that in all the best terms. It's just a great event to go to. Everybody should try to get to one of the games here if you have a chance in your lifetime. Detroit and Minnesota are places where Green Bay fans get a lot of abuse. **John Madden** talked about that, too. He said, "Even though you're competitors, there's kind of a graciousness that the people of Green Bay extend to other fans. It's more fun-loving banter, as opposed to mean-spirited viciousness—worried about your life kind of thing when you go somewhere else." I've talked to Packer fans who have gone to other games, especially in Minnesota and Detroit. Sometimes they were actually afraid to wear anything that signified the team they're rooting for. It's not that way in Green Bay. That's the small-town charm of Green Bay. It's people who just love the game and everything about it, and even love the competition of the other team showing up....

> **When former Olympic gold medal figure skater Peggy Fleming was stranded in New York following the September 11th attacks, she hitched a ride to her San Francisco home with John Madden on the Madden Cruiser, the custom bus that Madden travels in because of his fear of flying. They are neighbors in the Bay area.**

Don Majkowski was the quarterback before Brett Favre. On a play that ended Don Majkowski's career, he went down and was wheeled off the field, and that was the end of his playing career. Brett Favre came in as his back-up quarterback and the rest is history with Brett Favre. We actually brought Don Majkowski back to be interviewed for the film on a Sunday game a year ago. He had not been back for a game. As he walked around the field before the game, the fans were unbelievably gracious to him. He had a chance to take a final bow. He went around and shook hands, and it was as if he had never left. It had been ten or twelve years since his career-ending injury. His wife pulled me aside and whispered to me, "You've done something great for this man who left the game he loved—had to leave, not on his terms, but because of an injury—and you brought him back to say goodbye in a very personal and final way." It was neat to see....

I was shooting for one of the television stations at the last game Reggie White played in the stadium. At the end of the game, I was across the field on the visitors' side. I ran out on the field and came face-to-face with Reggie White. He put one knee down, and I put a knee down, and he got ready to give a prayer. I sat in the middle of a circle of all the players as Reggie did his final prayer in Lambeau Field. Just to sit there, as a television photographer, and to hear what was being said, and to hear the warmth he had, and the other players were there to join in the prayer and just seeing how humble this man was. How he gave respect to the team. Also, how he gave God all the credit for his ability. It was something very neat to see....

I was with Gilbert Brown one time on a television project. He was spending some of his free time going to one of the area prisons to visit the inmates there. He was going there on his day off to give a little talk. It was a scary-type prison setting. I went along as a television photographer and stood next to him as we walked down the cell block. At one end of the cell block, Gilbert looked over his shoulder in a very fatherly way and said to me, "First thing you want to do is get behind me, and I'll take care of you from here on out." He wasn't a man of a lot of words, but the words he used were very carefully picked and were very appropriate. It was interesting, in a small setting like that, to see how much he cared and thought about other people.

Ray Nitschke had already died before we did this **film** project, but I had interviewed him in the past. There was a big difference between Ray Nitschke, the player and Ray Nitschke, the person. He was an incredibly nice man off the field.

A lot of these players, no matter what their era, keep coming back to Green Bay. Bart Starr is really involved and comes back a lot. He stays involved in the community, involved in the area, not really a Green Bay native. He lives in Arizona, but is always very active and always comes back for things when they ask him. Their life and their history was such an important part of Green Bay that they still are very active with it. It's neat to see.

The good thing about Green Bay is that there are not as many distractions as there might be in New York or in Miami. In Green Bay, you've got to look long and hard to find trouble sometimes, and maybe that's the good thing about Green Bay. It is a town of small houses, and nice families—a real community.

When you go to Green Bay in January, there are not a lot of other things you can do other than concentrate on football, from the point of these players. It's amazing how many players stay there in the off-season to work out in the facility, or in the gym, and to be close to the coaches and the fitness people.

Inside The NFL on HBO is the longest running series of any kind of cable television.

WELCOME TO CHICAGO...WHERE THE LOCAL TIME IS ALWAYS 1985

CHET COPPOCK

Chicago-based Chet Coppock is regarded by many as the number-one sports talk radio host in America. He is heard on The Sporting News Radio Network.

Whenever you begin talking about the Packers and the Bears, you've got to begin with the two central figures in the rivalry—that's George Halas, who was belovedly and affectionately known as the 'old man' and Vince Lombardi.

The year that was most difficult for Lombardi, when it came to the Bears, was obviously 1963. Green Bay had won National Football League championships in '61 and '62, beating the Giants both years. They were seemingly indestructible. Even though, they had lost Paul Hornung to a National Football League gambling scandal, it was really very minor.

Beginning in 1963, the old man, Halas, had gone 17 years without winning a championship. It was almost a foregone conclusion that Green Bay would knock off the Bears in the old Western Division and go on to win their third consecutive championship.

The Bears were coming off a 9-2 season in 1962, and during the off-season, the old man hired as an assistant coach a guy from Miami, Jim Dooley. Dooley later became head coach of the Bears, and is remembered by most Packer fans as being a very dysfunctional head coach. The fact is Dooley had no chance to win whatsoever because, at that time, the Bears were just absolutely beyond awful when it came to acquiring personnel. Their drafting was abysmal.

Going back to the winter of 1963, the old man put Jim Dooley in charge of breaking down Green Bay's offensive tendencies. Essentially, Dooley lived with an old projector at 173 West Madison in

Chicago, which at that time was the Bears downtown office. He simply broke down everything Green Bay had done over the previous three years on offense. He knew exactly what Fuzzy Thurston was doing, what Jerry Kramer was doing, what Jim Ringo was doing, what Bob Skoronski was doing, what Jim Taylor was doing, Bart Starr, Max McGee—Dooley became a 'book of knowledge.'

The Bears created what was known as the buzz and read defense. One thing led to another. The buildup for Green Bay at that time was significantly greater than it is now. Over the years, with the decline of the Bears, and prior to that, the decline of the Packers under Bart Starr in the late seventies and early eighties, the rivalry is not nearly as big today for 25-year-old football players as it was back in 1963.

The Bears convened in Rensselaer, Indiana for camp, as they always did in those days. Their entire eight-week window of camp, and all six of their exhibition games, including one with Green Bay, were designed with one thing in mind—that was to beat Green Bay on opening day. I remember riding up on the train with the Bears. My father was very close to **George Halas**. My dad's business partner, one time, was Luke Johnsos, the old man's offensive coach.

Most people do not realize that the most remarkable football shrine is Lambeau Field, which is such a magnificent ball park. If you don't like the emerald-green grass and the sidelines at Lambeau Field, my advice is…become a hockey fan, or go watch soccer.

If I was taking somebody from Paraguay or North Korea and wanted to show them what football in America is all about, there are three venues I would take them to. One would be Tiger Stadium in Baton Rouge, which for a Saturday night game is just unmatched in terms of fan energy. Number two would obviously be Notre Dame Stadium in South Bend because of the remarkably pristine, traditional atmosphere of the Rock, the Four Horsemen. The third would be Lambeau Field.

> **The Chicago Bears wear blue and orange because those are the colors that team founder George Halas wore when he played for the University of Illinois.**

Without the presence of George Halas, and the fact that Halas lobbied the city fathers in Green Bay, back in the late fifties, when the Pack was playing at old City Stadium, there would have been no Lambeau Field. The old man was instrumental in keeping the Green Bay Packers alive. He recognized that while you had Chicago, you had New York, you had Detroit, you had San Francisco, this very quaint franchise at Green Bay was vital for the strength of this league. So, the old man, in '57 and '58, was in Green Bay on a regular basis lobbying the city fathers for the construction of Lambeau Field.

Move the clock up five years…the Bears take the train from downtown Chicago, up to Green Bay. They were probably 13-point underdogs, and they were given only a modest chance to win the ball game. They came out and put on one of the greatest defensive shows of football I have ever seen…or anybody has ever seen! They intercepted Bart Starr five times. They won the ball game 10-3. When the old man died in '83, I broke the story of the death of George Halas. Sid Luckman called me from the coach's bedside to tell me he had passed away. The first thing I thought about, ironically, was not that legacy of the old man or 226 coaching victories, but it was the football which always stood proudly in his office dated September 15, 1963, Bears 10—Green Bay 3, with the inscription, "Greatest team victory." When you contemplate the impact of George Halas coaching four separate tenures of ten years each, a total of forty years—for him to isolate that one ball game as the greatest team victory in and of itself makes a statement which is almost staggering in terms of depth and in terms of impact.

Now, the Bears have beaten Green Bay in the opener so Green Bay is looking up. The rematch is November 17, of 1963 in Chicago. It's literally impossible to describe without pulling out every cliché known to man the vibrancy in that ball park that day. The Bears-Packers, playing in old Wrigley Field, which was just as cozy as it could be, 48,000 fans. Who knows how many people were standing? I do recall that in all the years I've covered football and watched it as a fan, which would roughly be 48 years, I have never been in a ball park, and this includes the Bears' Super Bowl year, where the feeling of tension before a ball game was stiff, so dominate, almost suffocating. The Bears had gone 17 years without winning a title. If Green Bay won that game, they were going to win the Division. The Packers were playing without Bart Starr. Nevertheless, you had this gnawing feeling inside that somehow the Italian was going to beat the old man.

The opening kickoff, Roger LeClerc kicked off for the Bears. Herb Adderley, who wound up in the Pro Football Hall of Fame, fielded the opening kickoff and ran into a *freight train*, who wore #25 on his jersey, by the name of J. C. Caroline, who was one of the last great two-way football players. He hit him with one of the greatest open-field tackles I have ever seen. The eruption of sound in Wrigley Field was so shrill you would have sworn you were watching a Led Zeppelin concert. It set the tone for the Bears to go ahead and beat the Packers that day 26-7. The score does not begin to indicate just how dominating the Bears were. The bottom line is this—the Bears had taken the Packers and in one given year had held this offensive machine, the Packer Sweep, this tremendous offensive line, which were, in my opinion, the most underrated offensive line of all-time to a grand total of ten points in the two games.

That, in and of itself, for one given year, if not the greatest chapter, is certainly one of the two or three greatest in Chicago Bear history. The Bears go on to beat the Giants for the title. Really, the Bears won the championship on that given Sunday in November when they beat Green Bay.

I always say that game, in and of itself, was a greater team victory than the 10-3 game in '63. I remember the day before that ball game, Richie Petitbon, a hell of a defensive back out of LSU, appeared on Channel 2. That was very primitive television before there was all the cockiness and strutting and talking in rhymes, and he said, "I think we're going to beat them again, only worse." I remember the old man saying, "Geez, why the hell would he say that? Why would you feed Lombardi anything?" Again, the Bears went out and just literally crushed the living hell out of them....

I'll always remember the last game Bart Starr coached in Green Bay. He'd been there for 10 years. Bart was never really suited to be a head coach. As competitive as Bart was, he was too nice to be a head coach. He coached his last game at Soldier Field against Mike Ditka in '83. The Bears closed the year 8-8. You knew it was Bart's last game. The press in Green Bay and Milwaukee had been speculating for weeks that Bart was done, and you knew he was. When the game was over, I was on the sidelines. I was working for Channel 5 and would always go down and do stand-up at the end of the game. I did my stand-up about Bart Starr and Mike Ditka. The reason I did that was that as the ball game was winding down and the clock was running out, I had no interest in talking to any player in particular. I wanted to see what was going to transpire between Mike Ditka and Bart Starr.

When they met at midfield, the look on Bart's face was one of such sadness. The look on Mike's face was one that was equally as sad. I think what it was—very little was spoken between the two men, very little was said. I talked about this with Mike a number of times over the years. They didn't have to say anything. What mattered was the handshake between the two men. "I love you." Two great warriors saying their final farewells.

Two competitors, two guys going head-to-head, jaw to jaw, wanted to beat each other in the worst way, but yet the display of respect was so poignant, and so rich in faith, and so rich in mutual admiration. You couldn't help but be terribly, terribly moved. I have no idea what the final score was that day…can't begin to remember…don't know who scored touchdowns…don't know who intercepted passes…but I will never, even if I live to be 100, forget that handshake as being one of the emotional, totally poetic moments I have ever seen on a football field.

I don't think I was as moved by the Golden Gate Bridge or the first time I saw **Madison Square Garden**, or the first time I met **Muhammad Ali**—I don't think I was as moved as I was by that handshake. That's a pretty big statement, when you get right down to it. That's the beauty of this rivalry. And, the beauty of the Packers and

> **The official name of Boston Garden was Boston Madison Square Garden.**

> **In 1979 Muhammad Ali beat football player, Lyle Alzado, in an eight-round bout….Rich Kotite, former head coach of the Eagles and the Jets, was once Muhammad Ali's sparring partner in Miami.**

Bears. For those people who are a little bit older, the rivalry at one time was so fierce and so outrageous. These two teams hated each other, but it's kind of interesting over the years how guys like Paul Hornung and Jimmy Taylor and Ed O'Bradovich or Mike Ditka when they talk about the rivalry, the sense of love between all these guys is overwhelming. Once you're part of that rivalry, and that rivalry weights you at the hip, not unlike Ali-Frazier with their three-fight series, the first two in the Garden, and the third one in Manila. For me, it's something I grew up with. It's something I appreciate with a sense of almost religious reverence. It's something I treasure. I only wish that today's younger football players would look upon it the way Brett Favre does.

I'll give you a statement that nobody else will ever give you. You can talk about Halas. You can talk about Red Grange. You can talk about Bronko Nagurski, Gale Sayers, Dick Butkus, Mike Ditka, **Walter Payton**, Jim McMahon, Clarke Hinkle, Don Hutson, Bart Starr, Jimmy Taylor, Paul Hornung, the incredible volume of football players who have been involved in this series. There are really four defining individuals who are what the rivalry is all about. One is George Halas. Two is Curly Lambeau. Number three is Lombardi. Number four, the one single player that best exemplifies the rivalry, without question, is Brett Favre, because of his ability to win, his ability to shine within the structure of the rivalry, and his competitive drive every bit the equal of Halas, every bit the equal of Lombardi, every bit the equal of Ditka. Every bit the equal, if not greater, than the aforementioned individuals.

Hornung and those players would go to the **Playboy Club** and bust curfew, and Lombardi would know about it, but there wasn't a thing

---

In the last 30 years, the record for the most touchdown passes thrown by a non-quarterback is held by Walter Payton, with eight.

The late Bo Belinsky married 1965 Playboy Playmate of the Year, Jo Collins, in 1968. They were married for five years...Jimmy Connors married the 1977 Playmate of the Year, Patti McGuire in 1978. They are still married.

he could do about it…tough as he was. Doug Atkins called up Halas at four o'clock in the morning to complain about the offense. These two teams were so representative of an era of pro football. The game, over the years, has changed so dramatically. The game is not nearly as good now as it was in the sixties. Then, the players were allowed to play. The emphasis wasn't on situational football where you were running into a 350-pound nose tackle on first down, or going into a nickel defense or a dime defense. There was such strong identification. I hated Forest Gregg. Growing up, I hated Bart Starr. I couldn't stand Paul Hornung. Couldn't stand Jimmy Taylor. There was such passion. Now, Paul Hornung has been a friend for 35 years. Every year, I look forward to calling up Bob Harlan, who is the president of the Green Bay Packers and is one of the brightest men in pro football. It used to be fun for me, as a kid, to watch Hornung and Halas point fingers at each other.

Here you had this kid from Louisville, you talk about a hot guy, and I'm as straight as I can be, and you talk about Mick Jagger, you talk about Brad Pitt, you talk about Clark Gable, you talk about Joe Namath—when Hornung was in Chicago, if he would walk down Rush Street….There was a joke over the horn about a week ago, when he would walk down Rush Street, the way women would swoon in front of Paul Hornung was like watching Moses part the Red Sea. If you look up the words, 'chick magnet' you'd find a picture of Paul Hornung. Babes just swooned over this guy. Why not? He was a big, good looking guy. He won the Heisman Trophy. He had this gorgeous blond hair. If you don't think it was a treat for a young Chet Coppock, at the age of 20, to get loaded with Paul Hornung, guess again. You thought to yourself that you were getting loaded with one of the 'wise men.' That's the kind of guy he was.

The display of sadness when the old man died, October 31, '83, when I broke the story and beat Monday Night Football with the story by 17-18 minutes, coming out of Green Bay. People were just broken hearted. I'll never forget it. The people who called to console me from Green Bay were just amazing. I always knew the impact of the man was staggering. He was George Halas. When he died, even to this day, when you talk to Hornung and to all the people who were there on the field with him, when he coached, the way they speak of Halas is almost like they were speaking about God himself.

I saw the dirtiest play of all time in the Bear-Packer rivalry. I saw the greatest hit. The greatest hit was obviously J. C. Caroline's hit on Herb Adderley. In 1954, on the kickoff, George Connor, who was All-American at Notre Dame, and went to the Pro Football Hall of Fame, was a member of the Chicago Bears. He hit Veryl Switzer on the kickoff return. I remember the helmet flying one way, the football flying the other, and you thought Switzer's's rib cage was going to fly up in a different direction. It was so wicked, so violent. I was only five or six years old, and there was a stunned silence because people thought Switzer was dead.

Walter Payton cherished the rivalry, really cherished it. He got it from day one. It always amazed me. Here was this kid from Jackson State, who had played at an all-black school. But, he got it from day one. He knew what it meant. He understood what it meant. He played brilliantly against the Packers.

It was either '85 or '86, the Bears were playing Green Bay at Lambeau Field. This was a time in the rivalry that had really become very, very dark. There was such bad blood between Ditka and Forest Gregg. If Jerry Markbreit, who refereed that ball game did not move so swiftly to calm Ditka down, on the Bear sideline…McMahon threw the interception. Then, the Packers' Charles Martin picks up McMahon like a rag doll and slams him on the carpet. That ball park was headed toward a riot. Martin was wearing a towel that had a list of ball players he wanted to nail in that game. Number 9 was the most prominent on that list. If Markbreit had not moved in and immediately ejected Charles Martin and got him over to Green Bay's sideline, and cooled Ditka, and waved off a penalty that Jerry had immediately dropped without seeing the pick on Jim Covert, there would have been a riot to end all riots in that ball park that day. If Markbreit, who is arguably the greatest official I've ever seen, had not moved so swiftly, who knows what might have happened.

When you mention the name of Martin to ex-Green Bay players, you will get a universal sigh of contempt from them. He really violated the code. The code of the series has always been—you take your shot, I'll take my best shot. You like to believe there's a fine line. It was ugly back in the mid-eighties, and it stemmed from Forrest Gregg and Mike Ditka, and the fact that Forrest was always a little bit jealous of Mike because Mike was a tight end. Mike was a glamour boy. Ditka was the greatest tight end in pro football history. He could have been an All-Pro at middle linebacker, at weak-side linebacker, strong-side linebacker, strong safety, weak safety, probably offensive tackle, fullback, tailback and maybe even a quarterback—he was that talented. I think the jealousy Gregg had of Ditka and the fact that the Bears were dominating the rivalry made it ugly. I will never forget Mark Lee tackling Walter Payton about ten yards out of bounds at Lambeau Field and running him directly into the Bear bench. It was one of the most outrageously contemptible plays I have ever seen in my life....

In 1970, I went to a wrestling show in Chicago at the International Amphitheater with a friend of mine. Immediately afterward, we didn't have tickets, but we decided to drive up to Green Bay to see if we could get into the Bear-Packer game. We arrived at the Northland Hotel at around two in the morning, and remarkably, there was a room available. The drive from the Amphitheater on the south side of Chicago to Green Bay was about 240 miles. About 4:15 in the morning, the fire alarm went off. This was not the first time it had happened. I remember that Abe Gibron was a Bear line coach, and later their head coach. He came walking out in the corridor wearing just his underpants. It was like seeing the arrival of a glacier. Abe at that time had to be at least 325 pounds.

A year earlier, the first time an X-rated film was shown in Chicago was at the old Playboy theater, a movie called, "I Am Curious (Yellow)." I was there with my girlfriend. During the course of the movie, I'm hearing this loud snoring sound from the front row. Finally I looked up there and go, "That's Abe." At that time, I'm working for WFLD as a 20-year-old sportswriter and reporter. I walked down to the front row and go, "Abe, Abe, wake up." He wakes up and looks at me and goes, "Oh no, don't tell Halas I was here." That happened, ironically, during Green Bay week.

IT WAS IN *SPORTS ILLUSTRATED*, SO, HELL, FOR ALL I KNOW, IT COULD BE TRUE.

MIKE WIER

If you owned a restaurant, wouldn't it be nice if Sports Illustrated *ran a cover photo of two famous people eating in your establishment? That's exactly what happened to Mike Wier, owner of Kroll's West, a restaurant in the shadows of Lambeau Field. In 1997, S. I. featured Mike Holmgren and Brett Favre dining at Kroll's West.*

Mike Holmgren ate at our place quite often. In 1997, **Sports Illustrated** called me to ask permission to do a photo shoot at the restaurant. A few weeks later, they set up a shooting one afternoon with Coach and Brett. They did it right after lunch hour so it wasn't too busy and not too congested. The two of them shared a couple of brats and burgers, and S. I. got some nice pictures of them, one of which ended up on the cover.

John Brockington always ate two of our double cheese steaks. I don't know how anybody could ever do that. When the Packers used to play in Milwaukee, the players' bus would go down on Saturday. Just before the bus would leave the stadium, 10 or 15 players would stop in to pick up "to-go" boxes we'd have ready for them. John would always have two double cheese steaks and two malts—I just couldn't believe he could eat that much food. A lot of the Packer players pick up food "to go" after the practices. Once they're released from training camp and have homes in Green Bay, it's easy to pick up food on the way home. The Packer players and their families are here regularly. Once in a

Sports Illustrated **began in 1954 and its first swimsuit issue was in 1964. The** *Sports Illustrated* **swimsuit issue has 52 million readers, 16 million of them are females... 12 million more than normal.**

while, you'll see someone asking them for autographs, but most of the time, there's a pretty good respect for the players in our city.

There is a group of terminally-ill children that come every year from Tampa, Florida in February or March. Jerry Watch was a native of Wausau, Wisconsin who played football for Tampa. Several years ago, he called and said, "We have this group of people we're bringing up every year, and we take them to Wausau for the weekend, all children. We're looking for a place to stop for lunch before we go to the stadium for our tour." I said, "Jerry, we'd be happy to put the lunch on for you and your kids any time you want." We've made that an annual event. Last year, we had just under 100 terminally-ill children. They fly in terminally-ill children every year so the kids can experience snowmobiling, skiing and Wisconsin winter sports.

The football season is over when they bring the kids down for a stadium tour. They get to meet Bob Harlan and Mike Sherman. They spend a day in Green Bay and then they go to Wausau for a day and then they come back through Green Bay on the way home. Any of the Packer players that are in town usually end up having lunch with the kids here at the restaurant. Eugene Robinson has been here with them, and, in 2004, Ahman Green was here with them. There were a couple of defensive backs who came down, too. The players just hear that the kids are in town, or see them when they're touring the stadium. A lot of times, they'll walk in and sit with them and talk with them for a while and make them comfortable.

The Green Bay Packers are probably the most giving franchise in the whole National Football League. We're involved in so many things for children and non-profit organizations.

What's the toughest thing about being a Bears fan? Explaining to your father why you're ga,

FROM THE TROPICAL TUNDRA OF HAWAII

RODNEY YASUSHI HORIKAWA

Rodney Yasushi Horikawa grew up near Hono-lulu, HI, dreaming of playing for the Packers. He is now a resident of Madison, WI. He does not play for the Packers!

We got there as most eleven- and twelve-year-olds probably do even today—on foot, on bicycles. I don't recall how the word got out that a football game was about to start down at the Ka'ala Elementary School playground but we got wind of it, perhaps via the coconut wireless, and began to trickle over there: Nakahodo, Shintaku, the two Takita brothers, Ito Yoshida, the Yamamoto boys, Kiyabu, Hisanuma, Kurashige, Kaneshiro. We arrived in rubber slippers or often barefoot, our feet stained red by that iron-rich dirt that makes Wahiawa the pineapple capital of the world. The Ka'ala Elementary School playground: If push came to shove and I had to name a dominant image of my childhood, a metaphor for growing up, it just might be that place.

I wonder how many times in the mid-60s, incarnations of the Green Bay Packers, invoked by the dreams and desires of eleven and twelve year olds, made their appearance on streets, back lots and playgrounds across America. I really can't know. What I do know is that on many hot Hawaiian days on the Ka'ala Elementary School playground in the summer of '64, Lombardi's Packers took to the field. I know; I was there. I was part of that legendary team. And our beloved alter-egos possessed us completely: as Nitschke, we played with vicious intensity; as Taylor, we pounded ahead with reckless, punishing abandon; as Starr, we faked runs on third-and-short and threw deep to a streaking Brian Nakahodo running towards the red rubber slipper-check that, to a streaking Max McGee running a post pattern; as Hornung, we swept right with graceful patience, waiting for daylight to open, behind the pulling Jerry Kramer and Fuzzy Thurston (even though the latter appeared to be someone's dumb six-year-old brother whom we conscripted because we needed a body. Ever see Fuzzy cry after being shoved to the ground by Hornung because he was in the way? I did.).

When Herb Adderley was inducted into the Pro Football Hall of Fame in 1980, I recalled what was for me his most memorable moment. On a summer day in '64, we were playing this group of kids whom we detested from the other side of Wahiawa. Back then there was a class line between upper Wahiawa and lower Wahiawa. Those living in lower Wahiawa, and the kids who went to Ka'ala Elementary School, came from working class families. Upper Wahiawa, including Wahiawa Elementary School, was home to a group of arrogant snobs whose parents were doctors, lawyers and other professionals. They rode expensive, new bicycles and wore clothes from Duke's and Liberty House. We rarely played together but when we did it was war. Through football, we punished them for every slight, every smirk that was thrown our way when we passed on our reconstructed bikes and with our hand-me-down Cornet's and Ben Franklin shirts. The game that was played that one summer day in '64 was possibly the greatest Packers-Bears game ever. It was brutally fought. On the last play of the game, despite our home field advantage, the score was tied and the Bears were at our goal line. They threw a screen pass into the right flat. I intercepted it. Herb Adderley took it up the right sideline, along the chain link fence on Mahele Street, and scored! When you factor in the significance of that game and the impact it had historically on playground football lore in Wahiawa, hands down, it was Herb Adderley's greatest play. It absolutely guaranteed his admission into Canton 16 years later.

Today, I am living and working in Madison, Wisconsin. I came here to attend graduate school at the University of Wisconsin-Madison in 1977. The scholarship offer from UW-Madison was pretty good. In truth, however, I had excellent offers from graduate schools in other states, as well. In finally choosing UW-Madison, I can't say that being in Green Bay Packer country had no bearing on my final decision. I just can't say that.

My wife, Beth, is from Milwaukee. We met at a grad school party one fall night in 1977. What I distinctly remember from our very first conversation was a story she told me about living for a year in Green Bay. One day while shopping she ran into—physically ran into—Bart and Cherry Starr. She turned a corner and walked right into Bart carrying a bag of groceries. You know, I can't say that that story, and how Beth told it, had no bearing on me falling madly in love with her. I just can't say that.

What I can say is this: on game day in the fall I get out my Walkman radio, put on the headphones and tune into the Packer pre-game show hours before kick-off. I absolutely love NFL football. I follow several teams these days—Jets, Seahawks, Eagles. The Green Bay Packers, naturally, are in a special category. I never miss a Packer game. However, unlike some fanatical Packer fans—and there are many in these here parts—the Packer thing is not a "religion" for me. I mean, on game day I don't drive around with a Packer flag on my car. I don't paint my face green & gold and then go watch the games at raucous Packer bars even though there's practically one on every corner. I have a Packer baseball cap, a team jacket and a couple of GB sweatshirts but I wear them only occasionally. For me, the relationship I have with the Packers is more in terms of interacting with a close "family" member. It's a blood thing. It is something that flows long and deep in my veins. It's about unconditional love. I feel a profound, lifelong connection to and with the Green Bay Packers. And why not? I grew up on that pineapple strewn, frozen tundra that is the Ka'ala Elementary School playground. The great Lombardi teams of the 60's knew that field well. Some of their most critical games were played there. Their ghosts still linger on the grass along Mahele Street and Kilani Avenue. I see them every time I go back home. The Ka'ala Elementary School playground in Wahiawa on the island of Oahu had a profound bearing on the success and glory of the Packers during that mythic 1960-68 run. That I know with total certainty.

MARRIAGES ARE MADE IN HEAVEN... SO ARE THUNDER AND LIGHTNING

BILL HALL

Bill Hall was born in Ashland, Wisconsin and raised in Minnesota. Hall, 47, owns the Iron Horse Saloon in Hurley, Wisconsin.

My wife and I got married at halftime of a Packer-Viking game. There were over two hundred people there, and the judge who married us dressed in a ref's outfit. The game was tied at the half, and the Packers went on to win. I heard from almost everybody that it was the best wedding they'd ever been to. We had it right in the bar, and there was an even mix of Packer and Viking fans. I had the family members from Minnesota in their Viking stuff, but it was still a great wedding. I met my wife here in Hurley, and she was already a fan. I've made her more of one, just with me being such a big fan.

When we lived in Minnesota, every Sunday my dad would pack us in the car and we'd drive back to Ashland to watch the Packers on TV with the rest of the family. I can remember my grandpa and all my uncles just going crazy on the couch. This was the era of Ray Nitschke and all those great players. I just didn't understand exactly what was going on, but I grew to, and I loved every minute of it.

Growing up in Minnesota I got so much razzing about being a Packers fan. In the 70s when the Packers weren't faring so well, all you heard about were the Purple People Eaters. My dad, my brother and I were all die-hard Packer fans. I have a sister and another brother who, sadly, are Viking fans.

I try to make it to two days of training camp every year. Two years ago, a local radio station gave me a press pass to get inside the field. I remember standing next to Larry McCarren, with both of our arms crossed…it felt like I was one of the guys. I brought my helmet to get autographed, and it was great because Larry was one of my all-time favorites.

Up here where we live is a big snowmobile area. One year a friend of my son's gave him a purple Geo. It ran and everything, but I had this idea. I put a stripe on it and had Viking horns put on it. I parked it out front and charged people to hit this car with a sledgehammer. All proceeds went to the local snowmobile club. Somebody called Channel 12, and they did a story on it that went out all over the country. Next thing I know, I'm getting calls from Arizona, Florida, New York, people saying they saw me on TV bashing this Viking car. We raised $180! Part of the money came from me taking bids on smashing the windows. The Packers lost that day so there was a little more hatred than usual against the Vikings.…

I was in Atlanta visiting my cousin. It was October and I told him I wasn't about to miss the game. He took me to this bar and we walked in and there was Falcon stuff all over the walls. I asked the bartender if he'd mind turning on the Packer game. I was wearing my colors, of course. He looked at me and told me that I'd have to go downstairs. So I walked downstairs and the place was completely full of Packer fans! Before you knew it, we were all swapping stories of how we had become fans and where we're from-it was like a big family get-together!

I love the outdoor stadiums. Places like Minnesota are like watching games in a bubble. The cold is our ally, too. I've sent e-mail inviting players to my bar, but so far I haven't had any luck getting them to come. I'd love to take the whole offensive line out snowmobiling. I've got friends that rent them and I could set them all up, but I just haven't gotten them to come yet.

I've got a heart of gold and green blood. That's my story and I'm sticking to it!

SHORT STORIES FROM LONG MEMORIES

One of my bartenders is a Vikings fan. He's a good bartender and a good person, so we keep him around. But anytime I buy anything Packers related, he always decorates it with a little Vikings-something. A few years ago, when the Vikings were playing the Packers at Lambeau Field on Monday Night Football, we made a bet that if the Packers won, he'd work for free that night. If the Vikings won, I'd double his pay for that night. I was at the game on a just a miserable, cold, wet night...and the Vikings won. I called the bar around 11 that night and he was still there. I asked, "Who else is there?" He said, "No one, but I'm keeping the bar open until 2 since you're paying me double."

——SHIRLEY HAYES, owner, Big O Bar

I'm a teacher, so part of what I do is to try to make learning meaningful. Some kids struggle with addition, subtraction, multiplication, and division. When they would do it with the Packer stories they would find that it was really easy. I felt like I was building new Packer fans through the stories. The kids loved it. We had a Packer Super Bowl party where we gathered in the gym and the kids did the "Packerena." The kids made cheeseheads and decorated their doors, and it was just an all-around learning experience and they enjoyed it so much. Not only was there learning, but we were able to talk a lot about leadership and what makes a leader. We talked about what sportsmanship really means. I know Lombardi said "Winning isn't everything, it's the only thing." That was fine for a group of men, but I wanted the kids to see it a little differently.

——PATRICIA PLEUSS, 58, teacher, Wauwatosa

I have a big Packers collection it consists of some old and some modern memorabilia. I have one room-full plus a Packers bathroom. I have a second Packers room coming along nicely. I have official Packers locker room carpet that is very hard for a fan to get. Just happened to be in the right place at the right time. The Packers Pro Shop was having a tent sale, where they were selling all of these great Packer items at great prices. We were looking around, and my Mom noticed some carpet rolled up and away from the tent sale. She called me over and said, "Hey, isn't that the stadium carpet?" Sure enough it was. I found someone who confirmed that it was from the stadium. Apparently, they did some remodeling and some of the carpet they took up, they put out for sale. I bought a good size roll of it, and had two throw rugs cut out of it and saved the rest for future ideas....

My one share of Packers stock hangs on a wall along with numerous posters and pictures. I have several autographs—my most loved one would be the regulation Packers helmet signed by Ray Nitschke. My friend and I spent about two hours with Mr. Nitschke. As he signed for others, he let us try on his Super Bowl ring. We took a whole roll of pictures with him and not a one turned out. That was so disappointing. He was such a great person who talked and joked with us the whole time. I have several thousand Packers cards and dozens of magazines with Packers on the covers. I have been told that my collection is one of the biggest that most people have seen.

——RICK NELSON, Canton, Ohio

One of the Packer coaches, Greg Blache, who was a defensive line coach during the '96 Super Bowl year, came here to Philips to speak to the students at school. He and I struck up a friendship and he did a tremendous amount of things with our school district. After he left, Andy Reid, who is now the head coach of the Eagles, stepped into his role. Coach Reid was the quarterback coach. Several times he got me items signed by Brett Favre to give to students who had exemplified positive attitudes or behaviors. So there have been some wonderful gentlemen that I now consider friends.

Through the years I've really worked to make our middle school in Philips the Packer Middle School. Our rooms are completely decorated with Packer items. We live out in the country, and on top of our house we have a giant cheesehead, which we light up every night. For us, as with a lot of people here, the Packers are a way of life. There are several reasons the Packers are so popular everywhere. One reason was the fact that they were winning championships right when the NFL came to TV. I also think it's because they're still the little city in a big city era. And the fact that the Packers are owned by the community. To me all of those reasons make it the Disney World of professional sports.

——RANDY KUNSCH, 54, Phillips, Wisconsin

Mike Holmgren was riding his Harley in the MDA Packerland Ride in '97. It was in June, the summer after the Super Bowl. We were all hyped up. He stopped across the street, and his security came up and asked if he could use our restroom. They said, "He's not signing anything today, but he'll sign something for you." I had all kinds of Packer stuff here. I just couldn't think fast enough, so I said, "Just sign right there on my wall." He said, "You've got to be kidding me." I said, "No." It's still there…on a kitchen wall, but you can see it straight ahead when you walk in the front door. I put a Plexiglas cover over it, but it's fading a little bit anyway…just like he faded on us. That was a thrill.

If a player or coach writes a book, I try to get it signed by them if I can. Brett Favre was very nice to me. I waited in line about five hours for his autograph at Sam's. There was such a maze in the store. He already had stayed an hour over what he was scheduled to do. All of a sudden, they said, "That's it folks. No more." A lot of people left, but there were a few of us who were so close—I was 20 people away. We started singing, "We love you, Brett. Oh yes, we do." We just kept it up, and he got this twinkle in his eye, and he just waved us on up and signed our books. We thought that was pretty nice.…

When I first started cheerleading, learning the game, I remember our coach saying, "If the cheer doesn't have the word "go," "fight," or "win" in it, you can't use it." We were cheer "leaders." Now they just get up and do all these formations. We actually went up into the stands and got the people cheering. So, we considered ourselves cheer "leaders." There's such a difference now.

——BARBARA BROZEK PELNAR, 62, Kewaunee, Wisconsin

I've been to two games in Green Bay. One was a preseason game against Carolina last year. It was kind of neat; I got my tickets from Fuzzy Thurston. He's got a bar in Green Bay and acts as an unofficial ticket broker for people needing tickets. I got to go to his tailgate party, and it was really awe-inspiring being there with one of Vince

Lombardi's starting linemen. The other game I've been to in Green Bay was in December, 1985. It was the game called the "Snow Bowl." I have an uncle who is a law professor here in Michigan. He happened to be on sabbatical at UW-Madison. Someone hooked him up with tickets so I got to go to it with him. They played Tampa Bay, which made it more fun, since they were not prepared for that kind of weather. Steve Young was the Tampa Bay quarterback and John McKay was the coach. My dad and my uncle ended up going to the car early, but I stayed in my seat for the whole game.

Growing up in Michigan, I really can't say why I became a Packers fan. All of my other favorite sports teams are Michigan teams. I have a vague recollection of walking through the living room when I was real little and the TV being on. They were doing a close-up of Bart Starr, and for some reason that just connected with me. It was like "Bart Starr, that's really cool," and I've been a Packer fan ever since.

——**VINCE PRYGOSKI**, 40, Gaines, Michigan

When I was married to my ex-husband, he and his friends were real involved with the Packers. I became a fan because "If you can't beat them, you join them." But, once I did, I actually became more of a fan than he was. I just accelerated. It was very exciting for me. We started having Packer parties and going to Packer parties. His group of friends used to have Packer parties at particular local bars in town. Because of all the drunk-driving laws and the problems, it was safer and made more sense, so we started taking turns having parties at each other's homes. One of the parties we had was for Super Bowl XXXI, which the Packers won. All of our friends were with us in our home, and it was great. Every time the Packers would score, they'd pass around the bottle of peppermint schnapps and everyone would take a swig. Then it got to the point where—if they made a *good run*, we'd pass the bottle around! We had a great time partying—and we won that game…I think.

——**MARY R. ENDTHOFF**, Waukomis, Wisconsin

My first job was with Osco Drug when they were in downtown Green Bay. Where I lived, I could go across the street every day and watch the team practice. You could stand right behind Lombardi and watch. He told Jim Taylor where to put his feet. I'll never forget that. "You step

here, here and here." All they had to practice in was a pasture with a wire fence. At the most, you were only a few feet away from them. They'd line up, and Lombardi would tell the backs where to put their feet, how to walk, how to run. "Here, here and here"—very specific— that's how he did it. ...

From our house, we could watch the people go by on their way to the ball game. The girls would be all dressed up with their nylons and high heels, and it would five degrees or ten degrees. We'd go over there to the old stadium. At halftime, we'd all go down below to Bar 24, Willie Wood's number, which was underneath Section 19. That's where we'd all meet and sit there and drink beer until they kicked us out...which was normally late.

————**GENE MOSHER,** Post Lake, Wisconsin

The most memorable games for me are ones that have happened lately, within the last few years. One of them was the first Monday night game after 9/11. That game was being played at Lambeau Field and they were bringing in firemen from all around the area to take part in a ceremony before the game. They asked for volunteers to drive the buses to bring these folks to the game. I volunteered of course, and got picked to be one of the bus drivers. After we got there we found out that we were also going to be part of the ceremony. We actually got to go out on the field with the firemen, the Redskins and the Packers, to help hold the American flag. I thought it was just awesome being part of that.

The second most memorable game for me was when we played the 49ers in the 2002 playoffs. They kind of did the same thing and asked for volunteers to come out on the field to help hold the American flag. I was one of four bus drivers that got picked for that. I thought, "How awesome for me to be part of this twice." I could have gone up to my seat after that, but they said we could stay down on the field. Even though you couldn't see anything down there, I decided to stay on the field for the whole game. It was just unbelievable.

————**WENDY SMETANA,** Green Bay

I remember that great tackle that came from Iowa and played for the Lions—Alex Karras. I just can't believe he didn't make it into the

Hall of Fame. I mean the Golden Boy made it in, and he had a little gambling trouble, too. You know, Alex Karras was the only opposing player that Lombardi feared. When the Packers pulled that famous sweep to the right, Jerry Kramer and Fuzzy Thurston led the way. Kramer was a big guy, but Fuzzy was a short guy. Finally, his knee started going and he told Lombardi that he needed to either trade or draft a guard because he didn't know how much longer his knee was going to hold up. They drafted this guard, and on the opening day, Fuzzy's knee went out and this rookie got put in to play against Karras. Well, Karras had a groin injury that the Lions hadn't told the league about—they got fined for it later. When you've got a groin injury your lateral movement is not very good. So this rookie had a helluva game against Karras, and after the game, a reporter asked him how he did so well against Karras. This rookie says, "I guess he don't have so many moves anymore." Being in the same division, they had to play the Lions again, this time in Detroit. It turns out that Fuzzy gets hurt and can't start, so this rookie has to start again. The Packers win the toss and on the first play from scrimmage Karras just cold-cocks this kid. He's laying on the ground and Karras is standing over him. Finally the rookie opens his eyes and Karras says, "How do you like those moves, smart-ass?"

——LT. COLONEL HERBERT BARNES, retired

The Bears and the Packers are two sides of the same coin. The Bears and the Packers are old line teams, historic teams, hard hitting teams. Bear fans hate the Packers, but they respect them. I can never see a Bears-Vikings rivalry like the Bears-Packer rivalry. Even if the Vikings are beating you 50-0, you don't respect them. Honestly, if the Packers ever folded or moved, it would make me less of a Bears fan. Don't get me wrong, I still hate the Packers, but they make the game better just being there.

——CHRIS CIESLAK, 28, Life-long Bears fan, Chicago

The Chicago Cardinals won the championship back in 1947. I wanted an autographed picture of one of their players, Red Cochran, so I wrote to him. Red also had been an assistant coach of the Packers. I didn't know he lived in De Pere, believe it or not. I took the letter to the stadium and dropped it off. You can just address an envelope to someone and take it down to the stadium. About a week later, I get a call—it's Red Cochran. He said, "Hi Larry. I got your request for an autographed photo. I'd like to know what you want me to do with it. Do you want me to mail it to you?" I said, "Yeah, you can mail it to me." He said, "How about if I stop over?" Then, about ten minutes later…the doorbell rang…I opened the door, and here he was, at my door. I thanked him for bringing the picture to me and invited him down to my basement to see my Packer Room. He came in and looked around the basement. We had a couple of beers, and we must have talked for a couple of hours about old Packer stuff. His injury that knocked him out of football came from Curly Lambeau. It was pretty neat to have a player here in my basement.

——**LARRY PRIMEAU**, Packer memorabilia collector

Being a "Packer Backer" is awesome! We have had so much fun and have met and made lasting friendships with fans all over the country —and world. Seeing someone in a Packer shirt or hat immediately strikes up a conversation—especially when you are a long way from Wisconsin. When in Florida, I go to the "Fumble Inn" in Bradenton to watch the games. There is a large screen TV in the "Packer Room" and you feel at home with new Packer friends the minute you walk in. These Packer bars are in every state and a list can be obtained at www.southendzone.com. It is not unusual to meet Packer fans from six or seven different states at a single game in Green Bay. Then there are the opposing fans…they are so excited to get to Lambeau Field along with the whole game experience. We always have a good time with them and enjoy seeing them have a good time in Green Bay. We want them to feel welcome—that's what it's all about!

——**MARY JO LINK**, Minong, Wisconsin

This is our fourth year for the maze. It's computer-generated and GPS cut. It's cut very precise. We use a 25-horsepower compact tractor with a 48" rototiller on the back of it. We plant the corn in two directions, double plant it. Then we till the maze in. We actually cut a 48" path in the corn. The way we design it on the computer is the way it looks in the corn field when you do a flyover.

We started working with Channel 5-TV. We approached them on cutting the Channel 5 or CBS logo in the corn maze, being that they were the station that covered the pre-season games and the home games. We shot TV commercials with the corn maze in. They put the package together for us, got the rights to use the "G" for Green Bay and Brett Favre's "#4" and other Packer things. We track our people that come into maze by a card we give them. We get a lot of Illinois and Minnesota people.

We looked for a way to market it to get Green Bay as our main drawing area. The station did the legwork with the Packers and getting it all set up and getting the contracts in order. One dollar from every person who goes through the corn maze goes to the Packer Foundation. We had a Packer Day in 2003, when we had a player, Grey Ruegamer, backup center, come up. He knew farming. His dad was a veterinarian. He could talk to people. He was just a super guy.

Since it's the fourth time we've done a maze, we have it down pretty good. We had a good October, which is by far our best month for the maze. Weather has a lot to do with it. It's an outside event. Normally, we open that maze up the middle of July, but this year we didn't open it up until August 10. You lose a lot of people when you're not open for a month. Those people are hard to get back because they were probably tourists who were up here and aren't going to come back. We usually put a thousand people through on a weekend. You get rain on that weekend, and you lose that thousand people. This year, we lost 1,700 people just not being open as early as usual. There's nothing you can do about it. We closed at the end of October. Then, we harvested the corn. The guy we work with on the design is from Idaho, and he said, "We've got to do Brett Favre. Lambeau Field is going to be there forever. Brett Favre may not be." We will have another maze next year.

———**DENNIS SCHOPF**, owner of an incredible Packer corn maze at a dairy farm in Door County, 50 miles from Green Bay

TO BE CONTINUED!

We hope you have enjoyed the first annual *For Packers Fans Only.* You can be in next year's edition if you have a neat story. You can email it to printedpage@cox.net (put "Packers Fans" in the Subject line) or call the author directly at 602-738-5889.

Also, if you have stories about Wisconsin Badgers, Notre Dame, or nasty stories about the Chicago Bears, email them to printedpage@cox.net (put the appropriate team name in the Subject line).

For information on ordering more copies of *For Packers Fans Only,* as well as any of the author's other best-selling books, go to www.fandemonium.net.

Note: There were no actual Chicago Bears fans harmed during the making of this book...well maybe one, but the authorities don't know about that yet.

Twice the Packers have had the first overall pick in the NFL draft: Paul Hornung in 1957 and Randy Duncan in 1959. (Above) Iowa sophomore quarterback Randy Duncan gets his 1957 Rose Bowl Christmas wish with Jayne Mansfield. They may have been young, but they each had a good head on their shoulders. Randy still does.